CURRENT RESEARCH IN FILM: Audiences, Economics, and Law

Volume 1

CURRENT RESEARCH IN FILM: Audiences, Economics, and Law

Volume 1

Bruce A. Austin, ***Editor***
Rochester Institute of Technology

Ablex Publishing Corporation
Norwood, New Jersey 07648

Printed in the United States of America.

ISBN: 0–89391–269–7 ISSN: 0748–8580

Ablex Publishing Corporation
355 Chestnut Street
Norwood, New Jersey 07648

Contents

About the Contributors

Bruce A. Austin is an Associate Professor in the College of Liberal Arts, Rochester Institute of Technology.

Boris W. Becker is a Professor in the School of Business, Oregon State University, Corvallis.

David E. Bradbury, a doctoral student in the School of Communications at Temple University, is a Lecturer in Communications at Ursinus College.

Barbara Brewer is an MBA candidate in the School of Business, Oregon State University, Corvallis.

Bodie Dickerson is an Instructor in the School of Business, Oregon State University, Corvallis.

Olen J. Earnest's motion picture experience includes Vice President, Marketing Research for MCA, Inc./Universal Pictures. Prior to working for Universal Pictures he was Director of Worldwide Marketing Studies, Twentieth Century-Fox Film Corporation, where he was responsible for administration of the marketing research for *Star Wars*. Earnest was a programming executive for ABC Television and Paramount Television, and Assistant Professor of Psychology at Wichita State University. He is a graduate of Wichita State University and attended graduate school at Washington University, St. Louis.

Susan Tyler Eastman, an Associate Professor of Telecommunications at Indiana University, is editor and author of *Broadcast Programming: Strategies for Winning Television and Radio Audiences* with Sydney W. Head and Lewis Klein, and *Strategies for Broadcast and Cable Promotion* with Robert A. Klein.

John Fullerton is a Lecturer in Film Studies, Derbyshire College of Higher Education, Derby, England.

Thomas Guback is Research Professor of Communications, Institute of Communications Research, University of Illinois, Urbana. He is presently working on a book about the economic structure and policies of the American film industry.

Mary Beth Haralovich is a graduate of the University of Wisconsin–Madison and teaches film and television studies at Iowa State University. She has published on the film industry, film advertising, and genre and is currently working on a book-length study of the contemporary entertainment industry entitled *Hollywood Today*.

John L. Huffman (Ph.D., University of Iowa) is Professor and Director of the School of Journalism at Bowling Green State University.

Ian Jarvie (Ph.D., London School of Economics) is Professor of Philosophy at York University. He has made scholarly contributions to philosophy, the social sciences, and film studies. Books he has written include *The Revolution in Anthropology; Hong Kong, A Society in Transition; Movies and Society;* and *Movies as Social Criticism*. Forthcoming books include *Rationality and Relativism* and *Philosophy of Film*.

Garth S. Jowett is Director of the School of Communication at the University of Houston.

Rosemary Magee is an On-Line Systems Representative for Summit Information Systems, Corvallis, Oregon.

Robert S. Nemes is a masters student in the Department of Radio-Television-Film at Temple University.

Mitchell E. Shapiro is an Assistant Professor in the Department of Communication, University of Miami, Coral Gables, Florida.

Denise M. Trauth (Ph.D., University of Iowa) is an Associate Professor of Speech Communication and Chair of the Radio-Television-Film Program at Bowling Green State University.

Janet Wasko, an Assistant Professor at California State Polytechnic University, is author of *Movies and Money: Financing the American Film Industry*.

Wenmouth Williams, Jr. is an Associate Professor in the Department of Communication, Illinois State University.

Foreword

The study of movies and the motion picture medium has, over the years, made significant strides in gaining respect as an academic discipline and as an area for meaningful and significant scholarly inquiry. Largely, the approach of many film courses, texts, and journals has been aesthetic in nature, with important works produced advancing our understanding of film. However, this approach has often omitted, overlooked, or overtly discouraged other kinds of film research. *Current Research in Film* is intended to help broaden the scope of film scholarship by providing an outlet for researchers whose focus is on three non-traditional aspects of film: the film audience, motion picture economics, and legal concerns relevant to film as a mass medium. *CRF* is designed with the intent of providing a forum for scholarly research which does not mandate that authors twist their writing to fit the biases and traditions of film and communications journals. In addition, *CRF* offers contributors flexibility with regard to such issues as methodology and manuscript length.

In this, the inaugural volume of *Current Research in Film,* 12 original articles by respected scholars are presented. The topics and issues addressed cover a wide range, including case studies of the marketing of a particular film and of a particular film studio, examination of one form of film exhibition, a study of a contemporary method for film censorship, a historical analysis comparing attempts at suppression of motion pictures, a review and analysis of research on movie preferences, a study of the relationship between movie preferences and personal values, a field experiment examining audience expectations of a film as influenced by previews, a critical inquiry on the film industry and its accommodations to social forces, results of a survey reporting on new technologies and their effect on motion picture attendance, an investigation concerning the influence of new technologies on the American film industry's financial arrangements and export business, and an analysis of industry-government relations and aspects of international film distribution.

Subsequent volumes of *Current Research in Film* will continue to address these key areas of motion picture research. *CRF* will present innovative and important film research within these three levels on an annual basis. Potential contributors are invited and encouraged to write the Editor.

Bruce A. Austin

Rochester, New York
December, 1983

1
Star Wars: A Case Study of Motion Picture Marketing*

Olen J. Earnest

INTRODUCTION

Star Wars was the brainchild of George Lucas, the creator of *American Graffiti,* a film made for $750,000, which, at the time of *Star Wars'* release, was the eleventh largest grossing film in the United States. Lucas described the difficulty in getting *Star Wars* launched:

> I started out saying this is a fairly viable project (and) I thought it would make roughly $16 million. The thing is . . .if I spend $4.5 million, then on the advertising and the prints and everything another $4.5 million, there is a little bit of profit there, if it makes $16 million. I said this was a good venture, and I could take it to the studios. . . . When I went to one studio . . .I said this is what I'm going to do, it's Flash Gordon, it's adventure, it's exciting, sort of James Bond, and they said, no, we don't see it. So I went to [another studio] and got the same thing.
>
> I think I got $20,000 to write and direct *Graffiti* and they wanted me to do *Star Wars* for $25,000. I was asking half of what my friends were asking, and the studio thought I was asking for twice as much as I would get, and they said, no, no. It is too much money and we don't really think it is for us. So they threw it out the window (1, pp. 43–44).[1]

---

*This article is an expanded version of addresses for Advanced Management Research, Inc., Marketing Seminars in San Francisco, St. Louis, Chicago, and London, England, 1977–1979, and to the Market Research Society 22d Annual Conference, March 23, 1979, Brighton, England. The author wishes to express his appreciation to Sidney Ganis, Senior Vice President, Lucasfilm Ltd., and Thomas Castaneda for their assistance in the preparation of this article.

[1]By Paul Scanlon. From *Rolling Stone* #246, 8/25/77. By Straight Arrow Publishers, Inc.

After the two studios rejected the project, Lucas approached Alan Ladd, Jr., president of Twentieth Century-Fox Film Corporation, partly on the basis that the studio had produced the successful *Planet of the Apes* film series. Ladd liked the idea, perhaps even more because Lucas' asking price was a mere $10,000 to start the project. As Lucas remarked, in what must be one of the greatest understatements of all time, ''Fox said it's got potential, so they went with it, but nobody thought it was going to be a big hit'' (1, p.44).

In retrospect, of course, it may seem surprising that a film which would become one of the top grossing films in Hollywood history would be rejected by two major studios. On the contrary, Lucas' experience is a somewhat common one. What studio executives are presented on a regularly occurring basis is repeated in miniature in advertising test marketing—studio executives read film treatments and/or scripts and must decide, given estimates of production costs and the cost of advertising and marketing of the film, if the feature is commercially viable; while moviegoers, in test markets, read film descriptions, look at various advertising strategy ideas, then relate their perceptions of the film and reasons behind their interest or lack of interest in wanting to see a particular motion picture. Both studio executives and potential moviegoers may experience a similar difficulty, viz., an inability to imagine or visualize what will eventually appear on the screen.

It is often the case that certain film ideas and/or scripts are not easily visualized from the written word, especially original films with no prior familiarity, such as a best-selling book or award-winning play. Ultimately, the decision as to whether or not to make a film comes down to ''gut'' instinct and a belief in the vision and integrity of the film maker, essential aspects of the film creative process that sophisticated marketing tools cannot—and should not—attempt to replace.

Imagine, for example, a studio executive trying to evaluate the box office potential of a film described as being about an extraterrestrial three-feet high, stranded on Earth, lost and alone, who befriends a young boy. The film tells the story of their encounter, developing friendship, and shared adventures. Whereas one studio executive may think this sounds terribly juvenile and limited in appeal (hence, limited in its perceived box office potential), another may believe in the film maker's vision and ability to execute the story in an exciting manner—via special effects, fast-paced adventure, believable characters, and so on—thereby broadening the film's appeal.

Once the creative decision is made to proceed with the production of a motion picture, marketing research, marketing, and advertising work jointly to create an advertising, publicity, and promotional campaign for the film's release in the marketplace. Moviegoers' reactions to various concept descriptions and advertising strategy ideas provide creative guidelines for studio marketing and advertising departments in the development of a film's ultimate advertising campaign. As this article will explore, moviegoers' perceptions of science fiction films, in general, and *Star Wars,* specifically, presented certain stumbling blocks in the development of the film's advertising and marketing campaign. Ultimately, the genius of George Lucas spoke for itself in the fully realized film, and moviegoer reaction to the film was, as is always the case, the final arbiter of the motion picture's eventual success or failure.

What follows, then, is a description of issues encountered in the marketing of motion pictures and the interrelationship of George Lucas' creative genius, marketing research, marketing, and advertising in the pre-release, release, and post-release stages of *Star Wars*— all contributing synergistically to the creation and launch of a successful motion picture.

OVERVIEW OF ISSUES IN THE MARKETING OF MOTION PICTURES

A motion picture is a rather unique product confronted with unique marketing problems. First of all, it is a luxury product—no one needs it to maintain their health or well-being or to enhance their personal appearance. Until the advent of the videocassette and the videodisc, you could not take it home to repeatedly savor at your leisure, like television, radio, or records.

Second, a movie is best characterized as an impulse buy, wherein the decision to attend is made a very short time before point of purchase. A moviegoer selects a film from several alternative films available in the marketplace. A film's marketing and advertising efforts, via the variety of opening week media placements, attempt to capture the attention of this potential moviegoer and convince the moviegoer that this is a film to see. The goal is to attract a sufficiently large number of moviegoers, affording the film a successful opening weekend and providing the necessary word-of-mouth to sustain the film in the competitive marketplace over the long run.

Third, on the average, it is a product with an extremely short shelf-life and, in most instances, it is seen only one time. A film's average life expectancy in theaters, all markets considered, averages four to six weeks. Yet a studio's livelihood depends on introducing as many as 20 or more of these new products into the marketplace every year, with each picture typically opening in several hundred theaters, each vying for high penetration in a marketplace characterized by low, limited growth potential. Together, the eight major film studios release an average of fewer than 200 motion pictures into the market yearly. Each studio hopes to attract moviegoers in sufficient numbers to pay for production, advertising, and film print costs and to produce a profit.

There are far fewer films released today than in the so-called Golden Days of Hollywood, partially as a result of the Supreme Court antitrust decision, whereby the major film studios could no longer exert a vertical monopoly over production, distribution, and exhibition. Since the late 1940s the major studios have been prohibited from owning theater chain operations which served as a ready-made outlet for their product. In essence, the Paramount decision[2] has given the studios more control, as only the major film studios control production and distribution channels and only they can afford the high costs of advertising and marketing of a film. The result is fewer films, playing fewer theaters, with each film required to perform better and achieve as high a market share as possible, *as quickly as possible,* since growth potential in the long run is limited.

The majority of films are not blockbusters since different movies attract different audiences with dissimilar demographic characteristics and moviegoing interests. The film that crosses all age and sex groups—the blockbuster—is rare.

The film market is characterized by quick entry and quick exit and the majority of the box office gross must be made early—for there may well be no later. Box office drop-off averages 15 to 20 percent after the first week of release, even for a good film, and declines even more rapidly thereafter. Media buys, primarily television, achieve high reach and frequency, just prior to a film's opening, to create awareness of the film's existence in the marketplace. In an age of rapidly spiraling media costs, it is now the rule-of-thumb that media expenditures to launch a motion picture average two-thirds the cost of the movie. The break-even point is calculated as 2.5 times the cost of production. Thus, a $15 million film must usually earn some $37.5 million at the box office just to break even. Movie making and marketing is indeed a risky business, particularly in view of the fact that costly media buys are not continued throughout the run of the movie at the same levels as those bought for the opening week. And very quickly after its opening, a film itself must prove sufficiently entertaining to generate a word-of-mouth level that will allow the film to sustain itself in the marketplace with minimal media expenditures beyond newspaper advertising.

There are additional risk factors in this high risk market. First, is the choice of when to release a film. Traditionally there are three preferred release periods:

1. The summer months, when the most frequent moviegoing age groups, teens and those of college age, are out of school. This period, extending over three months, is one which has the greatest opportunity to maximize a film's box office potential.

---

[2]The Justice Department filed an antitrust suit against the major motion picture companies in 1938. In 1940, the government obtained a consent decree against five of the studios; the studios agreed to change certain exhibition and distribution practices while the government held a right to reinstitute the antitrust suit if it felt dissatisfied with the studios' efforts. In 1944, the Justice Department renewed its suit, claiming the studios constituted a monopoly by virtue of exerting complete control of the motion picture process—from production to distribution channels to ownership of theater chains (exhibition). The case, *United States* v. *Paramount Pictures, Inc., et al.*, was heard by the Supreme Court in 1949. Justice William Douglas wrote the majority opinion which resulted in the separation of production and exhibition when, by 1954, the major studios had totally divested themselves of their theater chains.

2. The Christmas holiday season, the second most preferred release period. However, this period is characterized by extremely high risk since it is crowded by the last minute rush to release a film before year's end in order to qualify for Academy Award nominations. Further, the holiday season itself is precisely the period in which the majority of box office must be accumulated since matinee business—so critical in the summer months—is lost once students return to school in early January.
3. The Easter holidays, again, where one must maximize box office potential very quickly or run into the onslaught of summer releases, if one is still fortunate enough to be a box office contender. During one of these heavy release periods, when often 25 to 30 major films premiere, it is not unusual for only two or three to dominate the market so completely that many films simply "get lost."

A fourth unique characteristic of motion pictures is that, unlike industrial and consumer package goods, there are no ongoing established brand leaders in the movie marketplace. When pre-testing a new package goods consumer product, marketing researchers have a clearer idea of the competition than those in the movie marketing business have. If one wishes to introduce a new shampoo, for example, the brand manager knows before the product is even created who the brand leaders are and what market shares they command. And when one gives consumers a new product to test, they can assess the product's benefits in terms of their immediate experience. They are likely to use shampoos already in use as a criterion against which they can compare the new product on a regular, if not daily, basis. The same cannot be said for a new movie, however. In consumer package goods testing—with an actual product in hand—marketing research can readily measure behavioral traits, i.e., actual product usage and the benefits derived therefrom. The majority of marketing research studies in the motion picture industry are conducted *before* the product, the movie, is completed. Studies, of necessity, must be conducted to produce guidelines for the development of the film's marketing and advertising strategy. But these studies measure moviegoer attitudes, not actual behavior, toward the still-to-be-released product. Behavioral measures—as, for instance, the likelihood of actually recommending the film to others or relating what films have actually been seen—cannot be utilized until the film is available for sneak preview or released in the marketplace.

Thus, the movie industry has few of the advantages of package goods market research. When pre-testing the various advertising strategies for a film, as much as six months to a year before release, market researchers often do not know—and certainly the potential moviegoer does not know—what the competition will be at the time of the film's release. Furthermore, what do moviegoers use as their standard of comparison to judge the advertising strategy presented to them in test markets? Since most people do not go to movies weekly or even monthly, their experiences with movies are much less immediate than in the case of package goods. If the advertising suggests that the film falls into a recognizable film type or genre, moviegoers will most likely fall back on their past experience with such films; if it stars a familiar actor or actress, then moviegoers may judge their interest in terms of their last moviegoing experience with that performer. Whether or not the moviegoer is favorably disposed toward science fiction will enter into interest in seeing a film that appears to fall into the science fiction genre. Similarly, if the moviegoer is a fan of Barbra Streisand, previous experience with her films, and satisfaction with her performances, will be a critical determinant of the desire to see a new movie in which she stars; additionally, another determinant will be perceptions as to whether or not her role in the forthcoming film conforms to moviegoer expectations of the type of role she is expected to play. For example, Streisand's role in *All Night Long* as a secondary, not leading, character, and as a passive rather than dominating, forthright character most frequently associated with her past screen performances, was in large measure related to fans' dissatisfaction with the film and their reluctance to recommend it. In addition, if the film is an original screenplay, the film will almost always look pale or imitative in comparative judgments, as moviegoers may compare the unknown against the known of their previous moviegoing experiences. As will be seen, the development of the advertising strategy for *Star Wars* was constantly faced with the fact that the last science fiction film against which moviegoers judged *Star Wars* was over 10 years old, Stanley Kubrick's monumental *2001: A Space Odyssey;* or the perceived quality of *Star Wars* was frequently judged against the television series, "Star Trek."

With this uncertain test environment a studio must plan a release schedule, arrange media buys to impact against a defined target audience (as, for example, moviegoers 18 to 34 years of age), and finalize an advertising and marketing strategy that will maximize awareness and attract moviegoers. Then the studio must deliver a film that entertains and sends moviegoers out spreading word-of-mouth in numbers sufficient to guarantee a viable competitive position at the box office in the first two or three weeks of release. And, for *Star Wars,* the competition indeed looked formidable. The major competition was led by:

- *The Deep,* the first major competitor which would go out in a very wide release pattern a month after *Star Wars. The Deep* was based on an established best-selling book, both in hardback and paperback, by the author of *Jaws,* whose film version was an established box-office hit and, at the time of *Star Wars'* release, the biggest grossing film in motion picture history;
- *Smokey and the Bandit,* starring Burt Reynolds, a bankable box office star in an all out action comedy;
- *Exorcist II: The Heretic,* a sequel to the extraordinarily successful original;

- *A Bridge Too Far,* featuring an all-star international cast including Robert Redford;
- *New York, New York,* starring Academy Award winning actress Liza Minnelli and directed by Martin Scorsese of *Taxi Driver* fame;
- *MacArthur,* featuring Gregory Peck; and
- *The Spy Who Loved Me,* another in the extremely successful James Bond film series, each of whose films surpassed the box office success of its predecessor.

STAR WARS' PRE-RELEASE MARKETING RESEARCH

More than a year before *Star Wars'* release a research program was initiated. A typical pre-release marketing research program proceeds as illustrated in Figure 1. Each form of testing's position in the triangle, and the width of the triangle, parallel the level of interest generated *and* the amount of information imparted by each about the film the moviegoer is being asked to judge. Thus,

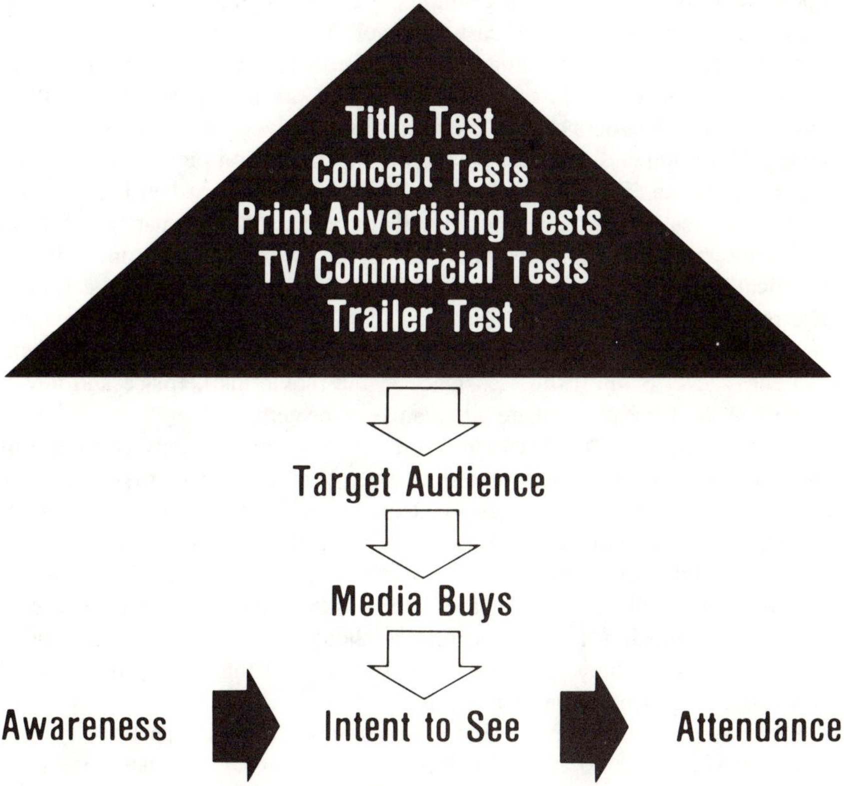

Figure 1
A Typical Marketing Research Program

titles alone give the moviegoer the least amount of information about a picture and generate the lowest level of interest in wanting to see the film. Going down the triangle, as more and more information is added, and especially as visual elements of the film are added, the moviegoers are able to form a more sound basis for their judgments in wanting to see the film. A theatrical trailer, then, typically generates the highest interest-in-seeing level because it shows the cast in the characters they will portray on screen, it is able to outline the story and its elements in greater detail, and, by showing extended scenes from the picture, the trailer gives the potential moviegoer a better idea of the film's production values.

The author's philosophy of marketing research stresses qualitative data over quantitative. The absolute value of an interest score, arrived at a year or so before a film's release, when both researchers and respondents do not have the opportunity for head-on comparisons with unknown competitive film advertising, is of less concern to the author—and other researchers—than determining precisely what each form of advertising communicates about a film, its story, characters, and elements. Does it position the film correctly and present a proper set of expectations of the type of film the moviegoer will see? It is not unusual for a print advertising strategy, for example, to elicit a high interest-in-seeing score (based on the presence in the cast of a well known actor or actress, perhaps) while totally miscommunicating what the film is about. As ultimately a film's performance and the word-of-mouth it develops are highly correlated with the expectations moviegoers have of the film prior to viewing, the aim of advertising strategy development is correct positioning of the motion picture. A qualitative research program aims, at each stage in the development of advertising strategy, to provide creative guidelines to advertising and marketing management. The goal is to arrive at a total advertising campaign (in print, television, radio, and theatrical trailer) that is internally consistent in its positioning of the film and externally consistent with the film itself. The presentation of this campaign in media buys aimed at a film's target audience must create both a sufficient awareness level of the film's existence in the movie marketplace and develop interest in the film to stimulate attendance at theaters.

In the market tests that help shape strategy, one not only starts learning about the potential audience for a film, i.e., whether the advertising generates interest in a particular market segment or across the spectrum of the potential moviegoing base audience, but elements of appeal may be discovered upon which to build from one stage of testing to another. Hopefully, elements are discovered that will broaden the base of the film's appeal, since a truly successful advertising campaign and motion picture should attempt to reach beyond the limited base of frequent moviegoers and attract the interest of the infrequent moviegoing segment of the population.

An advertising campaign that captures only a narrow aspect of a film will almost inevitably fail to attract the interest of a wider range of potential moviegoers. For example, when advertising strategies for *The Rose,* starring Bette

Midler, focused only on Midler, few moviegoers outside the rather narrow spectrum of Midler fans expressed interest in the film. Once a strategy was devised that told the story of a fascinating, complex character who had a dream of becoming "somebody," interest increased beyond moviegoers solely interested in the star. Therefore, a crucial guideline of advertising strategy development is: If strategy aims only for a narrow audience segment, it is unlikely that the film will appeal to a broader audience; and conversely, if the strategy incorporates elements offering the potential to broaden the base of the film's appeal, the narrow audience will still be attracted.

Finally, a marketing research program typically consists of interviews conducted in a one-on-one manner among moviegoers contacted in high traffic locations (shopping malls, for example). Potential interviewees are selected for certain demographic characteristics such as age, sex, moviegoing behavior, liking for a particular motion picture or a type of film, interest in a specific actor or actress, and the like. The interview then proceeds to determine interest in the film as generated by the particular form of advertising being tested, what specific perceptions of the film story are suggested, and, based on the moviegoer's perception of the story, what the interviewee thinks would or would not appeal about the movie. Quite often, when it is not necessary to present visual material to the moviegoer—as in the case of title tests or concept testing—interviewing is conducted by telephone with a random sample of moviegoers in a defined market area or areas. Typical sample sizes range from 100 to several hundred persons.

Title Test

The title, *Star Wars,* was tested more than a year before the film's release. This was the only title tested for the film. The purpose of the testing was to ascertain moviegoers' perceptions of the film conveyed by the title. By itself, the title generated little interest in seeing the film. The predominant theme conveyed by the title was that of a science fiction film centering on some kind of conflict in outer space. The word "wars" was interpreted against moviegoers' recent moviegoing experiences. Since moviegoers had been seeing such films as *Taxi Driver, Two Minute Warning,* and *Black Sunday,* it was not surprising that *Star Wars* communicated a generally unfavorable and violent impression of the film, particularily among female moviegoers. This initial study indicated, as well, that what was percieved as a science fiction film appealed to a limited audience, primarily young male moviegoers, ages 25 and under.

Concept Tests

Several *Star Wars* concepts were tested. At this stage the framework of the film was presented to moviegoers including a story outline, character names and descriptions, and a description of the film's special effects in order to uncover potential elements around which advertising strategies might be developed. In judging the film's title and the framework of the film outlined in concept tests, moviegoers fell back on their last or most recent experience with the science fiction film genre. Thus, the early stages of testing revealed major hurdles for the film's marketing plan. It soon became abundantly clear that the title and concepts generated two stereotypes of the film that only the film itself would be able to surmount successfully. First, that *Star Wars* was just another science fiction film. In 1977, moviegoers' experience with science fiction had been limited to few films of the genre—the most prominent of which was *2001: A Space Odyssey* and, secondarily, *Logan's Run*—and the "Star Trek" television series. In these concept tests, moviegoers judged what they thought *Star Wars* would be like based on stereotypes of science fiction formed by past experience. Typically, they indicated, science fiction films portrayed a future world overrun by space hardware and destructive technology and populated with inhuman aliens and robots. It was also felt that the genre stressed dazzling technological achievements over an involving story and human characters. While these aspects appealed to younger male moviegoers, few female or older male moviegoers over the age of 35 expressed interest.

Second, the concept descriptions outlined a somewhat disturbing element: *Star Wars* was perceived as a science fiction film that seemed more suited to juvenile, than to adult, tastes. Consider these character names and the basic plot description presented to respondents in one of the concepts: Luke Skywalker is a farm boy from a desert planet called Tatooine who suddenly finds himself in the middle of a galactic civil war. His allies include Ben Kenobi, a mystical old gent who is the last of a group called the Jedi knights, Princess Leia, one of the chief rebels opposing the Empire, two wisecracking robots, Artoo Detoo and See Threepio, Han Solo, a daredevil space pilot and his sidekick, Chewbacca, an eight-feet-tall anthropoid. This band of heroes is out to get Darth Vader, a former Jedi knight, and Grand Moff Tarkin, who run the Empire with a group of flunkies and storm troopers. The villains operate out of the Death Star, an enormous satellite designed to go around the galaxy destroying defiant planets unwilling to side with the Empire. The princess is held captive by Tarkin, and Luke's priority is to rescue her and thwart the Empire's attempts to control the galaxy.

Little wonder, then, that the film sounded juvenile in its appeal. As a basic plot point, a boy's efforts to rescue a princess, sounded terribly simplistic. But, this image of the film was exactly what George Lucas set out to achieve. In initiating the project, Lucas felt that the children of today do not have the fantasy life of those of previous generations. Children of today, he felt, lacked the exposure to westerns, the swashbuckling pirate movies, and the fantasy serials so popular in the 1930s and 1940s. At bottom, these film genres were fairy tales or myths with high adventure set in exotic far off lands which were always that place over the hill, be it Camelot, Sherwood Forest, Treasure Island, or the Land of Oz. The elements of these adventure tales were carried down to us, as well, through western films. An admitted fan of Flash Gordon and Buck Rogers and a strong advocate of outer space exploration, Lucas felt that outer space was a natural location for the story he had in mind. He felt such a story would give children of all ages a fantasy world that would get away from the hard facts of *2001* and take them to a romantic image of the future. Film makers had looked at the future from the hardware end of the telescope and now Lucas wanted to view it from the romantic angle—a future world with the romanticism of fairy tales, myths, and real heroes. Thus, by uniting the hardware of science fiction with the romantic fantasies of knights errant and damsels in distress, Lucas would show the world of space as a world filled with fun, fantasy, and adventure—*space fantasy,* not science fiction.

However, in concept tests the traditional stereotypes of science fiction and fairy tales dominated moviegoer images of what *Star Wars* seemed to be and the mainstream of moviegoers failed to combine, in their own imaginations, the elements of science fiction and fantasy and foresee what the film might contain. In the concept stage, one area was uncovered in the research that seemed capable of raising *Star Wars'* story to a level felt worthy of adult entertainment. This was the notion that Luke Skywalker's adventures might be a space-age version of the classic legend of Ulysses' *Odyssey.* Viewed in this context, the Princess' abduction reminded some moviegoers of the story of Helen of Troy. Relating the elements of Greek myths to those of *Star Wars* created a plot framework of epic proportions with a broad sweeping sense of adventure and a grandeur enhanced by the film's promised special effects. The recommendation was made to explore some variation of this theme in the print advertising strategy development.

Print Advertising Tests

Testing of several print advertising strategies for the film continued to show that greatest interest in the movie was expressed by men 25 and younger. However, two test ads, built around the Odyssey theme, positioned *Star Wars* as a quality film. Both ads displayed the copy, "An odyssey to the edge of your imagination and beyond, far beyond." This copy, in conjunction with the film title and appropriate visuals of the film characters and special effects, communicated a story of epic proportions, fast-moving adventure, and imaginative science fiction spectacle. This copy was used for the film's print teaser campaign. The film's final print campaign married the visual elements of one of the Odyssey ads, rearranged to emphasize the human aspect, with copy that is the actual on-screen introduction to the film, "A long time ago in a galaxy far, far away." This copy outlines in one brief statement George Lucas' concept of the film: the elements of all the heroic adventure tales that begin with the line, "A long time ago," combined with the visuals of the film's setting, "in a galaxy far, far away," to clearly communicate *space fantasy.*

Trailer Test

To start building awareness that *Star Wars* was coming, a theatrical trailer was readied for hundreds of theaters nationwide and released in December 1976, five months prior to the film's May 1977 opening date. This trailer was created some eight months before *Star Wars'* release; prepared this far in advance of the still incomplete film, the trailer did not contain many of the key special effects which were still being created, and the trailer was on the theater screens before John Williams finished the film's musical score. In market tests, the trailer conveyed elements of a fast-moving science fiction adventure more than a strong sense of story; and women continued to feel that it presented a typical science fiction film filled with space hardware and alien creatures. This potential problem area was addressed by, as earlier noted, a print advertisement that emphasized the film's human characters (prominently featuring Luke Skywalker and Princess Leia) in the foreground while relegating the hardware aspects to the background. Additionally, just prior to the film's opening, the *Star Wars* television campaign would include commercials incorporating the broader elements of the film, including human characters and relationships as well as the film's dazzling special effects, a sense of its fast-paced adventure, and the like.

Star Wars' Release

Due to complexity of the film's special effects and the deadline of bringing them to completion and preparing 70 millimeter Dolby™ stereo film prints to meet the release schedule, there was no opportunity to test market television commercials or sneak preview the film itself prior to release. At this point, the film had, therefore, unknown commercial status and was targeted for release on May 25, 1977. What has now become common practice—the release of a major film prior to June when the majority of younger moviegoers are out of school—was, in 1977, a rare occurrence. But the Twentieth Century-Fox marketing team placed their faith in Lucas' film and made the decision to release the film in a "window" in the market that avoided head-on confrontation with major June releases, thus allowing unchallenged entry into the movie marketplace. Furthermore, this release date allowed the opportunity—if the film opened successfully—to play throughout the summer months when one has the greatest chance to exploit maximum box-office potential. The film opened in 42 theaters in fewer than 30 cities across America with 70 millimeter Dolby™ stereo film prints in key markets. If the film's pre-eminence could be established in those markets, then, it was felt the film stood the best chance to gain momentum as it spread its release pattern in June and July.

It was clear from title testing, several concept tests, and print advertising strategy tests that all media should impact primarily against 12 to 24 year old moviegoers and, secondarily, against moviegoers ages 25 to 35. No network television campaign was planned due to the limited nature of the initial release pattern. Instead, local television spots were purchased on the basis of the projected release pattern, as it would have been foolish to buy network television, have people see a television commercial, and then not have the film available in a given area for several weeks. Again, as film is an impulse buy, the media buy for television has greatest impact at the time of release. Radio spots were purchased on contemporary stations which would attract the 12 to 24 year old primary target audience. An inexpensive, but potent, form of advertising was college newspaper advertising. Besides local newspaper advertising, print buys were placed in so-called "hip" publications such as *Rolling Stone*.

To determine the film's potential opening strength, a nationwide tracking study, conducted by telephone among a randomly drawn sample of moviegoers in the top 30 movie markets of the United States, was begun one month prior to opening to measure awareness of and interest-in-seeing the film. This type of study seeks to measure, in part, the impact of a film's advertising campaign upon moviegoers just prior to and following its release and their interest in seeing the film (if they have not already seen it). Moviegoers are asked—unprompted—what new movies they have heard about or have seen advertising for. The spontaneous level of recall of a film title is that film's *unaided* awareness level.

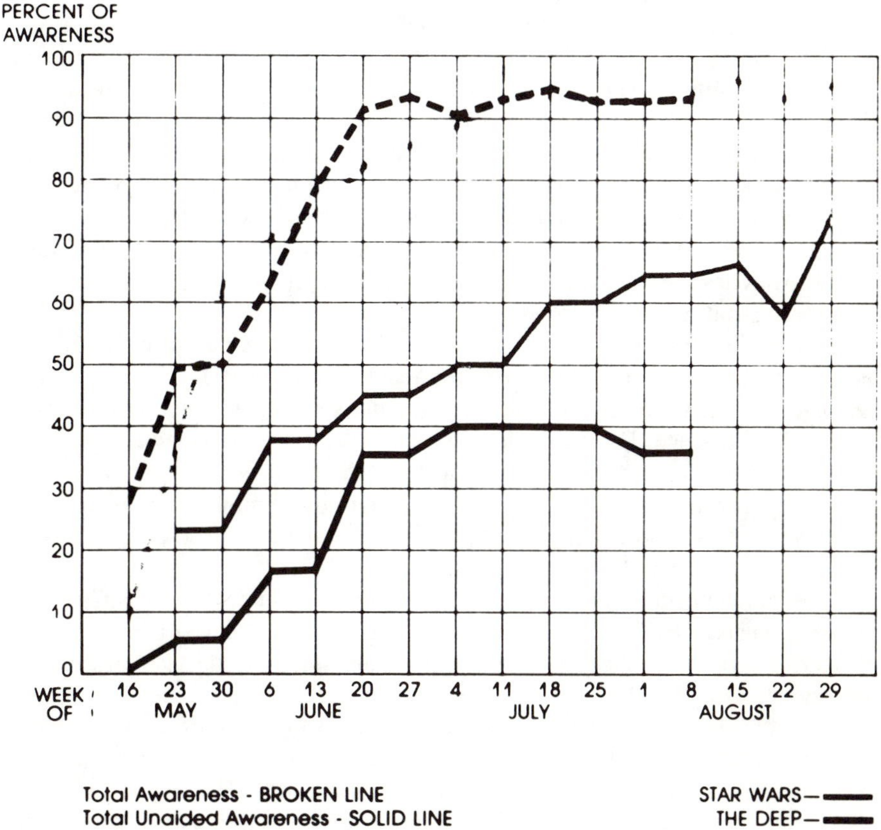

Figure 2
Moviegoer Awareness of Star Wars vs. The Deep

For all current films not named spontaneously, moviegoers are then read a list of titles and asked which they have heard of; this is termed *aided* awareness and, taken together, unaided and aided awareness yield the total awareness level for a motion picture among a nationwide sample of moviegoers. Such studies are routinely conducted on a weekly basis to provide an ongoing monitor of moviegoers' awareness of films, the specific sources of their awareness, and their interest in seeing current and forthcoming films. Figure 2 shows the awareness levels, both unaided and aided, for *Star Wars* as compared to *The Deep, Star Wars'* first major summer competitor. In order to successfully launch a motion picture, historical data shows that the effect of the pre-opening advertising campaign must create an awareness level of 60 percent or better at the time of a wide release in several hundred theaters. But *Star Wars* was scheduled for release in fewer than 50 theaters while *The Deep* would open in several hundred theaters. Still, awareness of *Star Wars* grew from approximately 10 percent at the beginning of May to 64 percent during opening week. Looking ahead for a moment, it can be seen that the most dramatic measure of *Star Wars'* awareness and eventual success was its unaided awareness level—or "share of mind"—among moviegoers. Still in a very limited release pattern, *Star Wars' unaided awareness level* crossed 40 percent—considered the threshold level for a major box-office breakthrough—the week that *The Deep* opened, rose steadily thereafter, and eventually surpassed 85 percent. Post-opening unaided awareness reflects the type of word-of-mouth a film receives. Thus, if a film fails to satisfy its audience and, therefore, generates mediocre to negative word-of-mouth, the film's unaided awareness level starts to plummet; this is the type of film that soon disappears from the marketplace.

Star Wars opened, then, on May 25, 1977, with a carefully coordinated advertising and promotional campaign strategically aimed at the target audience. As just illustrated, this first contact with the market achieved high awareness of *Star Wars'* presence. During opening week, *Time* magazine hailed *Star Wars* as "the movie of the year." *Star Wars* shattered theater house records in virtually every city in which it opened. Viewer reaction to the film in key markets found that *Star Wars'* word-of-mouth level (intent to "Definitely" recommend the film to friends) exceeded 90 percent.

A key element in a moviegoer's intent to recommend a film is the extent to which it meets or exceeds the expectations of the film the viewer carries into the theater. Moviegoers stated that the film transcended *all* the stereotypes and expectations they held prior to seeing the film, based on their previous experiences with science fiction films. For the first time in their moviegoing experience, the respondents reported, a so-called science fiction film was fun and lighthearted. And, even though it featured robots and future technology, audiences were captivated by the humorous and human relationship between the robots, C3PO and R2D2, who quickly became known as the Laurel and Hardy of the robot world. Another factor was the surprising frequency with which moviegoers used the words ''realistic'' and ''believable'' to describe the film. They cited the imagination that went into the film's making and they noted that space hardware looked real in the space environment created for the film. Even within the realm of fantasy, various elements of the film combined to create an atmosphere of realism and fun. And moviegoers reported a feeling of participation; the majority of respondents said they had never experienced such a feeling in a science fiction film before.

POST-RELEASE SURVEYS AND MARKETING STRATEGIES

It would have been easy to claim victory at this point, but *Star Wars* had all the major summer competition to face for its June and July wider release pattern. The film had to maintain the momentum created in the limited release pattern to secure its box-office position as other competitive films were released. Marketing studies were quickly undertaken to assess its box-office momentum in order to secure *Star Wars'* preeminence in the market.

The first post-release effort was directed toward assessing the difference in audience reactions among those who saw the film in 70 millimeter Dolby™ stereo versus those who did not. Dolby™ prints are expensive to manufacture, but the studio was committed to manufacturing more if survey results showed that viewing the film in stereo substantially enhanced audience reaction. The survey clearly showed that Dolby™ stereo was as important a dimension of the film as was the visual. Names and telephone numbers were collected from moviegoers attending *Star Wars* in both stereo and non-stereo equipped theaters in selected markets. Although all moviegoers rated the film, its characters, and elements at levels judged superior, the ratings among those who saw the film in stereo were directionally higher. And, when asked in what way, if any, did viewing *Star Wars* with stereophonic sound enhance enjoyment of the film, the majority described the sound and visual as interrelated dimensions which, they said, took the viewer beyond a passive moviegoing experience to one of active participation in the film. Consequently, more Dolby™ prints were ordered for distribution to meet the timetable of the wider release in July.

During the summer it was natural to expect large attendance by children, high school, and college age moviegoers. But did *Star Wars* have the potential to transcend this audience? Specifically, what was the awareness and interest in seeing *Star Wars* among men and women ages 35 and over? From a nationwide telephone survey, an untapped audience potential was discovered, particularly evident from favorable attitudes expressed toward seeing the film among infrequent moviegoers, ages 35 to 49. These potential moviegoers' reasons for not attending *Star Wars* were not associated with adverse perceptions of the movie. They indicated they were primarily deterred from attending by the long lines and crowds at theaters. With this information in hand, *and* with it becoming clear that

Star Wars had growth potential at the box office over a long period of time, the older, less frequent moviegoer became the target for the 1978 summer advertising campaign.

Another aspect of this survey reinforced the significance of penetrating deeper into this potential audience. Among those over 35 years who had seen *Star Wars,* more than half classified themselves as infrequent moviegoers, i.e., they attend a motion picture less often that once in two months. Then, another national survey showed that through the end of August, four out of every 10 moviegoers showing up at the box office had already seen *Star Wars* one or more times; repeat attendance ranged from once to over 40 times. Thus, at the end of the traditional summer moviegoing season, not only had *Star Wars* started tapping the difficult to reach infrequent moviegoer, but the film was generating exceptional levels of repeat viewing.

An important lesson was learned from tracking the box-office pattern of *Jaws,* at the time the number one grossing film in box office history. *Jaws'* box office fell dramatically following the summer moviegoing period. The number of *Jaws'* film prints was drastically reduced going into this normally deflated period at the box office and, concomitantly, advertising levels to support the film were reduced as well. Since it was apparent that theaters in key markets could easily sustain *Star Wars'* extended play, the studio provided the film prints the market would support and backed the film with attendant advertising, maintaining awareness that the film was still playing. The *Jaws* lesson was learned well as, in November 1977, six months after its initial release, *Star Wars* surpassed *Jaws* as the number one earning film in domestic motion picture history. Then, going into the Christmas holidays, *Star Wars* was treated as a brand new film and promoted with a fresh look and the same advertising support given other of the studio's Christmas releases.

At year's end, the film rental figures for *Star Wars vis-à-vis* its summer competitors (Table 1, below) clearly showed that the anticipated box office

Table 1
Film Rentals Through December 31, 1977[a]
(in millions)

Star Wars	$125.0
Smokey and the Bandit	35.8
The Deep	32.5
The Spy Who Loved Me	22.0
A Bridge Too Far	19.9
Exorcist II: The Heretic	14.0
Annie Hall	13.0
New York, New York	less than 10.0
MacArthur	less than 10.0

[a]*Variety,* 21st International Film Annual, May 17, 1978.

contest proved, ultimately, to be no contest at all. Buoyed by its extraordinary word-of-mouth levels, *Star Wars* outdistanced its nearest box office competition, *Smokey and the Bandit,* by almost $90 million.

In May 1978, one year after its initial release, *Star Wars* was still playing in almost 100 theaters and the film celebrated its first birthday, as an advertising strategy was being prepared for *Star Wars'* withdrawal from the movie marketplace. Its withdrawal was actually accomplished in two steps: one in the summer of 1978, and the second in the summer of 1979.

First, the 1978 strategy—its aim was to attract the over-35 moviegoer. With that audience in mind, a new print campaign was designed in tandem with a massive TV and radio blitz, the largest, most concentrated advertising campaign ever undertaken for a motion picture. The theme of this campaign was a reminder to older moviegoers of the fun of the Saturday matinee, Errol Flynn swashbuckling entertainment experiences of their younger moviegoing days—or how to be a kid again for two hours. At the heart of this campaign was a TV advertising schedule in which at least one *Star Wars* commercial was seen on every prime time television program on all three networks over a three-night period as well as network children's TV programs on a single Saturday morning. The radio campaign was mounted over an eight-day period that slotted at least one commercial per hour between 6:00 a.m. and midnight in every U.S. market. The total campaign had a target saturation of 55 million homes encompassing 150 million viewers and listeners. This strategy for *Star Wars'* media domination was planned with the precision and secrecy of a commando raid, starting with the research which identified the untapped audience potential, and continuing through the design and production of new commercials and buying media time before competitors, or even the networks themselves, knew what was afoot.

As to its success, *Star Wars'* opening weekend of the July 1978 re-release generated $10.2 million at the box office, at the time, a new motion picture industry record. A survey of over 7,000 moviegoers at theaters during the first weekend of this 1978 wide release showed that 54 percent had seen *Star Wars,* ranging from once to over 100 times, and of the 46 percent who had not seen *Star Wars,* the largest portion—almost three-fourths—was accounted for by the campaign's target audience. The weekend after this release, *Star Wars* established itself as the worldwide box office champion, surpassing *Jaws* again, internationally. At year's end *Star Wars* global profits exceeded $235 million after a $9.5 million initial production cost.

Intending to remain the undisputed box office victor, *Star Wars* was released again in August 1979 with a concentrated three-week schedule. Furthermore, this 1979 re-release was used to announce the forthcoming release of the next installment in the *Star Wars'* saga, *The Empire Strikes Back,* which wide segments of *Star Wars'* fans eagerly anticipated. Each print of *Star Wars* was tagged with a preview of scenes from *The Empire Strikes Back* with this fact prominently stated in the re-issue's advertising campaign. This re-issue was again backed by the same kind of multimillion dollar advertising campaign conducted for the 1978 summer release. This re-issue generated more than $10 million at the box office in its opening days and the re-issue, in total, added almost $25 million to its already record-breaking film rentals. A nationwide survey at the time of this re-issue showed loyal fans flocked to theaters—74 percent said they had seen *Star Wars* an average of almost four times, with wide segments claiming 90 or more viewings of the film.

Star Wars' rank as the all-time top-grossing film stood for more than five years until surpassed in January 1983 by *E.T. The Extra-Terrestrial.* At the time of this article's writing in late summer 1983 the third part of the *Star Wars* saga, *Return of the Jedi,* leads the summer box office amassing $127 million in film rentals in seven weeks of release. Based on head-to-head tracking study comparisons between *E.T.* and *Return of the Jedi* it is unlikely that *Jedi* can surpass the box office status of *E.T.* or *Star Wars,* but it has catapulted into the ranks of the top five films, thus placing the entire *Star Wars* trilogy among the most successful films in cinema history.

REFERENCES

1. Scanlon, Paul. "The Force Behind George Lucas." *Rolling Stone* 246, August 25, 1977, pp. 40–51.

2
Giving Them What They Want: Movie Audience Research Before 1950

Garth S. Jowett

> A movie audience is very sensitive. With little experience I could see, hear, and "feel" the reaction to each melodrama and comedy. Boredom was registered—even without comments or groans—as clearly as laughter demonstrated pleasure.
>
> Adolf Zukor (36, p. 42)

In recalling his early years as one of the true founders of the American motion picture industry, Adolf Zukor made constant references to his penchant for "watching" audiences as a means of gauging their reactions to the films that he and his competitors were producing. This habit had started in his 125th Street arcade as early as 1902, and then continued in his larger 14th Street enterprise where he kept a "box office" on the peep show machines, which "proved little except that the public wanted action, romance, and comedy" (36, p. 41). During his long life in the film industry, Zukor continued this practice, and as late as 1953 he was writing that "I feel out of touch unless I pay my money at box offices as I walk about the city and watch pictures with the audiences" (36, p. 43). It was no mere whim which caused Zukor to title his autobiography, *The Public is Never Wrong* (36).

Zukor's trust of his own instincts and observational abilities as an accurate measure of audience preferences was not unique in the motion picture industry. Even now, in an age of sophisticated research techniques, those movie and television executives who claim to have this mystical power are looked upon with awe by some, and disdain by critics who constantly wonder out loud as to who was responsible for the decision to make a certain film or television program. The fact is that no major American industry ever operated with so little research of its market as did the motion picture industry during the period of its greatest influence, from its early years until the mid-1950s.

The reasons for such strange industrial behavior are myriad; much of it has to do with the complex psychology of the founders of the industry whose immigrant backgrounds made them naturally distrustful of any outside authority—they were used to creating and running their own businesses—and their past successes were achieved with precisely the same combination of instinctual and business acumen. These new entertainment entrepreneurs viewed making movies as yet another business, nothing more, and certainly nothing less, and the self-reliant techniques that had made most of them comparatively wealthy in one situation could be trusted to work in another (11, 35).

Almost from the first exhibition dates, the movies were being subjected to close scrutiny because of their apparent influence on the audience; and the founders of the industry, while very proud of their accomplishments, were not eager to proclaim their success in terms of actual audience size. Thus the estimation of audience size and composition came from sources outside the industry, such as journalists, social workers, educators, clergymen and others with an interest in the social control of the new entertainment form (20, pp. 45–46). Clearly, given the mood of the social reformers, the fledgling industry was not going to trumpet the extent of its hold on the American public by providing statistical evidence to support assertions that too many Americans, particularly those under 17, were spending too much time in what Jane Addams called "The House of Dreams" (1, pp. 75–76).

The lack of audience studies coming from the motion picture industry itself can also be explained by the general internal disorganization of the various component activities which made up the entire industry. Who should be responsible for compiling such statistics—the studios, the distributors, or the exhibitors? And who would benefit the most from their accuracy or inaccuracy? Each segment obviously had their own need for audience figures, and more often than not, these statistics were manipulated according to who had the most to gain. (This is still a common practice throughout the industry.) Also, the very last thing that was on the minds of these industry pioneers was the cultural or social significance of their product. In any criticism of the industry for their lack of foresight in not undertaking audience studies, we should also consider the relatively unsophisticated nature of the behavioral sciences at the turn of the century, when empirical examination of the audience was not a normal practice. Certainly, there were no recorded incidents of social scientists requesting research funds from the studios to conduct such studies. (We can only surmise what the answers might have been!)

What is perhaps the most significant factor, and one which we tend to ignore, is that close scrutiny of the box office, combined with what sociologists today would call "unobtrusive observation" was as successful a technique for gauging audience preferences as any yet devised. It was upon this talent, real or imagined that the reputations and fortunes of most of the major Hollywood moguls were based. The biographies of Samuel Goldwyn (23), Irving Thalberg (31), and David Selznick (30), show that this was a skill commonly ascribed to movie executives at this level. Each was seen to have a unique gift for choosing the right properties for the right stars at the appropriate time. Of course there were failures, but these are generally considered to be exceptions and explained away by other, more mundane factors. In Hollywood the key to survival and power often lay in how much of this instinctual ability an executive was able to demonstrate.

The best-known example of such instinctive executive prerogative is the often-told story of Columbia's infamous president, Harry Cohn, who claimed that he had a "foolproof device for judging whether a picture is good or bad. If my fanny squirms, it's bad. If my fanny doesn't squirm, it's good. It's as simple as that." To which equally legendary screenwriter and wit Herman J. Mankiewicz uttered that infamous retort— "Imagine—the whole world wired to Harry Cohn's ass!" Mankiewicz's employment at Columbia was terminated (29, pp. 141–142).

In the face of such impeccable authority, and such obvious ego involvement, it is little wonder that there was almost no need for audience research. That would have to wait for a later period, when the movie industry found itself under siege from television and other newer entertainment diversions, and personal innate instincts were not enough in a world of statistical sampling techniques and computer projections, and budgets for individual films in excess of $50 million.

As late as 1947, Robert W. Chambers, a former director of research for the Motion Picture Association of America noted that: "From the standpoint of statistical knowledge, it has been said that the motion picture industry probably knows less about itself than any other major industry in the United States" (6, p. 169). The result of this failure to adequately document itself had led to a great many myths about the movie industry, and had created a long and seemingly unbridgeable gulf between the industry and well-meaning social scientists and others wishing to undertake research in this area. As an example, in the thirties and forties the estimated weekly attendance figures remained virtually unchanged for long periods of time, despite constant shifts in other areas of the economy. Also, within the industry there were disagreements regarding the actual size of the movie business, and so we are left with the old historical myth that movies were "America's Fifth Industry" (18, p. 123), or Will Hays' assertion that motion pictures stood "well among the first ten industries in this country" (14, p. 34). In fact, as Mae D. Huettig pointed out in 1944, "that in so far as size of industry is measured by dollar volume of business, the motion picture industry is not only not among the first ten, it is not even among the first forty" (16, p.55). Huettig ranked the motion picture industry 45th, behind less glamorous industries such as paper, pulp and related products, liquors, musical and scientific instruments, and cartage and storage. However, to be fair Huettig does point out that when compared to industries in other branches of the entertainment field, in 1939 motion picture corporations accounted for 78 percent of the gross income and 92 percent of the net income of the group (16, pp. 57–58).

To fill this information void, statistics about the motion picture industry were compiled by a wide variety of sources. For economic data the various branches of the federal government were useful, but when it came to audience statistics there were no such clearly defined centralized sources. For almost 40 years whatever audience research findings were made public were the result of private studies, undertaken by well-meaning academics, social workers, and social reformers seeking information in order to pressure for more stringent social control. Unfortunately, very little of this information specifically dealt with the tastes and movie preferences of the audience, and instead tended to concentrate on size and composition, and frequency of attendance; essentially those findings which could best be translated into direct social action. We are thus left to the generalized interpretations of the classic film histories of Robert Grau (12), Terry Ramsaye (26), and the more reliable Lewis Jacobs (17) for understanding the shifts in audience tastes in the early years. While each one of these books serves a purpose, they do not quote any empirical evidence, relying instead on interpreting broad trends to indicate the rise and fall of certain genres. Such interpretations suggest that the industry was responsive to audience tastes as measured at the box office, and that the movie industry's basic philosophy was to imitate success till the audience had its fill, and were ready to move onto something new. (It may be noted that even in this, the "sophisticated" age of motion picture marketing research, this credo still predominates!)

The movies were considered to be an exceptionally fascinating phenomenon by professional observers of the cultural and social scene. Never before had a form of recreational activity captured the imagination of the entire public the way this one had, and it was soon obvious that this was no passing fad, but an entertainment which seemed to provide a degree of psychological comfort as well as being a demonstrable "influence" on the lives of a significant portion of the audience. For this reason it represented for the new emerging "progressive" professions, such as social workers, academics, and municipal managers both an opportunity and a threat to the improvement of social and cultural conditions. For the Progressives, the focus of attention was the child, for children represented the potential for the future, and thus they were the objects of study pursuant to the introduction of relevant legislation aimed at improving social conditions. The movies very quickly became an integral part of the life of urban children, and they were therefore subjected to the same type of scrutiny and evaluation as any other "normal" activity. Except that the movies were not normal, in that they were seen as a potent socializing agent, putting forth "messages" which were considered to be predominantly antisocial. So, while the industry showed little concern for studying itself, there were others who were vitally interested in what "messages" were being sent, and what kinds of films the audience appeared to want.

In this early period there were studies of audience preferences, albeit minor and obscure, but they provided just a glimpse of what the American public liked in their motion picture fare. We begin with simple observations about the content of the short films shown at peep shows, and later in vaudeville houses and the first storefront nickelodeons. In general the public seemed to favor a combination of subjects. They were comfortable with what they were familiar with from their past entertainment experiences, such as vaudeville acts and melodrama (''Butterfly Dance,'' and ''The Bar Room''), while at the same time they were attracted to entirely novel visual excitements provided by the new projected medium, such as travelogues and newsreel-type features (''Venice, Showing Gondolas,'' and ''Kaiser Wilhelm Reviewing His Troops''). These were the actual titles of the short subjects shown during the first historical week at Koster and Bial's Music Hall in late April, 1896 (26, p. 237).

Exactly what the public thought of these films can only be gauged by the fact that it was upon these films that the foundation for the entire motion picture industry was built. Historians can argue about the question of how long audiences remained interested in this type of short subject, and whether or not the movies were used as ''chasers'' in vaudeville theaters (2), but these early films created the interest necessary to establish a solid audience base which ensured the success of the entire industry.

We also know that as separate viewing theaters were developed in the period after 1902, audience preferences did move away from the purely visual spectacle, and strong interest and identification began to develop for fictionalized melodrama with visual appeal. As the traditional audience for theatrical melodrama switched their allegiance to the motion picture, so did the early filmmakers utilize the elements of this stylized theatrical form as a staple ingredient in their own work. As A. Nicholas Vardac has pointed out, ''The conventions of realism of the legitimate stage were apparently in the process of breakdown, and the screen, with its unfailing reproduction of real life, was moving into the breach, taking over a ready-made and waiting audience'' (33, pp. 186–187). It was stories such as these, combined with the comedy-slapstick stories developed from the older vaudeville routines that constituted almost the entire content of movies in the period before 1915 (27).

One of the earliest studies made of movie audiences was conducted in 1916 by Ray Leroy Short (28) as part of the first known M.A. thesis on the motion picture industry. He submitted questionnaires to 1,000 Iowa City schoolchildren asking them ''what kind of moving pictures do you like best?'' Short's tabulation (Table 1) revealed some extremely interesting, and previously undocumented facts concerning the shift in preferences exhibited with age progression. In particular, the decline in popularity of both the Western and the War film, together with the increase in interest in ''love stories,'' ''tragedy,'' and ''scenic and clearly educational'' films as children became older was an interesting, if somewhat obvious fact. This pattern of preferences could be found elsewhere in popular culture, particular in popular reading matter, but this demonstration that such strong taste differentiation was already in operation could have been a

Table 1
% Table Based on 1,000 Written Answers from Iowa City School Children, Grades 5–12, to the Question "What Kind of Moving Pictures do You Like Best?"[a]

Kinds	9th	10th	11th	12th	13th	14th	15th	16th	17th	18th	19th	20th	
	(% of total by age in years)												
Exciting[b]	44.5	58.0	52.4	45.4	42.1	42.1	32.1	20.1	18.7	22.9	15.3	40.0	
Wild West	. . .	31.1	24.1	22.2	15.2	18.1	8.9	4.2	12.5	7.0	12.2	20.0	
War	22.3	7.6	17.2	8.3	8.5	8.8	4.5	4.2	1.2	1.4	. . .	. . .	
Detective/Adventure	11.1	11.6	6.4	5.6	11.1	8.8	10.5	8.3	5.0	11.1	. . .	20.0	
Excitement	11.1	7.7	3.7	9.3	7.3	6.4	8.2	3.4	. . .	3.4	3.1	. . .	
Comedy	22.2	26.8	30.8	36.9	39.7	35.1	35.1	33.3	35.0	26.4	36.5	. . .	
Love stories	11.1	. . .	3.7	5.6	8.5	13.6	16.4	25.9	22.8	29.4	30.2	20.0	
Scenic and clearly educational	11.1	. . .	2.7	4.6	3.6	4.0	6.0	9.1	14.8	12.9	12.0	20.0	
Historical	. . .	. . .	.9	. . .	. . .	.8	1.5	3.3	2.5	1.4	. . .	20.0	
Tragedy	. . .	1.8	.9	1.8	1.9	2.4	1.5	6.6	2.5	7.0	. . .	. . .	
Children's stories	11.1	11.5	6.4	1.8	.7	. . .	. . .	. . .	. . .	. . .	. . .	. . .	
All kinds	. . .	1.9	2.2	3.9	2.8	2.0	6.7	1.7	2.5	. . .	3.0	. . .	
Do not like motion pictures	. . .	. . .	. . .	. . .	.7	. . .	.7	. . .	1.2	. . .	3.0	. . .	
Like to act out pictures seen[c]	44.4	46.2	37.0	41.4	27.0	8.0	2.7	.8	. . .	. . .	. . .	. . .	
Number in age group	9	52	110	108	152	125	134	120	80	72	33	5	1,000 (Total)

[a]*Source:* Short (28, p. 45).
[b]Total of the four following classes; i.e., Wild West, War, Detective, and Excitement.
[c]Submitted to fifth to eighth grades only.

useful revelation to the motion picture industry, if it had taken any notice whatsoever of Short's research, which apparently it did not. (Unfortunately the major thrust of the thesis dealt with mechanisms of social control of the entertainment medium, thus making it certain that the industry would avoid reading it!)

In terms of attendance, Short found that more than 63 percent of the respondents had attended the movies in the prior week, with the average number of attendances of this group being 2.4 per child. As Short noted, with some concern, "one significant fact from the standpoint of school attendance is that practically 70 percent of all admissions were after seven p.m." (28, p. 45). The importance of the younger audience was always understood by the industry; after all it was very difficult for the theater managers to ignore the swarms of children passing through their doors at all hours of the day. Exactly how much of the audience was under 17 was a matter of some considerable conjecture, but no one ever disputed that it constituted the largest segment. This fact created a major problem for the industry which claimed that it essentially made films for adult audiences, and that the younger audience was therefore only incidental to its major target. The industry's public demeanor was, of course, a ploy to remove responsibility for the many claims then being made about "movie influence" (20, pp. 77–83).

The Reverend J. J. Phelan undertook a major study of the motion picture industry in Toledo, Ohio in 1919 as part of his graduate work. While the bulk of the study again deals with issues related to social control and morality, he quoted several surveys dealing with the preferences of schoolchildren. One Portland, Oregon study, done by President Foster of Reed College in 1914, showed that of the 2,647 answers from respondents from nine different grades to the question, "What kinds of pictures do you like best," 36 percent said "comedy," 16 percent said "war," and 15 percent preferred "cowboys and Indians." Unfortunately, we do not know how the age preferences were broken down (25, pp. 53–55). However, a 1918 study of 2,464 schoolchildren in Providence, R.I. was more conclusive (Table 2). Here again we find evidence of changes in preference

Table 2
Movie Preferences, Providence, RI, 1918[a]

Grade	5	6	7	8	Totals
Educational	195	183	317	312	1,007
Western	192	211	186	146	735
Comedy	85	90	99	100	364
Do Not Attend	20	44	47	45	156
Drama	25	34	36	44	139
Comic	5	19	10	29	63
Totals	522	581	695	676	2,464

[a]*Source:* Phelan (25, p. 52).

Table 3
Rural Motion Picture Preferences (1926), Responses (%) to "What Kind of Pictures Do You Like Best?"[a]

"Westerns"	47
"Educational pictures"	15
"Adventure," "pictures full of pep," "fast and exciting," "fight pictures," etc.	11
"Comedy"	10
"Artistic, including classics such as *Ben Hur*"	3.5
"Society pictures"	1.5
"Love stories"	0.2
Miscellaneous: "Cheerful pictures," "country pictures," "pictures with a good moral influence."	11.8

[a]*Source:* Jones and Conrad (19, p. 421).

as age increases, in a similar pattern to that found by Short in Iowa City (25, p. 52).

A much more detailed survey of "Rural Preferences in Motion Pictures" was undertaken in 1926 by Harold Ellis Jones and Herbert S. Conrad as an offshoot of their work on age and mental ability. They had initially used movies as a means of attracting subjects for their testing procedures, and later made them an integral part of the test program as a source of both verbal and pictorial content. Jones and Conrad soon discovered that the movies' "maximum usefulness can be developed only when they are adapted to the interests and preferences of the group which is being studied" (19, p. 419). They asked 200 people from four rural communities in Vermont and New Hampshire "What kind of pictures do you like best?" Responses reported by Jones and Conrad are displayed in Table 3.

The popularity of "westerns" was much higher than we have noticed elsewhere, and when asked which pictures they least preferred, the "great majority" answered "society pictures." As the researchers pointed out: "It is interesting to discover that the peaceful New England Farmer finds his chief satisfaction in stories of the frontier, while the life of Newport, Park Avenue, and Deauville fills him with boredom and resentment" (19, p. 421). Also of unusual interest was the fact that Harold Lloyd was almost twice as popular as Charlie Chaplin, which was due to the fact that "the exuberant and relatively external type of comedy is more readily appreciated than the subtler and psychologically more complex situations developed by Chaplin" (19, p. 423). This esoteric little study raises a very important question about the variation in regional preferences for motion pictures. While the industry did acknowledge such variations, because box-office returns were analyzed on a regional basis, the cultural reasons behind variations were never clearly understood.

In 1926, Alice Miller Mitchell undertook a study of the moviegoing habits of some 10,000 Chicago schoolchildren representing three groups: average public-school children, juvenile delinquents, and a specific group of children who had a certain degree of organized leadership in their lives, such as the Boy Scouts or the Girl Scouts (24, p. 6). Using a combination of written questionnaires and selected interviews, Mitchell put together a remarkable study, clearly influenced by the Chicago School of sociological research, under whose guidance the study was conducted. The results provided a detailed picture of how children used the movies as socializing devices, the role of the movies as part of the "normal" life of the child, and what the patterns of preference were for the various groups.

One basic finding was that 64.1 percent of the entire group of 10,052 children claimed to attend the movies once a week or more. The frequency rate varied from "eight to nine" times a week, (generally among the so-called "delinquent" segment of the sample), to "do not go" (1.7 percent), but as Mitchell pointed out: "The most outstanding factor which apparently influences the frequency of juvenile attendance at the movies is the degree to which some organized recreational interest enters into the life of the child. . . . Left to themselves the children apparently turn to the movies for entertainment" (24, p. 25).

Alice Miller Mitchell was one of the first to study how children select the movies they choose to see. An examination of her findings about this aspect of adolescent moviegoing provides interesting data on an almost totally neglected area of movie research (Table 4). The very minor input by parents in the choice of movies was confirmed by the numerous complaints voiced on this issue. The strength of the "title" as a drawing factor is surprising considering that titles were often misleading, while the "coming attractions" shown in the theaters were not as important as the industry seemed to think.

In Mitchell's chapter dealing with "movies children like," there is a clear indication of the variation in preference patterns with age, but her research provides the additional breakdown by sex, which reveals yet a further variation

Table 4
Method Used by Children in Selecting Movies They Attend (%)[a]

Method	Boys	Girls
Newspapers	21.2	24.7
Title of movie	18.3	18.9
Pictures in lobby of theaters	14.4	9.1
Actors or actresses in movies	8.5	13.3
Recommendation of friends	6.3	6.2
"Coming Attractions" trailers	3.6	2.7
Selected by parents	0.9	2.5
No special method	5.3	4.7

[a]*Source:* Mitchell (23, p. 161).

Table 5
Movie Preference by Age and Sex (%)[a]

	Grade School		High School	
Category	**Boys**	**Girls**	**Boys**	**Girls**
Westerns	34.0	20.2	7.5	6.5
Adventure	13.7	7.2	13.7	6.1
Comedy	11.4	16.5	13.0	10.3
Historical	2.0	4.6	12.9	10.6
Sports	5.3	3.7	11.9	8.0
Romance	4.7	13.3	7.0	22.8
Mystery	6.3	6.8	8.9	8.8
Tragedy	2.1	7.7	5.6	9.9
War	5.1	2.2	3.8	2.2
Educational	1.3	1.4	2.8	2.1

[a]*Source:* Mitchell (24, pp. 111–113).

in preference (Table 5). Once again we see that there is a definite decline in the interest in Westerns as children grow older, while girls clearly enjoy "romance" in their films to a much greater extent than boys. As Mitchell pointed out, "Girls also use the romance movie as a training course in the delicate art of loving and being loved" (24, p. 99). Mitchell's work has been largely ignored; however, her pioneering efforts in trying to discover what kinds of films children liked is still useful in giving us an historical perspective on shifting dimensions of taste.

It is a rather surprising fact that the most extensive series of studies ever undertaken on the impact of the motion picture on American life—The Payne Fund Studies—did not examine the preferences of moviegoers. Completed in 1933, the 12 studies which comprise this series include examinations of the content of movies (9), what children learn from the movies (15), and the patterns of attendance of children (8). None of the studies actually examined in any systematic fashion the preference patterns of their subjects. Herbert Blumer's two studies on "movies and conduct" and "movies, delinquency and crime" used a diary system which elicited information on the types of movies seen, but this information was not categorized systematically (3, 4).

In the mid-1920s, the sociologist Robert Lynd and his wife Helen visited "Middletown," which was in reality Muncie, Indiana. The classic study of life in Middle America which was the result of their research, includes a small, but significant section on the movie-going habits of Middletown's citizens. While "Westerns" were popular, and frequently shown, the Lynds noted that "comedy, heart interest, and adventure" comprised the bulk of what appeared on Middletown screens. Once again, the point is made that Harold Lloyd's comedies drew the largest crowds, with the next most popular category being the "sensational society films." (Apparently Middletown residents were not as provincial as their counterparts in Vermont and New Hampshire!) Westerns and "million dollar spectacles" (*The Hunchback of Notre Dame*) also attracted large audiences to the downtown movie houses (22, pp. 263–269). Middletown's movie preferences seemed to be as normal as any other small city in the nation.

There were few movie preference studies published during the thirties, with most of the research interest on the movies being centered on the aftermath of the publication of the Payne Fund Studies. Henry James Forman's selective misinterpretation of the actual findings of the original research in his much reprinted book, *Our Movie-Made Children* (10) captured the headlines, and attention was now shifted to the question of "movie influence," and more significantly, toward the development of a suitable means of social control (20, pp. 233–259). The little that did appear on the likes and dislikes of the American moviegoer were usually found in books such as Margaret Thorp's paen to the movie industry *America At the Movies* (32), in which she discussed in very general terms the American people's love affair with the screen. Of some disappointment was the failure of sociologists W. Lloyd Warner and Paul S. Lunt to examine motion picture preferences in their detailed study of "Yankee City" (Newburyport, Massachusetts), despite a detailed statistical analysis of the composition of the audience. Their interest in the movies as part of the recreational activities of "Yankee City" seems to assume that all types of movies were attended at the same rate, which was clearly not the case (34, pp. 412–419). Such assumptions about unvaried moviegoing were quite common in the period before 1950, despite constant evidence to the contrary.

It was during the thirties that the movie industry, now beset with the financial woes of the Depression, and saddled with the infamous "Code" worked out jointly between the Hays Office and the Catholic Legion of Decency, began to pay a little more attention to systematizing the feedback provided by exhibitors and patrons, but the major emphasis was still placed on box-office returns.

It was also during the thirties that the "sneak preview," complete with opinion cards to be filled out by those having just watched this extra bonus, became a standard method of judging the potential success or failure of a new release. The major problem with results obtained in this fashion was that too often the audience did not represent a true cross-section of the moviegoing public, especially if the preview was held in the Hollywood area; then the audience would often contain a large number of individuals with a particular interest in the film. Also, there was a tendency for only those who liked the movie to fill out the cards, thus skewing the results in a favorable direction. But, as pioneering audience researcher Leo Handel pointed out, sneak previews were at least a step in the direction of more scientific analysis (13, p. 9).

It is also true that the studios did actually analyze the fan mail sent to their stars. A top star expected about 3,000 letters a week (32, p. 96) and the studios carefully measured and weighed the amount of mail received as a means of gauging the rise or fall in popularity. Here again the danger was that only a small portion of the movie audience wrote letters, and these tended to be largely teenagers and younger women who sought such contact with their idols. But the studios used what was at hand, and many a star found his or her contract not renewed because of a decline in the amount of mail they received.

In the early forties the motion picture industry finally began to use a more sophisticated type of audience research, largely due to the efforts of Dr. George Gallup, who had formed Audience Research Inc. (ARI), headed initially by David Ogilvy. In 1937–39 ARI undertook 194 surveys for RKO president George Schaefer on the moviegoing habits of the American public, and the findings immediately destroyed several of the industry's long-held myths. Gallup's group estimated the weekly audience to be closer to 54 million than the 80 million which the industry had claimed for several years, and the total box office was $700 million, far short of the billion dollars claimed by the Hays Office. ARI also discovered that the long-held belief that females constituted a larger portion of the audience was not accurate, they constituted only 51 percent (a fact which many previous ''amateur'' studies had also established). But more significantly, certain films had much greater appeal for one sex or the other, and Hollywood was not taking advantage of this difference in preference. (An interesting sidelight was the discovery that women did not particularly like comedians. In films and on radio, comedians appealed to men twice as much as women.) Another interesting fact was that in 1940–41, ARI found that there was only a small audience outside of New York which wanted to see pictures about Hitler or the Nazis, confirming the low box-office returns on these films in this period before America's entry into the War (5, p. 73).

This ARI series of studies was among the first to point out that female moviegoers liked male and female stars equally well, but males overwhelmingly preferred male stars because of their much greater preference for ''action'' films. This psychological concept of ''identification'' had been articulated in several of the Payne Fund Studies and other research on movie effects, but Hollywood still did not seem to understand, or know how to market in light of this fact. To underscore this point the ARI research indicated that the number one boxoffice attraction in the U.S. in 1941 was Spencer Tracy, who appealed to men and women equally well (5, p. 73).

In 1945 Bosley Crowther published an article in the *New York Times Sunday Magazine* highlighting for his large audience some additional ARI findings, this time dealing directly with total audience preferences, not just those of children (7). The central finding is found in Table 6. (The table of proportions was tabulated against an index of 100, and with most individuals selecting more than one category, the total adds up to more than 100.) From the results of the thousands of responses to the ARI surveys, it was clearly established that the tastes of moviegoers were significantly stratified, and that there was a remarkable consistency of appeal within these stratifications. Again we find a consistent

Table 6
Movie Preferences (%) by Sex[a]

Category	Males	Females
Musicals	35	49
Light comedy	35	42
Serious drama	23	42
Excitement, adventure	39	25
Slapstick comedy	43	18
Army, navy, aviation	40	23
Detective, mystery	36	24
Romance, marriage	9	32
Westerns	16	7

[a]*Source:* Crowther (7, p. 45).

pattern of female dislike for westerns, and a strong preference for romance, musicals, and light and serious drama; while males liked slapstick comedy, action, and detective films. The relatively low rating for male preference for westerns was also consistent with previous surveys as we have seen above (7, p. 45).

In 1946, in the *Wall Street Journal,* another article on ARI appeared, this time dealing with the manner in which the movie industry was using audience research to market the ''perfect'' film. By this time ARI was offering a full research service beginning with a ''market-want-to-see'' survey, which evaluated the individual drawing power of the title, story and stars, followed by a test of these three elements combined. (ARI discovered that moviegoers liked one word titles.) After the film was released, ARI did ''shown-area'' penetration studies to give the studio some idea of total box-office potential. When combined with penetration studies done before the release, this helped to determine whether the film was living up to its potential. As an example, a high early penetration figure, followed by a low post-release one, indicated that the audience did not like the film as much as they initially thought they would, and the studio needed to give the movie a quick release.

Paul Lazarsfeld, one of the leaders in the developing field of communications research, conducted several motion picture studies through his Bureau of Applied Social Research at Columbia University in the period 1941–1950. Lazarsfeld was mainly interested in frequency of attendance relative to other media activities, particularly radio listening. In a 1947 special edition of *The Annals of the American Academy of Political and Social Science,* Lazarsfeld noted that the study of preferences in audience research was a controversial matter, and that in radio the issue of ''preferences'' had been all but discarded in favor of researching actual listening figures. He went on to point out the dangers of asking ''what movies do you like best'' when most respondents were uncertain about the precise definition of the categories being used (21, pp. 165–166).

Lazarsfeld felt that there were two opposed findings which could be generalized from his study of preferences in entertainment. It would seem logical that people would want to complement their own experiences, thus the city dweller seeks information about how rural people live, or "youngsters want to know what makes grown-ups tick." But this was not usually the case, for, as the experienced social scientist pointed out,

> People want mainly to hear about themselves. In all preference studies we find a strong element of projection. . . . Westerns are most popular in the Rocky Mountains. Old people like movies with a small-town setting and possibly with older heroes. Actually, this projective element in audience preferences is best documented in studies of magazine reading, but it seems to prevail in all mass media. (21, p. 166)

For Lazarsfeld it was unfortunate that on the issue of the study of movie audience preferences there had been no joining of the commercial and scientific interests, for, he noted,

> The movie producers certainly would profit from more detailed information of this kind. And certainly the scientist who is interested in personality and group differences could hardly find a better field in which to make an intensive study—a study of the kinds of movies various people like and why they like them. (21, p. 166)

The most significant research on audience preferences was done by Leo Handel's Motion Picture Research Bureau, which did most of its work for MGM. Handel, in his seminal summary of audience research, *Hollywood Looks At Its Audience* (13), notes the difficulty in creating categories of films which will provide meaningful data. "Westerns," as an example, may be cheap $100,000 class "B" pictures, or an expensive $3 million Technicolor extravaganza, yet both stories come under the heading *western*. Another problem is that most films do not clearly fall under one story type, but contain ingredients from many different types. Handel noted that both his work and that of ARI found that "it is the particular story rather than the story type which determines the interest," and that "the picture type which ranks lowest may be used in a top production with a great cast and an attractive title, and, if skillfully executed, may be an outstanding success at the boy office" (13, p. 119).

In 1943 Handel conducted a detailed series of preference studies, with 2,000 respondents in 45 towns across the country. The results of these surveys were summarized in his book. Each respondent was given the opportunity to choose the two story themes liked best and the two liked least, resulting in more than 8,000 comments for analysis. As shown in Table 7, the comedy complex is well in the lead, with the exception of "slapstick" comedy; while romantic themes were extremely popular with women, but rate rather low with men.

Table 7
Story Preferences (%) of Men and Women[a]

	Men		Women		Total	
	Likes	Dislikes	Likes	Dislikes	Likes	Dislikes
Sophisticated comedies	3.3	2.6	6.3	1.2	4.8	1.9
Family life comedies	2.9	1.0	4.2	.7	3.6	.9
Musical comedies	10.0	1.6	14.7	1.4	12.4	1.5
Just comedies	5.5	.8	4.5	1.7	5.0	1.3
Slapstick comedies	3.8	8.3	1.6	11.8	2.5	10.1
War pictures	15.4	4.7	7.1	9.0	11.2	6.9
Mystery, horror pictures	6.8	5.6	4.8	12.7	5.6	9.3
Historicals, biographies	6.3	5.9	5.2	3.8	5.8	4.8
Fantasies	1.0	6.9	1.3	4.5	1.2	5.6
Western pictures	6.9	7.4	1.5	14.4	4.2	11.0
Gangster, G-men pictures	5.8	5.6	1.8	12.7	3.8	9.3
Serious dramas	6.4	6.6	13.2	2.3	9.8	4.4
Love stories, romance	5.0	11.4	18.0	2.7	11.6	7.0
Sociall significant pictures	1.8	4.3	2.4	1.7	2.1	3.0
Adventure, action pictures	11.8	.7	4.7	1.5	8.2	1.1
Musicals (serious)	2.7	7.0	4.4	2.4	3.6	4.6
Child star pictures	.6	9.1	2.7	4.5	1.7	6.8
Wild animal pictures	1.6	5.0	.5	8.2	1.1	6.6
No preference	2.0	5.4	1.0	2.7	1.5	3.8
Other	.4	.1	.1	.1	.3	.1
Total	100.0	100.0	100.0	100.0	100.0	100.0

[a]*Source:* Handel (20, p. 124).

Somewhat surprisingly, serious drama rated much lower with men than with women, and women showed a strong dislike for westerns, gangster films, and horror and mystery films.

Handel was particularly interested in the audience response to war films, undoubtedly because his major client—MGM—was trying to gauge the market for such films in 1948, now that the war itself was over. Convinced by the statistics that men liked adventure, and therefore war films, he conducted a series of in-depth interviews to determine what women thought about war films beyond the obvious surface reasons such as aversion to fighting, or lack of self-identification for female members of the audience.

His findings showed that women expectedly had trouble with films that contained few women, but in 1948 there were still strong feelings of insecurity and a potential threat to marriage associated with war and the army. Women also preferred films in which the fighting was subordinate to the actual characterizations of the men who do the fighting (13, pp. 122–123). How much of Handel's research was actually used we might never know, but war movies after 1948 showed increased attention to the characterization of the soldiers, and a greater sensitivity to portraying the women in their lives, and the problems of the home front.

Leo Handel collected his research in his 1950 book *Hollywood Looks At Its Audience,* the publication of which occurred precisely at that point in time when the American audience for movies began to decline from their all-time per capita high in 1947 (20, p. 475). As the movie industry was forced to change in the face of television, combined with the inevitable shifts in the leisure tastes of the American people, it began to think about "marketing" its product in order to maximize its financial return. Also, as the making of television and the making of theatrical films blurred in the Hollywood studio operations, the more refined audience techniques from broadcasting were tried, not always with success. The study of film audience preferences is still a very imprecise "science," awaiting some genius who is able to make sense of the vagaries of American popular tastes. Whoever that person may be, their place in the pantheon of the motion picture industry is assured.

REFERENCES

1. Addams, Jane. *The Spirit of Youth and City Streets.* New York: Macmillan Company, 1909.
2. Allen, Robert C. *Vaudeville and Film 1895–1915: A Study in Media Interaction.* New York: Arno Press, 1980.
3. Blumer, Herbert. *Movies and Conduct.* New York: Macmillan Company, 1933.
4. Blumer, Herbert, and Philip Hauser. *Movies, Delinquency and Crime.* New York: Macmillan Company, 1933.
5. "Boy Meets Facts." *Time,* July 21, 1941, pp. 73–74.
6. Chambers, Robert W. "The Need for Statistical Research." *Annals of the American Academy of Political and Social Science* 254, November 1947, pp. 169–172.
7. Crowther, Bosley. "It's The Fans Who Make The Films." *New York Times Magazine,* June 24, 1945, pp. 14–16.
8. Dale, Edgar. *Children's Attendance at Motion Pictures.* New York: Macmillan Company, 1933.
9. Dale, Edgar. *The Content of Motion Pictures.* New York: Macmillan Company, 1933.
10. Forman, Henry James. *Our Movie-Made Children.* New York: Macmillan Company, 1933.
11. French, Philip. *The Movie Moguls.* Baltimore, MD: Penguin Books, 1971.
12. Grau, Robert. *The Theatre of Science.* 1914. Reprint. New York: Benjamin Blom, 1969.
13. Handel, Leo A. *Hollywood Looks At Its Audience.* Urbana, IL: University of Illinois Press, 1950.
14. Hays, Will H. *See and Hear.* Hollywood, CA: Motion Picture Producers and Distributors Association, 1929.
15. Holoday, Perry W., and George D. Stoddard. *Getting Ideas From the Movies.* New York: Macmillan Company, 1933.
16. Huettig, Mae D. *Economic Control of the Motion Picture Industry.* Philadelphia, PA: University of Pennsylvania Press, 1944.
17. Jacobs, Lewis. *The Rise of the American Film.* New York: Teacher's College Press, 1939.
18. Jobes, Gertrude. *Motion Picture Empire.* Hamden, CT: Archon Books, 1966.

19. Jones, Harold Ellis., and Herbert S. Conrad. ''Rural Preferences in Motion Pictures.'' *Journal of Social Psychology,* 1, 1930, pp. 419–423.
20. Jowett, Garth. *Film: The Democratic Art.* Boston, MA: Little, Brown and Company, 1976.
21. Lazarsfeld, Paul. ''Audience Research in the Movie Field.'' *Annals of the American Academy of Political and Social Sciences* 254, November 1947, pp. 160–168.
22. Lynd, Robert S., and Helen Merrell. *Middletown.* New York: Harcourt, Brace and World, 1929.
23. Marx, Arthur. *Goldwyn.* New York: W. W. Norton & Company, Inc., 1976.
24. Mitchell, Alice Miller. *Children and Movies.* Chicago: University of Chicago Press, 1929.
25. Phelan, Rev. J. J. *Motion Pictures in a Typical City.* Toledo, OH: Little Book Press, 1919.
26. Ramsaye, Terry. *A Million and One Nights.* New York: Simon and Schuster, 1926.
27. Sanderson, Richard A. *The Development of American Motion Picture Content and Techniques Prior to 1904.* New York: Arno Press, 1977.
28. Short, Ray Leroy. ''A Social Study of the Motion Picture.'' M.A. Thesis, Iowa State University, 1916.
29. Thomas, Bob. *King Cohn.* London: Barrie and Rockcliff, 1967.
30. Thomas, Bob. *Selznick.* New York: Doubleday & Company, 1970.
31. Thomas, Bob. *Thalberg.* New York: Doubleday & Company, 1969.
32. Thorp, Margaret. *America At The Movies.* New Haven, CT: Yale University Press, 1939.
33. Vardac, Nicholas. *Stage To Screen.* Cambridge, MA: Harvard University Press, 1949.
34. Warner, W. Lloyd, and Paul S. Lunt. *The Social Life of a Modern Community.* New Haven, CT: Yale University Press, 1941.
35. Zierold, Norman. *The Moguls.* New York: Coward-McCann, 1969.
36. Zukor, Adolph. *The Public is Never Wrong.* New York: G. P. Putnam's Sons, 1953.

3

The Influence of Personal Values on Movie Preferences

Boris W. Becker, Barbara Brewer, Bodie Dickerson and Rosemary Magee

Why do people prefer the types of films they do, and why do these preferences vary across types of individuals? A number of reports have suggested that preference for film types may be rooted in fundamental human characteristics.

Bettelheim, for example, emphasizes the role that movies have played in American culture. He sees movies as providing the myths and shared fantasies that create a tie between individuals and groups—a way to find some consensus in spite of great personal differences. The western was "a myth by which one could live and grow" (5). But, to some extent, the western now has been replaced by the science fiction film, a new myth for a new frontier. Indeed, Gene Roddenberry, producer of the *Star Trek* series, explicitly calls *Star Trek* the "wagon train to the stars" (6).

Many comments such as these have appeared, especially in the popular literature. Nonetheless, as Austin (1) has pointed out, few serious efforts have been made to identify the linkages between fundamental human characteristics and film preferences. The purpose of this exploratory study is to suggest, and test, the notion that film preference is related to and based on a most fundamental determinant of a person's attitudes and behaviors—personal values.

The identification of this relationship has important implications, both theoretical and practical. Relating film preference to personal values would allow integration of movie viewing into new and growing theories of choice behavior. Identifying determinants of movie preference and viewing would have powerful implications for film producers, particularly in the development of promotional campaigns to support their movies.

VALUES, ATTITUDES, AND BEHAVIOR

The study of human values has a long, if less than coherent, history. Since the early seventies, interest in the subject has risen and a number of essays and research studies have appeared. Extensive bibliographies and reviews can be found in Becker and Connor (3), Connor and Becker (8) and Rokeach (16).

Exactly what is meant by the term "values?" A reasonably clear consensus regarding a definition of values seems to be emerging among social scientists. Kluckhohn et al. (12, p. 389), defined "values" as "a conception, explicit or implicit . . .of the desirable which influences the selection from available modes, means and ends of action." Building upon this foundation, Rokeach (14, p. 124) defined values as "abstract ideals, positive or negative, not tied to any specific object or situation, representing a person's beliefs about modes of conduct and ideal terminal modes." Values, thus, are global beliefs that "transcendentally guide actions and judgments across specific objects and situations" (14, p. 160).

Values must be distinguished from attitudes, which focus on *specific* objects and situations. "An attitude is an orientation toward certain objects (including persons—others and oneself) or situations. . . . An attitude results from the application of a general value to concrete objects or situations" (19, p. 19). While values are fundamental in nature and few in number, attitudes are more ephemeral and as countless as are objects and situations in the world.

In brief, then, values may be conceived as global beliefs (about desirable modes of behavior and end-states) that underlie attitudinal and behavioral processes. Attitudes are cognitive and affective orientations towards specific objects and situations. Behavior, finally, is a manifestation of one's fundamental values and consequent attitudes.

As has been noted elsewhere, most examinations of values treat them as either an independent or dependent variable, that is, as either affecting or being affected by other variables (3). In this research, values are treated as an independent or predictor variable. Specifically, this study addresses the following question: Is preference for a type of film dependent upon the individual's values? Or, put another way, do personal values of individuals influence their film preferences?

LITERATURE REVIEW

Little is known about the effects of personal values on people's motion picture preferences. A small number of studies, however, have touched at the edges of this question, largely by looking at the influence of personal values on participation in other leisure activities.

Jackson (11) examined the relationship between values and leisure behavior in general. He found that value orientation affected both the individual's choice between work and leisure and the selection among leisure activities.

Urban (20) found that psychological characteristics apparently were more important than demographic or socioeconomic characteristics in predicting heavy magazine readership. Although she did not explicitly measure respondent values, she did find heavy magazine readership related to a strongly felt "need to know." Becker and Connor (4), surmising that this cognitive need may reflect a more basic value orientation, attempted to relate differences in personal values to mass media usage. They found many significant differences among the personal values of heavy users of television, magazines, and newspapers. The personal values of heavy magazine readers were almost the opposite of the values of heavy television watchers.

Additionally, Becker and Connor (2) investigated the personal values of heavy as opposed to light book readers. Their most interesting finding was that the values of male heavy book readers (10 or more books per year) are so different from those of the general population as to constitute essentially a distinct subculture.

Recent research by Otis (13) suggests that movie-viewing is related to fundamental personal characteristics. She found evidence of selective exposure to the film *Close Encounters*. People who chose to view that film exhibited a significantly greater belief in the existence of flying saucers than individuals viewing two unrelated films, *The Gauntlet* and *Saturday Night Fever*.

METHOD

Information on both personal values and movie preferences was collected as part of a larger investigation of values and consumer choice behavior. Subjects were seniors and graduate students enrolled in business classes at a western state university. Three entire classes were selected as a convenience sample; data were collected prior to any discussion of personal values, so as to minimize response bias.

One might argue that students, because of their homogeneity, represent a relatively uninteresting population from which to draw a sample. But, quite to the contrary, a relatively homogeneous sample provides a powerful test of possible values effects. If differences are found in a seemingly homogeneous group, even greater differences might be found in samples of greater heterogeneity.

Respondents were asked to rank order their top three movie preferences from among the following categories: comedy, drama, Disney-type, foreign, horror, musical, non-fiction, pornography, romance, science fiction, violent action, and western. To allow the fullest play of the respondents' values, and to minimize investigator-induced bias, no effort was made to further identify or specify each film genre. A respondent was defined as preferring a type of film if he or she ranked it among the top three choices. Three categories of films were selected for analysis—romance, science fiction, and violent action—since they showed sufficient variation in preference to allow statistically meaningful comparison.

Values were measured by means of the Rokeach Value Survey (RVS), Form D (15). The RVS is one of the most popular structured values instruments, reflecting as it does the Rokeachian concept of values referred to earlier. The RVS contains two sets of values, Terminal and Instrumental. "Terminal" values describe desirable states of the world, while "Instrumental" values describe desirable modes of conduct. Each set consists of a list of 18 distinct values. Within each set, the respondent arranges the 18 values in order of his or her preference. Subjects thus report two sets of 18 rank-ordered values. Standard procedures were employed in the administration of the instrument. Form D uses movable gummed labels, by which the respondent arranges his or her values in the preferred priority ranking. Information on the design of the RVS, together with data on validity, reliability and factorial structure, is available in Rokeach (15).

FINDINGS

Findings will be presented in sequence for the three types of film preferences to be related to values—romance, science fiction, and violent action.

Medians are used in all analyses, rather than means, since the RVS yields ordinally scaled data. "Rank Order" means the ranking of each value according to its median score; for example, the value with the lowest median score (most important) is ranked one, and so on through each set of 18. Because this is an exploratory study with a relatively small sample, the minimum level of statistical significance is set at 0.10.

Romance

Table 1 presents median scores, and rank orders for those medians, for those who preferred romantic films as compared to those who did not prefer romantic films.

Those who prefer romance ranked significantly higher than other respondents the terminal value "salvation" and the instrumental value "forgiving". The romance group ranked significantly lower the terminal values "a world of beauty" and "wisdom," as well as the instrumental values "broad-minded," "imaginative," and "independent."

Rokeach has identified, through factor analysis, several "values factors" that logically group together some of the 36 individual values. Both "imaginative" and "independent" are part of the factor he calls "competence versus religious morality." The romance group also ranked lower than the non-romance group the two other competence values: "intellectual" and "logical." Conversely, the romance group ranked higher than the non-romance group all the religious morality values: "salvation," "clean," "forgiving," "helpful."

Respondents who preferred romance ranked higher all the values on the

Table 1
Personal Values and Preference for Romance Films

Values	Romance (*n* = 25) Median	Rank	Non-Romance (*n* = 62) Median	Rank
Terminal Values				
A Comfortable Life	10.0	(12)	11.0	(11)
An Exciting Life	9.8	(10.5)	7.5	(7)
A Sense of Accomplishment	9.8	(10.5)	7.2	(6)
A World at Peace	9.3	(8)	11.7	(12)
World of Beauty	14.4	(16)	11.9	(13)[b]
Equality	12.1	(14)	13.5	(16)
Family Security	4.8	(1.5)	8.7	(10)
Freedom	7.4	(6)	5.3	(3)
Happiness	4.8	(1.5)	4.9	(1)
Inner Harmony	6.0	(3)	8.0	(9)
Mature Love	8.0	(7)	7.9	(8)
National Security	15.3	(18)	16.0	(17)
Pleasure	12.6	(15)	12.1	(14)
Salvation	11.3	(13)	17.0	(18)[a]
Self-Respect	6.4	(5)	5.0	(2)
Social Recognition	15.0	(17)	12.5	(15)
True Friendship	6.1	(4)	5.9	(4)
Wisdom	9.7	(9)	6.5	(5)[a]
Instrumental Values				
Ambitious	6.8	(4.5)	8.5	(8.5)
Broadminded	9.0	(8.5)	6.0	(3)[a]
Capable	6.8	(4.5)	6.9	(5)
Cheerful	8.7	(7)	9.5	(10)
Clean	12.7	(14)	14.1	(17)
Courageous	12.8	(15)	10.8	(12.5)
Forgiving	9.0	(8.5)	11.9	(15)[b]
Helpful	8.4	(6)	10.8	(12.5)
Honest	3.0	(1)	5.3	(1)
Imaginative	14.4	(17)	8.0	(7)[c]
Independent	11.0	(11.5)	6.8	(4)[a]
Intellectual	11.0	(11.5)	8.5	(8.5)
Logical	13.0	(16)	10.3	(11)
Loving	5.3	(3)	7.5	(6)
Obedient	16.0	(18)	16.9	(18)
Polite	10.2	(10)	12.5	(16)
Responsible	5.0	(2)	5.7	(2)
Self-Controlled	11.6	(13)	11.7	(14)

Terminal Values: Rank Correlation = .76 T-Stat = 4.61 $p = .01$
Instrumental Values: Rank Correlation = .60 T-Stat = 2.97 $p = .01$

[a]Significant by Median Test (X^2), $p < 0.10$
[b]Significant by Median Test (X^2), $p < 0.05$
[c]Significant by Median Test (X^2), $p < 0.01$

"self-constriction versus self-expansion" factor: "honest," "obedient," "polite," "self-controlled." There was no clear pattern on the self-expansion values, with the exception of "broadminded," which was ranked significantly lower by the romance group.

There was a clear distinction between the romance and non-romance groups on yet another factor, "inner versus other directedness." The romance group ranked higher the other-directed value "polite" and lower both inner-directed values: "courageous" and "independent."

The same clear pattern emerged with respect to Rokeach's "love versus respect" factor. The romance group ranked higher both love values, "mature love" and "loving," and lower both respect values, "social recognition" and "self respect."

Finally, the romance group ranked higher all four of the "family versus societal security" values: "family security," "ambitious," "capable," "responsible." The value "family security" is particularly interesting, because it was ranked 1.5 by the romance and 10 by the non-romance group. Two of the four societal security values, "a world of beauty," and "imaginative" were ranked significantly lower by the romance group.

Additionally, the romance group ranked higher the values "a world at peace," "inner harmony," and "cheerful." Ranked lower were "a sense of accomplishment," "an exciting life," and "freedom."

These findings are consistent with research conducted by Spaulding (18), who found that romanticism was strongly associated with religious orthodoxy. Additionally, he found that romanticism was characteristic of individuals to whom a family orientation was important.

The possibility occurs that the apparent differences in values, to some extent, reflect a greater preference for romance films on the part of females. To evaluate this possibility, a chi-square test was done on sex and romance preference. Results of that test indicate that preference for romantic films was independent of sex.

In summary, individuals who prefer romance films seem to have the following value profiles:

1. They have more traditionally religious value systems than those who do not prefer romance.
2. Their value systems are more self-constrictive and more other-directed.
3. Their values imply a greater concern with family than societal security, and a greater concern with other family-oriented values, such as love and affection, at the expense of respect-oriented values.

Science Fiction

Table 2 presents data on personal values of individuals who prefer science fiction movies as compared with those who do not. Those who prefer science

Table 2
Personal Values and Preference for Science Fiction Films

Values	Science Fiction (n = 31) Median	Science Fiction (n = 31) Rank	Non-Science Fiction (n = 56) Median	Non-Science Fiction (n = 56) Rank
Terminal Values				
A Comfortable Life	12.0	(13)	10.1	(11)[a]
An Exciting Life	3.0	(7)	8.2	(8)
A Sense of Accomplishment	9.0	(10)	8.0	(7)
A World at Peace	9.3	(11)	11.8	(12)
World of Beauty	11.6	(12)	13.6	(15)[a]
Equality	12.8	(15)	13.3	(14)
Family Security	8.9	(9)	7.0	(5.5)
Freedom	5.0	(2)	6.8	(4)
Happiness	3.8	(1)	5.5	(1.5)
Inner Harmony	8.8	(8)	7.0	(5.5)
Mature Love	7.6	(6)	8.3	(9)
National Security	16.0	(17)	15.8	(17)
Pleasure	12.7	(14)	11.9	(13)
Salvation	16.9	(18)	16.0	(18)
Self-Respect	6.2	(4)	5.5	(1.5)
Social Recognition	14.1	(16)	13.8	(16)
True Friendship	6.8	(5)	5.8	(3)
Wisdom	5.3	(3)	8.5	(10)
Instrumental Values				
Ambitious	9.8	(10)	6.3	(3)[b]
Broadminded	6.0	(3)	7.3	(6)
Capable	8.8	(8)	6.5	(4)
Cheerful	7.4	(5)	9.3	(8)
Clean	14.4	(17)	13.3	(17)
Courageous	12.6	(16)	10.9	(13)
Forgiving	11.4	(13)	10.7	(12)
Helpful	10.6	(12)	10.1	(10)
Honest	4.2	(1)	5.6	(2)
Imaginative	8.3	(7)	10.5	(11)
Independent	7.6	(6)	7.8	(7)
Intellectual	9.0	(9)	9.5	(9)
Logical	10.3	(11)	11.3	(15)
Loving	6.0	(3)	7.3	(5)
Obedient	16.9	(18)	16.4	(18)
Polite	12.1	(15)	12.2	(16)
Responsible	6.0	(3)	5.3	(1)
Self-Controlled	12.1	(14)	11.0	(14)

Terminal Values: Rank Correlation = .88 T-Stat = 7.38 $p = .01$
Instrumental Values: Rank Correlation = .86 T-Stat = 6.61 $p = .01$

[a]Significant by Median Test (X^2), $p < 0.10$
[b]Significant by Median Test (X^2), $p < 0.01$

fiction films ranked significantly higher the terminal value "a world of beauty," and significantly lower the terminal value "a comfortable life," and the instrumental value "ambitious."

"A world of beauty" is part of the "societal versus family security" factor, as is "imaginative," which is also ranked much higher by science fiction devotees. Those preferring science fiction films ranked lower all four family security values: "family security," "ambitious," "capable," and "responsible."

The pattern for the "competence versus religious morality" factor was essentially the opposite of that for the romance group. While the differences between those who do and do not like science fiction were not as marked as in the case of romance films, the pattern is highly consistent. The science fiction group ranks higher all the competence values ("imaginative," "independent," "intellectual," "logical"), and lower the religious morality values ("salvation," "clean," "forgiving," "helpful").

In common with the romance group, the science fiction group emphasizes those values on the love end of the "love versus respect" factor. Albeit somewhat marginally, the science fiction group ranked higher both "mature love" and "loving," and ranked lower "social recognition" and "self-respect."

Additionally, the science fiction group clearly ranked higher the terminal values "freedom," "happiness," and "wisdom," together with the instrumental values "broadminded" and "honest."

A chi-square analysis suggests that, in the case of science fiction films, preference was related to sex of respondent, with males showing the greater interest in this genre. Rokeach has suggested that different values may lead to the very same behavior, and that seems to be true with respect to a preference for science fiction films. Males who preferred science fiction films ranked higher than did females who preferred science fiction films the values "freedom" (M–1; F–8) and "logical" (M–10; F–16.5). Female sci-fi fans ranked higher than male fans "inner harmony" (F–2.5; M–9.5) and "forgiving" (F–7.5; M–9.5).

In summary, individuals who prefer science fiction films have a value system somewhat less distinctive than do those who prefer romance. Respondents who preferred science fiction exhibited the following value profiles.

1. The science fiction group tends to rank the competence values higher than does the non-science fiction group, at the expense of traditional religious values, which they rank lower.
2. Their value systems place less emphasis on family security and more on societal security.
3. They rank as more important those values relating to love than values relating to respect.

Violent Action

The notion of what constitutes "violence" may have depended largely on the perspective of the beholder. Violence ranges from a cartoon character being

Table 3
Personal Values and Preference for Violent Action Films

Values	Violent Action (n = 34) Median	Rank	Non-Violent Action (n = 27) Median	Rank
Terminal Values				
A Comfortable Life	9.5	(9.5)	11.0	(12)
An Exciting Life	7.0	(7)	10.3	(11)[b]
A Sense of Accomplishment	6.3	(3.5)	8.3	(8)
A World at Peace	13.5	(14)	9.0	(9)
World of Beauty	12.8	(13)	14.1	(16)
Equality	14.5	(16)	12.3	(14)[a]
Family Security	8.5	(8)	6.0	(3)
Freedom	4.8	(2)	6.9	(4.5)
Happiness	3.5	(1)	7.8	(7)
Inner Harmony	10.0	(11)	6.9	(4.5)
Mature Love	6.3	(5)	9.8	(10)
National Security	15.5	(17)	15.9	(18)
Pleasure	11.7	(12)	12.2	(13)
Salvation	16.0	(18)	15.0	(17)
Self-Respect	6.7	(6)	4.4	(1)
Social Recognition	14.0	(15)	13.7	(15)
True Friendship	6.3	(3.5)	5.6	(2)
Wisdom	9.5	(9.5)	7.6	(6)
Instrumental Values				
Ambitious	8.0	(6)	5.9	(4)
Broadminded	6.5	(4.5)	7.1	(6)
Capable	6.5	(4.5)	6.9	(5)
Cheerful	8.5	(8.5)	9.4	(9)
Clean	11.5	(15)	13.6	(16)
Courageous	10.5	(12.5)	11.8	(13)
Forgiving	12.5	(17)	8.8	(7)[c]
Helpful	10.5	(12.5)	9.3	(8)
Honest	5.7	(1)	3.0	(1)
Imaginative	8.2	(7)	14.3	(17)
Independent	6.0	(3)	9.8	(10)
Intellectual	8.5	(8.5)	10.0	(11)
Logical	10.0	(11)	13.0	(15)
Loving	8.8	(10)	5.7	(3)
Obedient	16.8	(16)	15.9	(18)
Polite	11.0	(14)	12.1	(14)
Responsible	5.8	(2)	4.6	(2)
Self-Controlled	11.9	(16)	10.8	(12)

Terminal Values: Rank Correlation = .73 T-Stat = 4.33 p = .01
Instrumental Values: Rank Correlation = .63 T-Stat = 3.19 p = .01

[a]Significant by Median Test (X^2), $p < 0.10$
[b]Significant by Median Test (X^2), $p < 0.05$
[c]Significant by Median Test (X^2), $p < 0.01$

flattened paper-thin by a steamroller, to aerial war scenes, to graphic close-ups of gruesome murders. Violence is likely to be an integral part of other movie categories, particularly science fiction, western, and horror. For this reason the "non-violence" preference group was defined by a different method from that used for the other genres. To be placed in the "non-violence" group, the respondent's top three categories had to exclude the four categories of violent action, science fiction, western, and horror. This procedure, necessarily, reduced the sample size for values comparison; the violent action group consisted of 34 individuals and the non-violent group 27.

Table 3 presents data on the values of those who prefer violent action films as compared to those who do not. Those who prefer violent action, not surprisingly, ranked the terminal value "an exciting life" significantly higher than those in the non-violence group. The violent action group ranked significantly lower the terminal value "equality" and the instrumental value "forgiving."

Those in the violent action group ranked higher all four of Rokeach's "immediate versus delayed gratification" values: "a comfortable life," "an exciting life," "pleasure," "clean." Conversely, they ranked lower three of the four "delayed gratification" values: "inner harmony," "wisdom," "self-controlled."

A similarly almost perfect division occurred on the "competence versus religious morality" factor. The violent action group ranked higher all four competence values ("imaginative," "independent," "intellectual," "logical") and lower three of the four religious morality values ("salvation," "forgiving," "helpful").

Additionally, the violent action group ranked higher the values, "a sense of accomplishment," "a world of beauty," "happiness," and "mature love." They ranked lower "a world at peace," "family security," "self-respect," and "loving."

The significantly lower evaluation of "equality" by the violent action group is particularly interesting in light of research on the effects of television violence. Gerbner (9, p. 195) has suggested that media violence may be a means of enforcing acceptance of social inequality. Whether the same effect can be attributed to movies is an interesting conjecture and a point for future research.

In this instance, there is again a significant difference in preference for violent action films by sex of respondents; far more men than women prefer this genre.

In summary, moviegoers who prefer violent action would seem to have the following value profile:

1. They emphasize immediate as opposed to deferred gratification.
2. They are more concerned with competence values, and less with values related to religious morality.

Cross-Category Comparisons

In an attempt to focus more clearly on inter-group value differences, the values of groups who prefer each of the three genres were compared against each other. Responses were sorted to eliminate overlaps in preference.

The greatest contrast in personal values occurred when those who prefer science fiction were compared to those who preferred violent action films. A statistically significant difference was found in the evaluation of nine values, and the rank correlation between the entire value systems of these two groups is the lowest of any comparison made. Those who prefer science fiction ranked higher societal values and delayed gratification. The violent action group, on the other hand, ranked higher competence, immediate gratification, and family security values.

Comparing the romance with the violent action group, the former clearly still ranked higher the religious morality, self-constriction and other-directed values. The violent action group ranked higher the competence, immediate gratification, self-expansion, and inner-directed values.

Finally, contrasting the romance and science fiction groups showed again that the former group ranked higher those values involving religious morality, self-constriction, and family security. Those who prefer science fiction ranked higher the competence values.

This "finer-grained" comparison essentially reinforced the findings obtained when each group simply was compared to all other respondents. Some value differences appear very consistent, regardless of the nature of the comparison being made. The implications of these differences are discussed in the following section.

DISCUSSION

Personal values clearly have an effect upon individuals' preferences for types of movies. Those who prefer romance movies have the most distinctive value systems as compared to those with other preferences examined here. The rank correlations of their entire value systems with those who prefer the other two genres are the lowest and there are numerous interesting differences in individual values and values factors.

To recapitulate, those who preferred romance films, as compared either to the remainder of the sample or to those who preferred other specific genres, emphasized the values related to religious morality, family security, and self-constriction. Those who preferred science fiction emphasized values of societal security and competence, while those who preferred violent action emphasized even more highly the competence values together with immediate gratification.

These results are interesting both for theoretical and practical reasons. First, as indicated in the introduction to this article, little is known about the fundamental motives that determine movie preference and, by implication, movie choice behavior. If values are as fundamental as scholars such as Kluckhohn and Rokeach suggest, then a valuable insight has been gained into the motives of moviegoers. Additionally, research on the influence of values on movie preferences can be related to the growing body of knowledge on personal values and human behavior. Recent papers by Carman (7) and Gutman (10) have formulated theoretical models of consumer choice behavior, in which personal values play an important role.

This research also presents intriguing implications for managerial decision-making. If film producers can identify the fundamental values of individuals who prefer different film genres, then promotional campaigns for specific types of films can be designed to appeal to those values. Thus, romance films can be promoted using (perhaps surprisingly) appeals to religious morality or family security. Science fiction films can be promoted as appealing to people who have strong "competence" values—a high need to know and understand. Beyond those fairly obvious implications, more ambitious efforts can be made to segment the film market on the basis of values differences.

For example, the group that preferred romance exhibited a value profile remarkably similar to the value profile found by Becker and Connor for heavy television viewers (4, pp. 38–39). This correspondence suggests that television may be a particularly appropriate advertising vehicle in reaching those people who prefer romance films. If print media are to be used in promoting a romance film, vehicles that are read by heavy television viewers, such as *TV Guide* or *Soap Opera Digest,* might be particularly appropriate. Further, the themes or campaign platforms used in the television advertising could be designed to appeal to the values of the romance group. Similarly, those who preferred science fiction had values quite dissimilar to television viewers and more similar to that of magazine readers; again the implications for media selection and copy platforms are obvious.

CONCLUSION

Personal values are fundamental, parsimonious bases of both attitude and behavior. The findings of this study suggest that personal values influence individuals' movie preferences. The value systems of individuals who prefer romance, science fiction, or violent actions films are different in many regards. Knowledge of these differences will both contribute to theoretical understanding of moviegoing behavior and to managerial decision-making by film producers.

This investigation suggests a number of possibilities for further research. First, the sample population consisted of college students, a very homogeneous group. A larger, and preferably probability-based, sample would allow greater generalizability of the findings. A larger sample would also allow finer-grained distinctions; for example, do values of black females who prefer romance differ from those of black females who do not prefer romance? The modest sample size of the present study did not allow subdivision of the respondents.

Second, the labels or genre offered as choices to respondents were based upon a review of the literature and upon the investigators' preconceptions. An extremely interesting question is the underlying dimensionality of film types. It is entirely possible that viewers, or segments of the viewing population, do not classify films according to the classification employed in this study. There do exist techniques for identifying the fundamental dimensions of "perceptual maps" by which individuals organize stimuli about them. One such technique, non-metric multidimensional scaling (17), may be particularly appropriate to the film classification problem.

This study is an exploratory effort. Nonetheless to find many interesting and often statistically significant differences with a sample of modest size suggests that additional research is warranted. The question of personal values and film preference is complex and interesting. Much remains to be done—only the tip of the iceberg has been sighted.

REFERENCES

1. Austin, Bruce A. "The Motion Picture Audience: A Neglected Aspect of Film Research." Paper presented at the Ohio University Film Conference, April 1982, available in ERIC ED 214 211.
2. Becker, Boris W. and Patrick E. Connor. "The Influence of Personal Values on Book Reading Behavior." *Journal of Library Administration* 3 (1), Spring 1982, pp. 13–23.
3. Becker, Boris W. and Patrick E. Connor. "On the Status and Promise of Values Research." Paper presented at the annual meeting of the Academy of Management, August 1979.
4. Becker, Boris W. and Patrick E. Connor. "Personal Values of the Heavy User of Mass Media." *Journal of Advertising Research* 21 (5), October 1981, pp. 37–43.
5. Bettelheim, Bruno. "The Art of Moving Pictures." *Harpers,* October 1981, pp. 80–83.
6. Blair, Karin. "The Garden in the Machine: The Why of Star Trek." *Journal of Popular Culture* 13 (2), Fall 1979, pp. 310–319.
7. Carman, James M. "Values and Consumption Patterns: A Closed Loop." In Keith Hunt (Ed.) *Advances in Consumer Research,* Volume 1. Ann Arbor, MI: Association for Consumer Research, 1977, pp. 401–407.
8. Connor, Patrick E. and Boris W. Becker. "Values and the Organization: Suggestions for Research." *Academy of Management Journal* 18 (3), September 1975, pp. 550–561.
9. Gerbner, George, Larry Gross, Nancy Signorielli, Michael Morgan and Marilyn Jackson-Beeck. "The Demonstration of Power: Violence Profile No. 10." *Journal of Communication* 29 (3), Summer 1979, pp. 177–196.
10. Gutman, Jonathon. "A Means-End Chain Model Based on Consumer Categorization Processes." *Journal of Marketing* 46 (2), Spring 1982, pp. 60–72.
11. Jackson, Royal G. "A Preliminary Bicultural Study of Value Orientations and Leisure Attitudes." *Journal of Leisure Research* 5 (4), Fall 1973, pp. 10–22.
12. Kluckhohn, Clyde, and others. "Values and Value-Orientation in the Theory of Action." In Talcott Parsons and Edward A. Shils (eds.) *Toward a General Theory of Action.* Cambridge, MA: Harvard University Press, 1951, pp. 388–433.

13. Otis, Laura. "Selective Exposure to the Film Close Encounters." *Journal of Psychology* 101, 1979, pp. 293–295.
14. Rokeach, Milton. *Beliefs, Attitudes and Values.* San Francisco, CA: Jossey-Bass, 1968.
15. Rokeach, Milton. *The Nature of Human Values.* New York: Free Press, 1973.
16. Rokeach, Milton. *Understanding Human Values: Individual and Societal.* New York: Free Press, 1979.
17. Romney, A. Kimball, Roger N. Shepard and Sara Beth Nerlove. *Multidimensional Scaling: Theory and Applications in the Behavioral Sciences,* 2 Volumes. New York: Seminar Press, 1972.
18. Spaulding, Charles B. "The Romantic Love Complex in American Culture." *Sociology and Social Research* 55 (1), October 1970, pp. 82–100.
19. Theodorson, G. A. and A. G. Theodorson. *A Modern Dictionary of Sociology.* New York: Thomas Y. Cromwill, 1969.
20. Urban, Christine D. "Correlates of Magazine Readership." *Journal of Advertising Research.* 20 (4), August 1980, pp. 73–84.

4

Influences of Previews on Movie Viewers' Expectations

Susan Tyler Eastman, David E. Bradbury, and Robert S. Nemes

Previews of upcoming movies are a significant element in motion picture marketing strategy. Previews seek to influence the process of selection among movies by commending exciting components of a film to the public (6, 12). Gantz and Eastman (9) surveyed television viewers about the influence of promotional materials on television program choices, and some research has looked into the influence of previews on theatrical movie attendance decisions. Austin (4) reported that about half of the audience planned in advance to attend, while the remainder decided on moviegoing before selecting a specific film. Newspaper ads, word-of-mouth and TV ads have been shown to influence the selection of movies (3, 5), and Hungerford (10) examined the salience of television commercials in attendance decisions. Daly (7), however, found that nearly half of moviegoers learn about a movie at the last minute. In one unusual experiment, Burzynski and Bayer (6) experimentally tested the influence of overheard conversations about films, finding that what was overheard before a screening may affect the viewer's appreciation of a movie. Although writers have pointed to the influence of previews on attendance, they have rarely touched on the possible influence of different types of previews on the audience's reaction to the movie. If audiences use previews in deciding whether to attend a movie, they may accommodate a film in part according to the length and format of the preview they see.

Before a feature film premieres, audience expectations may be shaped by theatrical previews screened during earlier theater attendance or by commercial advertisements on television. A new theatrical release is typically announced to the public by means of a short preview, called a "trailer," weeks or even months before the release date of the film. The National Screen Service (NSS) is the sole nationwide distributor of trailers and printed accessories (posters, photographs and other displays). Publicly held, NSS operates nine branch offices in the U.S. and ships about 20,000 trailers a week to about 13,000 U.S. movie theaters (see

11, 13). Very short announcements called "teasers" sometimes precede regular trailers. Teasers are generally intended for showing in combination with trailers for other upcoming movies. A regular trailer then replaces the teaser as the release date of the movie approaches. Typically, teasers are 90 feet long (one minute) while trailers range from 150 to 275 feet (just over two minutes to just under five minutes). Trailers begin appearing on theater movie screens about four weeks prior to release of a film.

Theatrical previews, however, frequently appear to oversell aspects of the content of a particular film, and managers of movie theaters regularly deal with angry patrons when viewing produces a marked disparity between their expectations and the actual content of films (2). One of the few published studies touching on previews reported that audience members expressed a strong desire for greater honesty in film advertising; as one respondent put it, "When movies are so overblown, they tend to be a letdown" (1). Burzynski and Bayer (6) found that exposure to positive, negative or no prior information in conversations overheard before entering a movie theater may affect audience members' appreciation of a subsequently-viewed movie (though their "positive" and "negative" experimental groups showed no significant difference when compared to a control group, leaving ambiguity in their findings). Inaccurate film promotion in previews may create a minor social irritation that is compounded by its perceived frequent occurrence. The escalating cost of movie theater tickets, of course, and any dissatisfaction with recently seen movies may contribute to patron irritation. Previews, then, comprise another unstudied element of the moviegoing context, mutually influencing perception of a feature film and being influenced at the same time by the viewer's prior experience with previews.

This study examined audience expectations about one feature film during its regional premiere to analyze the effects of the movie's previews on audience expectations about the content of film and their degree of satisfaction of expectations after viewing the entire film. The field test was conducted in a first-run commercial suburban theater by manipulating the previews for *Thief* shown to attending audiences during the regional opening on three successive testing nights (weeknights). One audience was shown a teaser (N=49), another a trailer (N=54) and the third no preview at all (N=31) before the screening of *Thief*. The third group functioned as a control group to permit weighing the differences in expectations between seeing a preview for *Thief* and not seeing any preview.

Thief, a high-tech crime motion picture directed by Michael Mann (also director of the Emmy-winning TV movie, *The Jericho Mile*), stars James Caan as ex-con who aspires to a dream life formed during his 11 years in prison (*Newsweek,* March 30, 1981, p. 82). He uses safecracking as the means to his goal of a glamorous life complete with wife and child, cars, clothes and money; he then finds he must fight to preserve his independence from "the organization," eventually giving up the wife, child and possessions to attain his greater dream, freedom. The movie focuses on the technical processes of the crimes and the strained relationships between the thieves, their fences and their pursuers, the police. *Thief*'s plot depends on the continual rebuilding of suspense after repeated eruptions of violence (explosions, gunfire, car chases and more explosions). The previews, as might be expected, capture the episodes of violence, excluding the long periods of narrative build-up that occupy most of the film and are the director's *tour de force*.

Based on previous findings (1, 2, 6, 14, 15), it was hypothesized (a) that the viewing of previews for *Thief* would significantly heighten audience expectation on six content dimensions; (b) that those viewers exposed to the longer form of the preview (the trailer) would report greater strength of expectations after seeing the preview than those seeing the shorter preview (the teaser); and (c) that the audiences seeing a preview for the film would have greater unfulfilled expectations after seeing the actual movie than the audience that did not see a preview.

METHOD

In this field experiment, three different treatments were administered to three sets of patrons in a commercial theater. One audience saw only a teaser for *Thief*, one saw a trailer, and one was not exposed to any previews (control group). Questionnaires assessed audience expectations on Likert scales ("strongly disagree" to "strongly agree") to six statements about violence, suspense, suffering, action, romance and adult sexual content in the movie, based on dimensions identified by Dengler (8). The teaser (90 seconds) and trailer (126 seconds), industry-generated promotional previews obtained from National Screen Service, were scheduled immediately before the main attraction, *Thief*.

The three-page, tri-colored, self-administered form was distributed with pencils when the two experimental groups entered the seating area. Each page was collected by aisle attendants after they asked that it be filled out (identified by color). Demographic items appeared at the end of the last page. One page was collected before the screening began, one after seeing the preview, and one after seeing the entire film. Sixty-five percent of the available audience on the first two nights completed all three pages of the questionnaire. The control group received a two-page questionnaire as they entered the theater; they filled out the first page before seeing the movie and the last page after the movie was shown. Approximately half returned codable pages as they left the theater.

On the first and second pages of the three-part questionnaires, patrons were asked to indicate the extent to which they agreed or disagreed with the six statements reflecting their perceived expectations of the amount of suspense, suffering, action, violence, romance and adult sexual content in the movie. Statements used the form: "I expect this movie to have a lot of violence." On the third page, the format of the item-statements was altered to "The amount of suspense in this movie was———," and viewers were asked to respond on a five-step scale ranging from "less than expected" to "more than expected." The change in format and scale permitted comparison of all three groups on the third questionnaire as well as comparison of page one (disagree/agree) to page two (disagree/agree) for the two treated groups and across all three groups on page one. It did not allow for a direct statistical comparison between the third scale (less/more than expected) and the first/second scale (disagree/agree), although it permitted comparison of all groups with a neutral position (3.00 on the Likert-type expectation scale).

Since a limited number of television advertisements had aired before the film's theatrical premiere, the influence of this variable was assessed statistically by creating a subgroup of those audience members who recalled seeing TV ads for *Thief*. The reading of newspaper ads and critical reviews was not assessed. Since the movie was just opening, the first-night audience was not likely to have chosen to attend based on peer comment, although word-of-mouth might have influenced some patrons on the following two nights. At a minimum, patrons would attend expecting a soon-to-be-released feature film produced by a major studio. Once into the theater, wall posters for *Thief* told the star and the crime (safecracking) while hinting at the high-tech filming style.

RESULTS

Comparisons among the three audiences showed no significant differences in demographic composition on items measuring age, education and frequency of attending movie theaters. Examination of the means for all six dimensions on the first and second pages of items completed by the "preview" group, using a MANOVA design, showed an increase in expectations for the entire treated group between the first set of items (base-line measure, pre-preview) and the second set of items (post-preview but pre-movie). This supported the first hypothesis that seeing a preview would generate increased expectations in audiences—although a bias created by testing might account for some of the increase.

As is reported in Table 1, t-tests showed significant differences on four of the six dimensions tested. The means for responses to items measuring "suspense," "suffering," "violence" and "romance" were significantly different after viewing the preview, but the means for "action" and "adult sexual content" were not. This response pattern suggests that seeing a preview may have initially increased the audience's expectations, focusing their attention on four significantly different dimensions.

A (matched) t-test comparing the two experimental groups showed no significant difference in expectations on the second questionnaire or on the post-test (administered after screening the movie), failing to support the second hypothesis that the length of the preview would generate stronger expectations on

Table 1
Comparison of Expectations Before and After Viewing Previews and Comparison of Realizations of Expectations in the Movie

Content Category	Group *n* of Control = 31 *n* of Treated = 103	Expectations	Realizations (Compare to 3.00)
Suspense	Control	Pre-preview = 3.80	3.58
	Treated	Post-preview = 4.22[a]	3.40
Suffering	Control	Pre-preview = 2.08	3.39
	Treated	Post-preview = 3.06[a]	3.44[a]
Action	Control	Pre-preview = 4.37	3.81[a]
	Treated	Post-preview = 4.62	3.50[a]
Violence	Control	Pre-preview = 3.41	4.16[a]
	Treated	Post-preview = 4.20[a]	3.84[a]
Romance	Control	Pre-preview = 2.59	2.06[b]
	Treated	Post-preview = 3.03[a]	1.96[b]
Adult Sexual Content	Control	Pre-preview = 2.81	1.90[b]
	Treated	Post-preview = 2.87	1.75[b]

[a]Significant at .05 level.
[b]Significant at .05 level with negative direction.

the six dimensions. The two experimental groups were combined, therefore, in subsequent analyses, creating a treated group of 103 who saw a preview and a control group of 31 who did not. A test comparing the small subgroup (N=7) that recalled seeing a TV ad for *Thief* showed no differences from the overall sample.

The control was compared to the treated group on the base line measure. No significant difference was found between groups on expectations of the movie on the six dimensions we measured.

Finally, t-tests compared the realization of expectations in the movie (third set of items) with a neutral score (3.0 on the less/more than expected scale). Neutral responses indicated that the movie exactly met audience expectations (had neither less nor more than expected); a score exceeding the neutral point (3.1–5.0) meant the movie had more of some particular content than the viewer expected; a score below neutral (1.0–2.9) meant the movie had less than the viewer expected on some dimension. Table 1 shows a significant difference between expectations and the actual film for both the treated and control groups on four of the six dimensions and a significant difference on a fifth dimension, "suffering," for the treated group only. "Suspense" was not significant for either group. The means for "romance" and "adult sexual content" were lower than the neutral point, indicating that the movie had less of these content dimensions than the audience expected, irrespective of whether they saw a preview. All other significant expectations were in a positive direction, meaning the movie contained more than the patron anticipated. Thus, the third hypothesis was not supported.

DISCUSSION

These findings showed that these movie audiences reported higher expectations on four of six dimensions after seeing a preview. The length of the preview, however, created virtually no difference in expectations in this experiment. This may have occurred because the two treatments were too similar in length and style; greater differences between teasers and trailers might produce another finding in future research. All patrons expected less action and violence in the movie *Thief* than they actually experienced while they also expected more romance and adult sexual content than they actually found. In addition to the trailer, the audience's expectations may have been set by their experience of moviegoing in general and by the types of roles the star played in other films. Less compelling, yet perhaps plausible, explanations would include: the audience's experience with that director (relatively unknown), that movie theater (general audience schedule) or the posters in the entryway (unlikely since the posters focused on safecracking and did not show a female figure).

The patrons who saw a preview showed stronger expectations of ''suffering'' after seeing a preview, while also perceiving even more suffering in the movie than they anticipated. On this dimension, then, viewing a preview appeared to create greater expectations that suffering would be a major movie element, while it in fact was not; viewers who saw a preview found significantly more suffering than they anticipated. This seems to indicate that the previews for the movie *Thief* were not an accurate indicator of the motion picture's content.

The length of a preview, and by assumption, its quantities of various types of content, did not significantly alter audience expectations. This suggests that the brief teaser for this film captured as much of the content of the actual movie as the longer trailer (with the same degree of accuracy). This finding may not generalize to teasers and trailers for other movies, especially those in other genres.

In general, then, this field experiment showed that previews may generate expectations of content that are not fulfilled by viewing the movie. There is some indication that previews may add to or reinforce aspects of the expectations the audience possesses when entering the movie theater. Whether the expectations acquired earlier were generated by the title of the movie, its stars, word-of-mouth publicity (as shown by Burzynski and Bayer, 6) or general social conditions (the historical milieu), cannot be assessed from a study of a single movie, but might be examined in tests of expectations across several films. Although this study found that trailers had at least a short-term effect on expectations, generalization from this study is necessarily limited because of the large number of confounding variables and the use of a restricted form of self-report in a manipulated field setting.

REFERENCES

1. Audienscope. "Report on Pre-Release Preferences of Moviegoers for December, 1976 Features." *Film Bulletin* 45, 1976, pp. 4–6.
2. Audienscope. "Moviegoers Tell What Pleases Them . . . What Turns Them Off." *Film Bulletin* 46, 1977, pp. 2–30.
3. Austin, Bruce A. "Portrait of a Cult Film Audience: *The Rocky Horror Picture Show.*" *Journal of Communication* 31, Spring 1981, pp. 43–54.
4. Austin, Bruce A. "Portrait of a Contemporary Drive-In Movie Theater Audience." Paper presented to the International Communication Association Convention, May 1983, Dallas, TX.
5. Austin, Bruce A. "The Motion Picture Audience: A Neglected Aspect of Film Research." In *The Film Audience: An International Bibliography of Research with Annotations and an Essay*. Metuchen, NJ: Scarecrow Press, 1983.
6. Burzynski, Michael H. and Dewey J. Bayer. "The Effect of Positive and Negative Prior Information on Motion Picture Appreciation." *Journal of Social Psychology* 101, 1977, pp. 215–218.
7. Daly, David A. *A Comparison of Exhibition and Distribution Patterns in Three Recent Feature Motion Pictures*. New York: Arno Press, 1980.
8. Dengler, Ralph. "The Language of Film Titles." *Journal of Communication* 25, Summer 1975, pp. 51–60.
9. Gantz, Walter and Susan Tyler Eastman. "Viewer Uses of Promotional Media to Find Out About Television Programs." *Journal of Broadcasting 27, Summer 1983, pp. 269–277.*
10. Hungerford, Chris. "A Survey of Los Angeles Theater Attendance of Two Motion Pictures Which were Advertised on Television." M.A. thesis, University of Southern California, 1955.
11. Lazarus, Paul N. "National Screen Service Corporation," pp. 234–236. In William A. Bluem and Jason E. Squire, *The Movie Business*. New York: Hastings House, 1972.
12. Mayer, Michael F. *The Film Industries: Practical Business/Legal Problems in Production, Distribution, and Exhibition,* 2d ed. New York: Hastings House, 1978.
13. Michel, Martin. "National Screen Service," pp. 373–377. In Jason E. Squire, *The Movie Business Book*. Englewood Cliffs, NJ: Prentice-Hall, 1983.
14. Silvey, Robert and Judy Kenyon. "Why You Go to the Cinema." *Films and Filming* 11, June 1965, pp. 4–5.
15. Ward, Phillip R. "The Consensus Mind of Moviegoers." *Film Bulletin* 45, 1976, p. 4.

5

The Development and Decline of the Drive-In Movie Theater

Bruce A. Austin

In America, with the advent of the automobile, a plethora of ancillary industries was spawned; a virtual car culture. The root beer and hamburger stands and billboards that populate the highways—in fact, even the highways as we now know them—came about in large part as a response by business interests to tap the mobile consumer's wallet. In addition to these, other industries developed later, once the car became more than simply a mode of transportation. Thus we saw the rise of custom car shops, their parts suppliers, and mechanics/artists, who built and serviced the kandy-kolored tangerine-flake streamline babies (101). And, half a century ago, in the midst of a catastrophic economic depression, a prescient entrepreneur developed the drive-in movie theater. At first a curiosity and later a point of moral concern, the "passion pits" or "parking lots for petters" have nevertheless endured as a form of film exhibition and today, in their golden anniversary, account for 21 percent of all U.S. movie theaters (41, p. 30A). Little, however, has been written in a comprehensive fashion about this form of film exhibition. This article examines the development, growth, and contemporary status of the U.S. drive-in movie theater. In addition to the historical overview of this form of exhibition, results of a field study involving personal interviews with patrons for one drive-in are reported, thereby painting an empirical portrait of a current drive-in movie theater audience.

THE FIRST DRIVE-IN

The innovation of indoor film exhibition occurred virtually simultaneously around much of the globe. In contrast, however, the development and exploitation of the outdoor form of movie exhibition "was unquestionably an American phenomenon" (51, p. 234). Anecdotal reports, often touting Yankee ingenuity, refer to farmers who stretched bed sheets between telephone poles on which to project movies as enterprising entrepreneurs who ''launched an era'' (36, p. 136). Such stories no doubt contain elements of truth but also represent only isolated, unorganized novelties—the stuff of legends, perhaps, but not meaningful in the sense of the development of an industry. Reports found in numerous sources indicate that the innovation of what might truly be called the first drive-in movie theater is credited to a chemical manufacturer named Richard Milton Hollingshead, Jr. (see 5, 7, 12, 16, 22, 23, 25, 31, 66, 68, 90). Along with his cousin, Warren Willis Smith, they formed a company, Park-In Theatres, Inc.

In early June, 1933, Hollingshead opened his drive-in movie theater in Camden, New Jersey. A modest initial effort, the theater contained seven semicircular rows of parking spaces with 50-feet wide aisles. It accommodated some 400 cars, each parked on a 5-percent grade. The first film projected on the 60-feet wide screen was *Wife Beware* starring Adolphe Menjou; there were three shows an evening. Sound for the film was possible due to the RCA Victor Company's newly perfected directional sound system, similar to the one used in Radio City Music Hall. Early press reports called the drive-in ''a colosseum for movie-minded motorists'' (7) while later ones described it in almost suspicious terms as ''an elaborate scheme designed to make the patron feel that the movie theater is his natural home'' (94, p. 61).

As history would show, Hollingshead correctly believed that the drive-in would be attractive to the public since it combined ''the two luxuries which he felt that people in a depression would give up last—automobiles and movies'' (54, p. 352). Convenience and informality, it seems, were other incentives which portended success for the drive-in as a business. An August 1933 story in *Business Week* reported that Hollingshead ''thought people would enjoy movies where they could dress as they please, smoke, talk, and eat supper at the same time'' (25).

TECHNICAL AND LEGAL CONCERNS

For the drive-in to grow and prosper, various technical problems had to be confronted and overcome. Physical construction of the screen tower and projection room, building of auto ramps and their maintenance, and other matters needed to be attended to (34). An initial concern was that of the location of the drive-in. Beyond the physical space requirements for accommodating automobiles, drive-in operators needed to locate optimally their sites for the convenience of their patrons. This resulted in consideration of traffic patterns and access roads (34). Early reports also recommended construction of drive-ins near laboring class rather than white-collar communities (16, p. 154), given what was thought to be the theaters' audience.

Flaherty described the early drive-in sound system (34, p. 69):

> The first drive-ins were primitive affairs and depended on a "blast system" to distribute sound to the cars. Powerful loud speakers were hung on the screen tower and on poles placed around the ramp area. With this method patrons nearest the speakers had too high a level of sound, and people in adjoining houses and farms could also hear the sound.

With the introduction of the "In-Car" speaker by RCA Victor in 1941, this problem was largely resolved—at least temporarily.

In 1953 Downs noted that among the possible technical changes to come was "the use of autonomous electronic sound receivers instead of loudspeakers connected to posts" (16, p. 161). By the 1970s his suggestion was being adopted as a means for helping the drive-in prosper (see 83, 84); in 1982 it was estimated that some 20 to 30 percent of all drive-ins had converted to low-power AM radio carrier current sound systems (18). A number of companies presently offer such systems under various product names including: "Cinema Radio" (New York), Radio Systems, Inc. (Edgemont, PA), "Tune-A-Movie" by Loc Rad, Inc. (Tucson, AZ), "Radio-Cine" by LPB, Inc. (Frazer, PA), "Cine-fi International" (Los Angeles), and "Polecate Radio Sound" (Redondo Beach, CA). Such systems typically involve wiring the theater lot with underground cables; patrons use their AM car radios to tune in the film soundtrack which is emitted from the underground cables in a quasi-broadcast fashion (see 18, 32, 37). Drive-in radio sound offers the advantages of eliminating replacement, maintenance, and repair of speakers and poles as well as improved sound quality (18). At the same time, however, without speaker posts automobiles may not be distributed efficiently over the parking lot (37) and signal "spillover" may disturb nearby residents by interfering with their home television and radio receivers (18). Moreover, the signal leakage might provide incentive for and "free admission" to nonpaying patrons parked adjacent to the theater with the sound they would not have had were it not for the radio sound system.

Other technical requirements which had to be met by the early drive-in operators included: screen luminance, heat dissipation, projection optics, projector mechanisms, and weather-proofing (see 81, pp. 94–105 for an early report; for more contemporary information see 37). Downs suggested in 1953 the possibility of developing "some method of showing films when there is still some daylight, or perhaps even full daylight" (16, p. 161). This, of course, would put ozoners on an equal footing with hardtops in terms of the number of screenings which could be offered daily. Screen technology became increasingly important to drive-in operators as expanding numbers of suburban multiplexes stiffened competition among film exhibitors and as complaints concerning the screening of R- and X-rated movies at drive-ins increased (discussed below). Efforts at developing a true "daylight containment" screen were redoubled during the mid-1970s in the hope of producing a brighter image—or at least one comparable with the indoor screens—while at the same time containing the image to only paying customers (see 20, 71, 75) and ensuring the life of the drive-in form of exhibition (84). Currently, in 1983, the Protolite Screen is the result of these efforts. Plotkin describes the Protolite screen as being made of stainless steel, its surface "composed of thousands of tiny convex and concave mirror elements" which are optically designed to permit "the control of the image so the surface can maximize the image quality for virtually any viewing situation." Protolite is promoted as being long-wearing, three to four times brighter and offering better contrast color and sharpness than present screens. The image quality is good enough for projection at any time—not just after dusk. The screen itself allows for three different images to be projected on a single screen with each image confined to a designated section of the drive-in, thus offering the multiplex option to outdoor theaters while preserving their single screen. Finally, Protolite contains the image to just the theater so that movies can be exhibited without regard to nonpatrons (79, pp. 64–65).

The issue of drive-in screen image containment is not limited to technological, economic, or competitive concerns—it encompasses legal issues as well. Early on, drive-ins were faced with such legal matters as zoning regulations, allegations that they caused traffic hazards, "and even occasional charges by moralists of contributing to the delinquency of minors" (62, p. 402). More recently private action and pressure have been brought against drive-in exhibitors regarding local zoning and public nuisance laws (82, pp. 151, 160–161). Perhaps the most benign level of such nuisance law actions involved the closing of theaters by a specified time, although this had the clear potential for hurting business by reducing the number of times a film might be shown, limiting the number of features exhibited (e.g., double or triple bills), or eliminating dusk to dawn movie marathons held at drive-ins. More serious are the nuisance actions concerning drive-in theaters whose screen is visible to nonpatrons (e.g., where the screen can be viewed from adjacent roadways). In particular, the exhibition of R- and X-rated pictures at drive-ins has been the focus of attention: "Some local legislators seem to believe that the playing of certain films at these drive-ins comprises a 'public nuisance' against which localities can legislate" (64, p. 145). Despite Mayer's assertion that such action "seems a most dubious proposition in view of the First Amendment rights that are affected" (64, p. 145), numerous such incidents have taken place. In 1974 the Baltimore County Council voted unanimously to prohibit drive-ins from showing X-rated movies on screens which could be seen by the nonpaying public with the result that "drive-in owners will have to erect expensive fencing or switch to more subdued fare" (69). In Berlin, Connecticut the town closed a drive-in because of a 20-feet hole in the fence around the theater which had been installed to block the screen from nonpatrons; a Federal judge ordered the reopening of the drive-in, however, based on First and Fourteenth Amendment arguments (17). Most recently, at the time of this writing, the theater manager and projectionist at the Miami Cruise-In

Theatre near Dayton, Ohio, were arrested on charges of pandering obscenity for screening the X-rated *Sexual Heights* in July, 1983 (99).

A final legal concern to be discussed here involves patent law. Hollingshead went so far as to patent the three key components of the drive-in: a fan, or clam-shell, shaped parking lot, terraced parking rows, and earthen ramps which tilted the cars upward (16, p. 153; 31, p. 89; 90, p. 102). Using this patent as his company's key asset, Park-In Theatres offered blueprints and franchises to other exhibitors. In return the exhibitors paid a flat fee of $1,000 and a 5 percent royalty on their gross receipts (31, p. 89). Slowly, resistance and then outright refusal to this franchising plan built. In a spate of suits, Park-In Theatres brought to court nonpaying exhibitors (see, e.g., *Park-In Theatres, Inc.* v. *Paramount-Richards Theatres et al.* 81 F. Supp. 466, 90 F. Supp. 727, 90 F. Supp. 730, 185 F. 2d 407, 71 SCt 1017; *Park-In Theatres, Inc.* v. *Ochs et al.* 75 F. Supp. 504, 75 F. Supp. 506; *Park-In Theatres, Inc.* v. *Waters et al.* 185 F. 2d 193; *Park-In Theatres, Inc.* v. *Perkins et al.* 190 F. 2d 137; *Park-In Theatres, Inc.* v. *Rogers et al.* 130 F. 2d 745). The Loew's Drive-In Theatre chain finally broke Hollingshead's franchise by refusing to pay the royalties; Loew's claimed that Hollingshead did not hold a patentable invention (16, p. 153; 31, p. 89). Although a lower court ruled in favor of Hollingshead's suit for unpaid royalities and patent infringement, this ruling was overturned by a Federal Circuit Court (see *Park-In Theatres, Inc.* v. *Loew's Drive-In Theatres* 70 F. Supp. 880 and 174 F. 2d 547) and the Supreme Court refused to hear an appeal (see *Park-In Theatres, Inc.* v. *Loew's Drive-In Theatres* 70 SCt 68, 338 U.S. 822) (16, p. 153; 31, pp. 89–90; 90, p. 102). The Court ruled that Hollingshead's inventions were landscaping and architecture and were therefore not patentable. By 1951, when the legal entanglements had been settled and Hollingshead's monopoly was broken by judicial decision, imitators were relieved of extra economic burdens.

THE GROWTH OF THE DRIVE-IN

Although the early drive-in movie theaters may have "catered to the American dream of mobility" (59, p. 53), they were not an instant success—at least not in terms of widespread adoption or diffusion. By the end of World War II one author estimated that there were "only some 60" drive-ins nationwide (62, p. 401) while the Sindlinger Company placed the number at 300 (86, p. 41). Following World War II, however, the drive-in form of exhibition experienced rapid growth. Downs (16, p. 153) attributes this expansion to three factors: "the rise in automobile ownership and use; the high level of general prosperity . . . and the particular features of drive-in theaters." Clearly, the curtailment of consumer automobile production and gas rationing which occurred during the war slowed the drive-in's development. When these restrictions were lifted, though, Americans enthusiastically took to the road. Between 1946 and

1952 consumption of gasoline by U.S. motorists increased 63 percent while during the same time span the number of drive-ins jumped to 3,276 (86, p. 41).

The postwar prosperity also brought population migration from the cities to the developing suburbs (see 92). Since even a modest-sized drive-in requires some 10 to 15 acres of land, their construction was impossible in the densely populated urban centers. The suburbs offered both physical and population availability to exhibitors with the potential for high profits. Investors found construction and operating costs relatively inexpensive, damage to the physical plant minimal, and high concession sales possible (21). By 1954 the Council of Motion Picture Organizations (COMPO) was identifying the drive-in as accounting for one of three "significant changes" in the pattern of movie attendance. Based on data gathered by Sindlinger, COMPO reported that drive-ins "accounted for almost half of the weekly motion picture attendance during the months of July and August for the years from 1952 through 1954" (11, p. 2). *Business Week* stated that about 20 percent of the total U.S. movie box-office gross was attributable to drive-ins (26, p. 129; see also 50, p. 47); other authors put the figure closer to 25 percent (see 90, p. 31). Table 1 displays data from 1948 to 1976 relevant to both the number of drive-ins in operation and the percentage of film revenues they accounted for. These data indicate that drive-ins did not account for one-fifth or more of the U.S. film revenues until the close of the 1950s and that the percentage of revenues earned by drive-ins peaked in the mid-1960s, declining steadily thereafter. Still, articles and photo essays in popular periodicals reporting the boom in drive-in construction and attendance were abundant (see 19, 26, 31, 33, 47, 49, 90, 92, 97). In 1941 the largest U.S. drive-in

Table 1
Film Revenues Accounted for by U.S. Drive-Ins

Year	Number of U.S. Drive-Ins[a]	% of All U.S. Theaters that were Drive-Ins[b]	% of All U.S. Film Revenues by Drive-Ins[c]
1948	820	4.5	2.9
1954	4,062	21.3	16.2
1958	4,700	29.4	19.9
1963	3,550	27.7	24.0
1967	4,900	27.4	24.4
1972	2,790	26.4	22.7
1973	3,800	25.9	22.4[d]
1974	3,772	24.5	22.1[d]
1975	3,801	23.8	21.8[d]
1976	3,800	23.8[c]	21.5[d]

[a]From Sterling and Haight (89, pp. 35–36) except 1976 which is from Gertner (39, p. 31A).
[b]From Morton Research Corporation (67, p. 16).
[c]Calculated from Sterling and Haight (89).
[d]Estimates by Morton (67).

was located outside of Evanston, Illinois and had room for 1,500 cars (28). Seven years later a drive-in in Asbury Park, New Jersey, was opened which could accommodate 500 cars and 25 airplanes; an airstrip adjoined the theater and planes could taxi to a ramp which faced the screen (35). By the late 1950s the 28-acre All-Weather Drive-In Theater was opened in Copiague, New York. This theater featured space for 2,500 cars, an air-conditioned indoor theater seating 1,500, a cafeteria, and an amusement park and playground (see 9 and 65). With the development of such a "Colossal Drive-In," Hine's 1952 prediction of thousands of customers attending one drive-in by the 1980s became a reality (see 49, p. 11). Even terrain, it seems, would not deter the committed drive-in investor. In hilly San Francisco, Robert L. Lippert, owner of the Lippert Theater chain, overcame the lack of flat, open land large enough for a drive-in with an amphitheater design and built a terraced drive-in holding 554 cars (27).

Downs' reference to "the particular features of drive-in theaters" (16, p. 153) and Handel's comment on drive-ins' distinctive characteristic of offering patrons "privileges" of convenience (48, p. 211) as reasons for the rapid growth of drive-ins are easily verified by the kinds of innovations and gimmicks used by drive-in operators to make their businesses more attractive. The Theatre Owners of America distributed a 14-page booklet detailing "ticket-selling ideas for drive-in theatre showmen" in 1958; 59 individual ideas "for promotion and exploitation" were detailed (91). A St. Louis operator of an indoor-outdoor theater featured two screens, one of which was specifically designed for showing 3-D movies to drive-in patrons (63); the Multiscope (80) and Autoscope (22) systems provided for individual screens for individual autos; the management of Phoenix's Cinema Park Drive-In installed a system of propeller blades throughout their lot which dispersed water as a fine mist thus acting almost like air conditioning (30); a Tennessee drive-in installed a while-you-wait laundry service as an additional inducement to customers (76). Most popular among the gimmicks offered to drive-in moviegoers were those which would encourage and make convenient attendance by the entire family. One author described the drive-in as a "total entertainment service" (62, p. 406). Thus, at different drive-ins one could find such extra features as playgrounds, shuffleboard, horseshoes, miniature golf and driving ranges, wading pools and swimming pools, baby bottle warmers, fireworks, pet facilities, and laundromats (see 5, 16, 31, 33, 36, 47, 49, 62, 66, 81, 90). All of this led *Commonweal* to conclude in a 1956 article (47): "As the whole family is frequently in tow, the drive-in has a graphic way of underlining the vehemence of the human desire to be entertained at all hazards." Three years before Downs (16), Luther identified 10 "advantages of drive-ins" which are in part analogous to Downs' reference to "the particular features" of drive-ins. Among the 10 Luther itemizes are: drive-ins "boast the world's largest screens," offer "a wide variety of subsidiary attractions" (as noted above), are "handy for the aged and handicapped," are less costly in terms of admissions and ancillary (e.g., parking) expenses, and provide privacy for the patron. Luther also notes some "limitations" of the drive-in including: "the battle with the elements," "claims that drive-ins are becoming driving hazards," and public acceptance which, however, "has happily proved to be less formidable than some of the other factors" (61, pp. 42–43).

While the innovation of the drive-in was uniquely American, its adoption was not limited to U.S. exhibitors. Thompson wrote that "nationally, the success of the drive-in theater chains was keyed to two factors: climate and driver registration" (93, p. 47). These two factors also suggest disadvantages in countries with intemperate climates and smaller driving populations (as well as the attendant economics of automobile ownership). Horton asserted "that the drive-in never caught on as more than a curiosity in Europe" due to the lack of wide open spaces, high land prices, and differences between the European and American attitude toward the use of automobiles (51, p. 238). Yet foreign drive-ins have been more than a mere curiosity. The first non-U.S. drive-in, the Metro Drive-In Cine, located outside of Rome, opened at the end of August 1957 and was operated by the American theater chain, Loews (81). The Metro had room for some 750 cars and 250 scooters, sent bilingual dialogue through its sound system, and was equipped for winter operation (19, 81, 92). Loews also had a 1,400 car twin drive-in in Sydney, Australia and opened a 1,000 car theater in Perth on April 20, 1957 (81, p. 93; see also 13 and 92). Between July 1956 and July 1957, 21 drive-ins opened in Australia and by the close of the 1950s there were some 50 Australian drive-ins (81). Denmark opened its first drive-in outside of Copenhagen in 1961 with space for 550 cars and used "a tiny transistor radio set for sound" which was supplied to each car (14)—a piece of technology which, as noted above, was not to become popular in the U.S. until much later. In Canada there were more than 100 drive-ins by 1952 and, during the same year box-office receipts were up 32 percent for the ozoners while hardtops showed only a 9 percent gain (8). So popular were Canadian drive-ins that a 1949 report stated that construction of at least 30 new ones were planned by various exhibitors, including seven by the nation's largest chain, Famous Players Canadian Corp. (24). Despite the scarcity of land, 18 drive-ins were squeezed into West Germany (56). Moreover, in 1977 and 1978 these drive-ins were reported as attracting the most patrons (38) and were among the theaters which were doing the best business (100), a distinct upturn from 1976 when half the drive-ins were reported as "deep in the red" and "only still in existence because they belong to huge cinema chains like Olympic or UFA" (56). Drive-ins could also be found in such countries as Rhodesia, Egypt, Venezuela, and Iraq, according to a 1951 UNESCO report (98).

In 1976, when television was introduced in South Africa, drive-ins, especially, were hit hard: "the fall-off in family trade was especially steep." To combat TV's impact the South African drive-ins shifted their admission procedure from a per person charge of 85 cents to a flat rate of $2.30 a vehicle (87).

In the U.S. the available literature on the effect of television on drive-ins is somewhat ambiguous. The drive-in movie-viewing experience has been described in terms virtually analogous to that of the televiewing situation: "seeing a movie in an automobile is like having a private box in an indoor theater. . . . A drive-in is not one theater: it is a series of separate theaters . . . united only by the single screen and the refreshment stand at the rear of the lot" (16, p. 149). Another writer noted that "for the audience the drive-in has many of the conveniences of television" (21, p. 104) and that it "proved a unique means for bringing back some of the 'lost audience' " in the 1950s (21, p. 104; see also 16 and 50). A key reason for the success of drive-ins, according to one author, was that "they are the answer to parents who want to take in the movies, but can't leave their children alone at home" (31, p. 22). Another writer went so far as to conclude that, during the time of TV's introduction and widespread adoption, "the fifties were the golden era for drive-ins" (51, p. 235). As Table 1 reports, though, the sixties were more profitable for drive-ins than the fifties; Table 1 does not, of course, factor in nostalgia as part of its data.

Some observers contended that the drive-in was, in fact, what saved movie exhibition from TV's impact. Motion Picture Association of America president Eric Johnston was quoted in 1952 as saying that "drive-ins more than make-up for the total seats lost through the closedown of theaters" (50, p. 47). A Sindlinger study found that from 1946 to April 1953—when television was first being adopted—5,038 theaters closed, of which 4,696 were hardtops (23.8 percent of all four-wallers) and 342 were drive-ins (11.4 percent of all drive-ins) (86, p. 39). Undeniably TV affected movie attendance with but "one shining exception," the drive-in, according to *Business Week* (50, p. 46). A 1955 audience study reported that drive-in audiences were affected to a much greater degree by television advertising for films than hardtop audiences; TV ads proved to be nearly twice as powerful in influencing attendance among drive-in movie patrons (52, p. 115). This finding may not be surprising, however, when the results of another 1955 study are consulted: the Sindlinger Company found that the average drive-in theater audience had a higher ratio of TV owners than the four-wall audience (85, p. 38). Moreover, in 1953, while 41 percent of all four-wall theaters remained open "only because profits from concessions [were] greater than losses on admissions" the comparable figure for drive-ins was 28 percent (86, p. 74).

Other writers have suggested that drive-ins were not immune to "the radical changes the industry had undergone" following the *Paramount* decision and the introduction of television (53, p. 367). Sindlinger's study noted that "although the Drive-In Theatre [*sic*] meets some of the changes in people's habits . . . it does not appear to be an Exhibitor's panacea" (86, p. 44). By the 1960s television was firmly entrenched and, some writers asserted, TV, along with other factors, "meant death for many drive-ins" (51, p. 235); but the data in Table 1 do not support this conclusion. The 1953 Sindlinger report to the industry noted that 1950 was the peak year for new drive-in construction and that since then new construction had declined and the number of drive-ins which went out of business had increased (86, p. 42). At present, the ever-increasing diffusion and adoption of various cable and pay TV services poses another threat to the movie industry. Yet at least one exhibitor, Robert W. Selig, vice president of Pacific Theatres, has asserted that his circuit of drive-ins "would survive as a prospering alternative" to this latest form of TV competition (95, p. 5).

Just as television threatened the motion picture industry as a whole, the drive-in provoked anxiety and concern among walk-in operators. In his analysis of marketing aspects of drive-ins, which he called a "bright new star in the exhibition field," Luther maintained that drive-ins were "a post-war development which is perhaps second only to that of television in terms of its effects on conventional theater exhibition" (61, pp. 41–42). Still, when first introduced the drive-in was widely regarded as "an experimental novelty confined to warm-weather locations" (49, p. 8; see also 34, p. 72). Sindlinger, as late as 1953, reported that their data showed that "about a third of those who attended a Drive-In [*sic*] for the first time—usually attracted by its novelty—do not return, preferring the 4-Wall Theatre" (86, p. 43). One year later, in a report to COMPO, Sindlinger reiterated their claim: "On a national basis, the drive-in theatre does not appear to be in direct competition with the 4-wall theatre, for, as the attendance and gross of the drive-in commences to climb in June to a peak in August, so does the attendance and gross of the 4-wall theatre" (11, p. 8). Other contemporaneous accounts, however, were not as sanguine. Conant wrote that "the rivalry of the drive-in" acted as one factor accounting for the closing of many smaller, independent theaters in the 1950s (10, p. 172). The Morton Research Corporation, after reviewing longitudinal economic data, reported that "over the long run," drive-ins "made substantial inroads into indoor theaters, however since 1967 the outdoor theater has been losing ground." However, Morton noted, drive-ins "account for a larger share of business in less urbanized areas of the country" (67, pp. 14, 24). The 1972 data analyzed by Morton showed that drive-in revenues as a percentage of total motion picture revenues by state ranged from a low of 5.8 percent for New York to a high of 52 percent for Maine (67, p. 34). East South Central states (Kentucky, Tennessee, Alabama, and Mississippi) accounted for the largest share of total film revenues by drive-ins while the Middle Atlantic states (New York, New Jersey, and Pennsylvania) accounted for the smallest share (67, p. 33).

To combat the threat of the drive-in, indoor exhibitors and film distributors took action. The major film producer-distributors, for instance, did not begin leasing films to drive-ins until 1938, and only then "largely because of the development of in-car speaker sound" (93, p. 47). Carl Goldman, executive director of Theatre Owners of New England, recalled the resistance of the majors to distributing their films to drive-ins. RKO, he said, was the first major to sell to drive-ins since "they had a big backlog of pictures" and drive-ins were thought to be "a passing fancy. . . . MGM was the last major to sell to the drive-ins"

(77). Conant recounts two instances of collusion among film distributors: on one occasion the eight largest distributors together refused to allow a drive-in to bid for a movie on first run; the second case involved five distributors who conspired in assigning to a drive-in unreasonably long clearance after first run (10, pp. 146–147). In short, indoor operators demanded run and clearance protection/priority over the drive-ins from distributors; distributors "appeared reluctant to show any largesse in their dealings with the drive-ins, since these strange new customers may buy films as little as five months out of the year" (61, p. 44). "In order to obtain 'equitable' runs and clearance, and 'reasonable' rental terms," drive-in operators responded by threatening legal action under the Sherman Act or the "theater-by-theater, picture-by-picture" provisions of the *Paramount* case (61, p. 45). This evidence tends to belie *Business Week*'s 1949 report that "the indoor and outdoor houses are on a competitive footing" for first run films (97, p. 45).

Recent reports suggest some change has occurred in the film booking and distribution practices for drive-ins (43, p. 70). The Pacific Theatre chain in California, which operates some 100 drive-ins, for instance, plays primarily first-run general audience pictures and thus is directly competitive with the walk-ins (42, p. 7). Steve Flynn of United Artists Eastern Theatres maintains that the key to keeping the drive-in audience is "geared solely to product and location" with the film-booking trend leaning away from teen exploitation and toward first run fare (59, p. 53). Still, when drive-ins are allowed shorter playing time commitments than hardtops, this remains a point of confrontation and contention. A 1978 article in *Variety* noted that Chicago drive-ins were permitted to book films for four weeks while the indoor theaters had to take them for eight weeks (45). This situation occurred not necessarily out of distributor motives for fair play, even-handedness, or to make up for previous transgressions. Instead, distributors found that they were "faced with a dearth of theatres available to play new product in" (44). More important, *Variety* reported, the "majors began to realize that because drive-ins attract an entirely different audience, hardtop pictures could play both outlets without hurting the latter's receipts, and at the same time increase their film co.'s profits" (44). The antagonism and rivalry between indoor and outdoor exhibitors and film distributors may, in the final analysis, be settled by forces outside of the exhibitors' control. Recently Raymond J. McCafferty, executive vice president and general sales manager at Twentieth Century-Fox, noted that drive-ins accounted for only 5 percent of Fox's total billings and that "the cable situation is far more important to us than drive-ins" (93, p. 48).

One clear effect of the problem of film distribution to drive-ins was the quality and recency of pictures exhibited. In 1953 one observer wrote: "The general feeling seems to be that drive-in patrons are not greatly concerned with the age of pictures; they seem to be content with second and third run pictures" (34, p. 71). Another reporter had noted earlier that "it doesn't seem to make much of a difference what kind of pictures are shown, because drive-in fans are far less choosy than the indoor variety'' (31, p. 85). In the fifties, with drive-in operators attempting to draw the entire family, the screen content reflected this. But with changes in the 1960s and 1970s, such as the development of the suburban multiplex and other factors, ''family fare at the drive-in gave way to teenage exploitation films as mom and dad sat at home watching TV'' (59, p. 53). In 1966 Bert Pirosh, an executive with Pacific Drive-Ins, stated: ''We get some of the so-called important pictures first run. We get all of the junk offered as first run because of the type of service we have.'' He went on to note, however, ''we get our patrons in on all our junk . . . so why stick them with something good'' (78, pp. 15, 18).

Although today, according to *Boxoffice,* ''the trend in drive-ins seems to be away from teenage sub-run exploitation films and towards first-run fare of all types'' (59, p. 53), the exploitation fare so often associated with the drive-in had at least one important consequence for film producers. The drive-in has been credited with providing an exhibition outlet for the product of smaller, independent film producers and distributors such as American International Pictures, a ''relatively late comer to the movie business [which] initially thrived by taking advantage of a totally new market, the drive-in theatre'' (88, p. 243). For Crown International Pictures, drive-ins once represented more than 50 percent of the market for their pictures but now account for only 30 to 35 percent of its bookings due to the decline in drive-ins (96).

THE FUTURE OF DRIVE-IN EXHIBITION

As with other aspects of the drive-in, the outlook for this form of exhibition appears somewhat ambiguous, with some reports suggesting stabilization and no expansion and others indicating that the death knell has been sounded. Jobes, for instance, wrote that following the *Paramount* consent decree the drive-in, along with indoor theaters, ''suffered from the radical changes the industry had undergone'' (53, p. 367; see also 62, pp. 402–404).

In 1958 a realtor was quoted as saying, ''The future of major theatre buildings lies with the drive-in, not the closed job'' (92, p. 17). While clearly self-serving, this statement today indicates perhaps the key factor in the decline of the ozoners—the price of real estate. Given the land requirements needed for a drive-in, new construction is virtually out of the question (see 57, 77). In 1976 the U.S. Department of Commerce forecast that ''it is doubtful there will be any appreciable increase [in the number of drive-ins] in the future due to rising land costs and stricter zoning regulations'' (cited in 70, p. 68). Existing drive-in operators today are finding that either outright sale of their land or its development for shopping malls or industrial locations provide powerful and attractive incentives to get out of the film exhibition business (see 42, p. 4). *Variety* reported that in New England states many drive-ins were closing due to "the escalating price of land in desirable locations" (77). Jerome Schlanger, vice president of the Budco Quality Theatres chain, indicated that Budco was selling off its 11 drive-ins located in New Jersey, Pennsylvania, and Delaware. He cited as the company's reasons for the move high operating expenses, increased competition from indoor multiplexes, and "soaring real estate values." "The drive-in business," Schlanger was quoted as saying, "is still good, but you can often make more money selling the property" (57). The majority, if not the consensus, opinion concerning the future of U.S. drive-ins has perhaps been best summarized by Frederic A. Danz, board chairman of the Sterling Recreation Organization in Bellevue, Washington: "All exhibitors, of course, are seeing the gradual demise of the drive-in theatre. Suburban real estate values make them prohibitive" (1, p. 23; see also 58).

Still, an optimistic view remains among some drive-in operators. In a 1981 speech to the Motion Picture and Television Controllers Association, Robert Selig, the vice president of Pacific Theatres, which owns about 100 drive-in screens, stated: "We read here and there that the drive-in theatre is doomed, that the value of the land is more valuable than the theatre operation but we haven't found a more productive use of the real estate" (46). He also contended that drive-ins did better business than hardtops in the 1981 summer (95, p. 5). And Steven Flynn of United Artists Eastern Theatres notes: "I don't think the drive-in will ever die. There will always be a drive-in audience. The successful ones will continue to be successful and those that aren't will become real estate" (59, p. 53; see also 15 and 29).

Weather, too, is an important consideration impinging upon the profitability of drive-in operations (95). Unlike hardtops which can remain open for business year-round, topless theaters in cooler climates usually shut down for the winter months. And, while direct operating costs also cease, such sunk costs as land taxes do not. As Milton Shapiro, president of Sameric Theatres, noted, "Indoor cinemas have a 52-week season, and you don't have to buy 11–20 acres of ground to build them" (57). According to Giles' research, drive-ins located in sunny California "are relatively prosperous . . . compared with the rest of the country" but even there, "it is probably only a matter of time until most owners sell or convert their real estate to other uses" (42 and 43).

Competition with the hardtop multiplexes is another reason for suggesting the decline of topless theaters (see 57, 59). Budco Theatres' Schlanger states that "a drive-in, with its single screen, must have a picture doing very well every week" (57). In part the multiplex concern is addressed by the development of the Protolite Screen, discussed above. Also, multiple screen drive-ins have been constructed to meet the indoor competition head-to-head. Plotkin reports that as of 1983 there were 212 multiple screen drive-ins: 162 twins, 30 triplexes, 14 quadriplexes, two fiveplexes, and four sixplexes. His research indicates that twinning was the most profitable for the drive-in since it increased revenues 30 to

50 percent. Adding a third screen results in a 10 to 20 percent increase in revenues. And "additional screens beyond three probably only contribute 5–10 percent more revenue at the box office and concession stand" (79, p. 65).

Other factors also militate against a rosy outlook for the drive-in. Plotkin recently itemized 10 reasons for the decline of the drive-in (79), some of which have already been discussed above. He suggests that the growth and spread of the population resulted in light problems which affected the image on the screen. Along with the population invasion came hardtop theaters which captured the suburban audience once "owned" by the drive-in. Giles' research confirmed this: the "degree of urbanization of a region does tend to negatively affect drive-in strength" (42, p. 6). Changes in lifestyle among teens affected the drive-in; Plotkin suggests that they no longer hang out at drive-ins, now preferring shopping malls, video arcades, etc. Other factors identified by Plotkin include the less comfortable environment of the drive-in (no air-conditioning) and the drive-in's no longer functioning as a "passion pit" because of "the advent of vans and a different attitude toward sex" (79, p. 64).

The Morton Research Corporation's exhaustive economic analysis of the film industry noted that "drive-in movies are beginning to lose ground" and forecast a decline of 0.3 percent a year in the percentage of film revenues earned by drive-ins (see Table 1) (67, pp. 2, 16). Still, doom and gloom may not be a definitive prognosis for all drive-ins. Horton suggested a "mini-recovery" for both hardtops and drive-ins but presents only largely anecdotal evidence (51, pp. 237–238). Thompson reports the 1982 opening of a six-screen drive-in outside of Houston—the "I-45"—which can accommodate 3,000 cars (93, p. 46). To help support their facilities during nonscreening hours, some operators have turned their lots into daytime flea markets, auction sites, and meeting grounds. Moreover, if audiences can be drawn, drive-ins tend to have relatively heavy concession sales. Estimates of refreshment sales are high (for early reports see 12, p. 22; 16, p. 161; 62, p. 401). Morton reports that, in fact, drive-ins "depend more heavily on concession sales" than walk-ins (67, p. 14). In 1972, for instance, 10.3 percent of hardtop revenues came from concession sales; for drive-ins the comparable figure was 19.7 percent (67, p. 17).

Jowett and Linton wrote that the drive-in "is an acceptable alternative form of movie experience; in fact, it is the only form of moviegoing for many of the population" (55, p. 95). The accumulated evidence, however, strongly suggests diminished prosperity for the drive-ins. With few exceptions, attendance and revenues are down and expenses and liabilities are up. Perhaps the most optimistic forecast would suggest that the drive-in has hit a plateau. New construction will be extremely limited and may balance the number of closings found in, especially, less hospitable, more populated climates. Predictions calling for the complete demise of the drive-in, however, are probably erroneous. The unique conveniences offered by drive-ins for the family especially may make continued operation viable, at least in some areas. A 1982 Newspaper

Advertising Bureau telephone survey of Americans and Canadians found that a majority of both groups said they wanted to go to the movies more frequently than they do presently. More important, though, was the finding that "the more young children at home, especially of ages six and under, the more likely [the respondents] were to say they would like to go to the movies more than they do now" (72, p. 22).

PREVIOUS RESEARCH ON THE DRIVE-IN AUDIENCE

Given the almost legendary status of the drive-in, anecdotal and apocryphal reports about its audience abound. Few scientific inquiries have been conducted, however, and none have been published since 1960. Jowett and Linton suggest that "the drive-in movie offers another type of collective moviegoing experience" (55, p. 95). This seems to have been recognized very early on in the development of the drive-in. A 1949 *Business Week* article reported that Hollywood moviemakers felt that drive-ins appealed to a distinctly different audience than walk-ins (97, p. 44).

One social aggregate that the drive-in was thought to appeal to was the overweight, the elderly, the infirm, and the physically handicapped. Such individuals, it was believed, might not normally attend walk-in movies due to inconvenience, their discomfort in conventional theater seats, or inability to "cope with crowds, jostling or standing in line" (see 5, p. 18; 12, p. 68; 16, p. 150; 28; 31; 97, p. 44). The outdoor theater, it was speculated, also attracted "people who are extremely health conscious" (12, p. 68). The informality of the drive-in, it was said, made them attractive to individuals who disliked having to get dressed up to go to the movies (12, p. 68; 28).

Early armchair analysis suggested that the largest proportion of the drive-in's first audience was the family—in particular young, moderate income, non-white collar families with small children (see 12, p. 68; 16; 28; 31, p. 22; 61; 90; 97). By 1966 one West Coast exhibitor noted that his chain drew "a double, a twin audience." One part was composed of teens, "the young 20's and other daters" (78, p. 15)—the "young romantics" (97, p. 44). The second portion was the lower-middle class family (78, p. 15). Given this exhibitor's sense of his audience's composition, this affected his film booking policy. Since he felt "the drive-in audience is comparatively an unsophisticated audience," he avoided screening "class pictures," "nudies," or "so-called art pictures" (78, pp. 15, 17).

Some of the informal observations about the composition of the drive-in audience, of course, were reasonably accurate and were confirmed by systematic research. In 1950 Handel suggested that because drive-ins "provide a rather novel form of entertainment," their audience may have distinct characteristics. Drive-ins, he wrote, "create new business. . . . A large portion of the drive-in theater audience is composed of regular movie-goers who would not have attended a conventional theater on the day of the drive-in theater attendance.'' Still, he wrote, ''it may be some time until this new medium establishes its own attendance patterns and motivations'' (48, pp. 210–211). At the same time as Handel, Luther concluded that his audience research showed that drive-ins ''offer a type of entertainment which is considered by patrons to be more of a supplement to, than a substitute for, the entertainment offered by conventional theaters'' (61, p. 46). The results of Britt's 1960 survey led him to conclude that ''the drive-in audience was noticeably different from the general population'' (6, p. 102).

A 1953 study by Sindlinger reported that ''the principal appeal of the Drive-In is to dating couples, family groups with small children, and to vacationists'' (86, p. 43). That more than half the drive-in audience was composed of the family group—two adults plus a child or children—was confirmed by research conducted in 1949 (61, p. 45), 1950 (62, p. 409), 1957 (73, pp. 10, 104), and 1959 (6). According to one study, the family as the predominant attendance relationship unit for drive-ins may be even more pronounced today than it was 30 years ago. One of the largest U.S. drive-in circuits, Pacific Theatres, commissioned an audience study which was conducted by the Stanford Research Institute (79, p. 64). Pacific's vice president, Robert W. Selig, reported that the results of this study indicated that fully 72 percent of those attending California drive-ins ''were classified as young married couples with two or more children who couldn't afford to go out and pay for a babysitter'' (84; see also 59 and 95). Selig also resurrected some old chestnuts: ''He says remaining segments of the drive-in going population includes [*sic*] the handicapped, the elderly, and those who simply don't want to get dressed up to go to an indoor show'' (84).

Regardless of the precise composition of the attendance unit, the attendance unit most frequently encountered at walk-ins prior to 1960 (and still true today) was two persons (48, p. 113; 60, p. 30); drive-ins, it has been found, were attended by larger groups. In two separate studies reported by Luther, an average of 3.45 and 3.28 persons a car was found (62, p. 409; 61, p. 45). The Opinion Research Corporation's (ORC) 1957 study found that while 32 percent of the hardtop admissions were accounted for by groups of three or more people, the comparable figure for drive-ins was 57 percent (73). Handel's preliminary inquiry found that an attendance unit of four persons ''is encountered most frequently'' (48, p. 211), a finding corroborated by a 1957 ORC poll (reported in 55, p. 84).

According to the literature, the 1950s drive-in audience went to the movies quite frequently, with an average attendance ranging from 2.3 to 5.2 times a month according to Luther (61, p. 45; 62, p. 409). Additionally, at least half of those surveyed reported they attended drive-ins a majority of the time and one-third said they attended no other type of theater during the summer (62, p. 409). By 1957 the drive-in attendance experience was widespread; 72 percent of those polled by the ORC had been to a drive-in and the last time they went to the movies, 35 percent went to a drive-in (73, p. 103; 74, p. 23). Luther's 1949 study found that the vast majority—67 percent—of his sample had no preference for any particular theater (61, p. 46). By 1955, though, Sindlinger reported the following: 54 percent of their sample preferred four-wall theaters, 30 percent preferred drive-ins, and 16 percent expressed no preference (computed from data in 85, p. 17). Further, females consistently reported a preference for conventional theaters over drive-ins (85, p. 17). Two years later, the ORC found a nearly even distribution of preference responses among those who reported having attended a drive-in: 32 percent preferred hardtops, 30 percent preferred drive-ins, and 10 percent checked the "no choice" option in response to the question, "If the same movie were playing at a regular theater and at a drive-in, where would you prefer to see it?" (73, pp. 103–105; 74, p. 23). Differences in these findings more likely indicate differential wording of the questions than point to any kind of trend or shift in public preferences for one kind of theater over another. Finally, in terms of attitudinal issues, Luther reported that 60 percent of his sample believed that movies at drive-ins "were either not as good, or were less desirable because they were older than those pictures available at conventional theaters" (61, p. 46).

Britt's 1960 study at least in part challenged the armchair analysis of drive-in patrons which typified them as blue collar. His respondents "generally had better jobs, higher income, more education, more children, more home ownership, more cars, more major appliances, and more conveniences" than the general population (6, p. 102). However, a 1978 report of a study conducted by the Leo Burnett advertising agency found clearly contradictory data to those reported by Britt. The 1978 report indicated that "while the heavy filmgoer is socially active, confident, future-oriented, financially stable, and career-minded, the drive-in patron tends to be a dissatisfied lonely blue collar worker with financial worries" (reported in 44).

AUDIENCE RESEARCH IN CONTEXT

The conceptual and research value of examining film audiences in the context of their movie experience has been suggested by Austin (3). He drew an analogy stating that the valid interpretation of data on film audiences, as with nonverbal communication, was dependent upon analysis of the context in which it occurs. Moviegoing is embedded within such contexts as the physical ambience of the theater, the form of exhibition, the type of film being screened, the attendance unit, and so on. Moreover, these contexts are themselves both interactive and mutually dependent (i.e., there is contextual layering); the implication for audience research is that such contextual layering needs to be taken into account when describing or analyzing the film audience. As far back as 1950

Handel wrote that "the place of exhibition itself may be the object of intense research studies" (48, p. 208).

Contextual research on the film audience requires that data on a wide variety of variables be collected. By itself, the results of research on one audience's composition offers descriptive information about that audience. While such descriptive information may be of interest and value for its own sake, its significance and benefit to the larger body of film audience research lies in the broader form of comparative analysis. By gathering such information on individual film audience contexts, comparisons among contexts is made possible and identification of the unique and shared attributes of film audiences can be clarified. Thus, while individual empirical portraits of one film audience context provide insight, such research gains meaningfulness when integrated and juxtaposed with the results of other context studies.

Research on the drive-in audience, while never prolific (as the pages above suggest), came to a standstill after Britt's 1960 report. Nevertheless, even today, the drive-in "is the only form of moviegoing for many of the population" (55, p. 95). And, since 1960, changes in important social, economic, and industry practices have occurred which may have caused a reshaping of the drive-in audience. Use of the automobile and driving habits changed following the gas crunch of 1973. Childbearing patterns have been in flux. Entertainment options—particularly home entertainment activities—have increased, and with them, presumably, entertainment habits have changed. The development of the suburban multiplex offers multiple screens and a variety of film-types, including those formerly restricted largely to drive-ins. The remainder of this article specifically addresses itself to the findings of a field study for which personal interviews with drive-in theater patrons were conducted.[1] In addition to reporting the results of the drive-in study, comparative data on two other film contexts are also presented when appropriate: a contemporary cult film audience (2) and an art film theater audience (4). Data on the cult film audience were collected by means of personal interviews with patrons waiting on line at a theater for the cult film in late 1979. Data for the art film audience were gathered by means of a mail questionnaire in 1982. Both studies were conducted in Rochester, New York.

PORTRAIT OF A CONTEMPORARY DRIVE-IN AUDIENCE

Personal interviews with a total of 607 patrons for one Rochester, New York drive-in theater comprise the sample for this study. The interviews were conducted on weekends (Friday, Saturday, and Sunday) during October 1981,

---

[1]An earlier report of these data was presented at the International Communication Association conference, May, 1983, Dallas, Texas.

and April, May, and June 1982. Altogether interviews were conducted on 21 separate dates. Patrons were interviewed only once even if they attended on subsequent evenings. Fewer than 30 patrons refused to be interviewed.

Patron interviews occurred prior to the screening of the first film. The interviewers were college juniors and seniors enrolled in mass communications courses who had been trained in interview techniques. They used a prepared 33-item questionnaire consisting of open- and closed-ended questions. Responses to the open-ended questions were content classified by the author. A strict probability sample for this field study was not possible.

The respondents were asked how often they attended drive-in theaters. An eight-point response scale ranging from "never to almost never" to "more than four times a month" was provided. For the sample as a whole the mean (and median) drive-in attendance was once a month. Using the responses to this question, the sample was divided into three groups. "Infrequent" drive-in goers were those respondents who reported drive-in attendance of once in two to six months or fewer (n = 257); "Occasional" drive-in goers were those respondents reporting drive-in attendance of once or twice a month (n = 229); "Frequent" drive-in goers were those respondents reporting drive-in attendance of three times a month or greater (n = 116). Subsequent data analysis with these three groups was performed using chi-square for nominal level and the Kruskal-Wallis one-way analysis of variance test for ordinal level variables. When significant differences were found using the Kruskal-Wallis test, post hoc analysis employed the Mann-Whitney *U*-test.

As a check for differential attendance patterns between the three attendance groups, as well as the meaningfulness of the categories, the respondents were asked, "All in all, about what percentage of the time do you go to drive-in movie theaters as compared to walk-in movie theaters?" An eight-point response scale ranging from "ten percent of the time" to "all of the time" was provided. Results of the Kruskal-Wallis test indicated a highly significant difference ($p < .001$) between the three groups: post hoc analysis revealed that the differences between all groups (by pairs) was significant. As would be expected, Frequents attended drive-ins most often and Infrequents least often. The respondents were also asked, "Suppose there was a movie you wanted to see and it was playing at both a drive-in and a walk-in theater. Which type of theater would you go to, all things equal?" For the sample as a whole, 76.5 percent selected the drive-in option. Cross-tabulation of the data found that preference for the drive-in increased in a linear fashion from Infrequents to Frequents and that the differences between groups were significant ($X^2 = 35.84$, $df = 2$, $p < .0001$, Cramer's $V = .25$). Among the Infrequents 64.8 percent said they would go to the drive-in while 82.4 percent of the Occasionals and 90.4 percent of the Frequents selected the drive-in option. By way of comparison, the art film audience overwhelmingly (98 percent) reported that they both preferred and actually attended walk-ins to drive-ins.

Table 2
Who Attends the Drive-In with Whom[a]

	% Infrequents (n = 253)	% Occasionals (n = 227)	% Frequents (n = 113)	% Total (n = 593)
Opposite-sex friend	41.5	40.5	40.7	41.0
Family	17.0	15.9	17.7	16.7
Spouse	15.0	15.9	21.2	16.5
Mixed-sex group	11.9	15.0	8.8	12.5
Same-sex friend	7.5	7.5	5.3	7.1
Same-sex group	5.5	1.8	6.2	4.2
Alone	1.6	3.5	0.0	2.0

[a]$X^2 = 15.55$, $df = 12$, $p = .213$.

The participants were asked how many people accompanied them on the evening they were interviewed and the relationship of those persons. For the sample as a whole the size of the attendance unit ranged from one to 14. Overall the mean size of the attendance unit was 2.66 persons and the median 2.23 persons (including the respondent). No significant difference ($X^2 = 1.68$, $p = .432$) was found among audience aggregates for the size of the attendance group. These data indicate that the size of the attendance unit has diminished by about one person since Luther, Handel, and the ORC reported their research in the 1950s. The drive-in attendance unit was slightly larger in size than that of the art film audience (a mean of 2.16 and a median of 1.91); the cult film attendance unit, however, was much larger (a mean of 4.67 persons, a median of 3.15) than the drive-in attendance unit.

Luther, Britt, and others, as reported in the literature review, found that the family group was the most prevalent attendance aggregate in their studies. In the present sample, however, the family group accounted for only 16.7 percent of those interviewed. Table 2 shows that the most common relationship of the respondents' companion was an opposite sex friend, followed by the family, spouse, mixed-sex group (more than two persons), same-sex friend, same-sex group, and alone. No significant difference among attendance groups was found regarding the relationship of the respondents' companion. The couple (spouse or opposite-sex friend) was also the most common attendance relationship found for art film patrons while the cult film attracted mixed-sex and male groups most often.

Males comprised 57.9 percent of the sample and the three attendance groups did not differ significantly as to sex of the respondents ($X^2 = 0.63$, $df = 2$, $p = .728$). For the sample as a whole the average age was 24 years (median age was 22.1 years); no significant difference ($p = .271$) among attendance groups was found. Thirty-three percent of the sample reported being married and no significant difference for marital status was found among the three attendance

Table 3
Occupations of the Drive-In Audience[a]

	% Infrequents (n = 247)	% Occasionals (n = 220)	% Frequents (n = 110)	% Total (n = 577)
Blue & pink collar[b]	34.0	39.5	40.9	37.4
High school student	14.6	14.1	13.6	14.2
College student	13.0	12.3	7.3	11.6
White collar	14.6	7.7	9.1	10.9
Skilled	10.5	8.6	9.1	9.5
Unemployed	4.5	8.2	13.6	7.6
Homemaker	2.4	4.5	4.5	3.6
Professional	5.3	3.2	0.9	3.6
Artist	1.2	1.8	0.9	1.4

[a]$X^2 = 24.57$, $df = 16$, $p = .078$.
[b]Including clerical and unskilled.

groups ($X^2 = 0.02$, $df = 2$, $p = .991$). Also, the three groups did not differ as to the number of children in their families ($p = .674$). Nearly similar proportions of males and females were also found to attend both the cult and art film. However, cult moviegoers were somewhat younger than drive-in patrons (an average of 19.3 years) and art film patrons were considerably older (an average of 49.7 years).

The respondents' occupation is reported in Table 3. More than one-third of the sample was employed in blue collar (e.g., factory and production-line work) or pink collar (e.g., secretarial, waitress) jobs. No significant difference among the attendance groups was found. Examination across the rows of Table 3 reveals that the percentage of blue and pink collar workers and respondents reporting being unemployed increases with frequency of drive-in attendance. Just the reverse is true for persons in the two student categories. These findings appear to suggest agreement, to at least a limited extent, with those reported in the Leo Burnett study. Frequent drive-in goers tend to hold less prestigious jobs than those who attend the drive-in less often. Table 4 displays data on the drive-in audience's occupation as reported by Sindlinger in 1955, Britt in 1959, and the present findings. As may be seen, the (combined) percentage of professionals and white collar job holders has remained relatively constant. The present study found nearly triple the percentage of unemployed persons as compared to 1955; this may reflect the present unemployment rate rather than indicating a trend, however. The present study also found that the percentage of drive-in audience members holding blue and pink collar jobs has doubled since the Sindlinger and Britt studies. Conversely, the percentage of drive-in moviegoers reporting skilled and semi-skilled occupations has dropped since these earlier reports.

The respondents were asked to report the highest level of education they had completed. The mean response for the sample as a whole was "completed

Table 4
Occupational Profile of the Drive-In Movie-Goer (%)

	1955[a]	1959[b]	1982
Professional and semi-professional	3.8	11	3.6
White collar	8.9	c	10.9
Students	16.0	c	25.8
Housewives/homemaker	19.3	c	3.6
Skilled and semi-skilled	16.3	21	9.5
Manager, proprietor	3.5	21	c
Farmer, farm managers	14.5	14	c
Service, sales, clerical, and unskilled	15.7	13	37.4
Unemployed	2.7	c	7.6

[a]From Sindlinger (85, p. 37).
[b]From Britt (6, p. 101).
[c]Data not reported in these categories.

high school.'' The Kruskal-Wallis test found a significant difference (p = .005) in education among the three attendance groups with Infrequents reporting the most and Frequents the least amount of education. Post hoc analysis revealed that the difference between Infrequents and Occasionals and between Infrequents and Frequents was significant; the difference in education between Occasionals and Frequents was not significant ($p > .05$). Table 5 reports data on the educational level of drive-in patrons from 1955, 1959, and the present study. Comparisons between these data are made problematic due to differences in the coding categories, especially in the case of Britt's research. Comparing just the 1955 and 1982 data, the general trend shown is a higher level of education which, no doubt, reflects a general population trend.

The present findings on education may also be compared to the cult film and art film audiences. The cult film audience was by and large composed of

Table 5
Educational Profile of the Drive-In Movie-Goer (%)

	1955[a]	1959[b,c]	1982
Completed College and Above	3.9	32	13.2
Attended College	7.6		23.0
Completed High School	33.3	46	39.6
Attended High School	37.4		21.6
Completed Grade School	17.3 (both rows)	17	1.3
Attended Grade School			1.0
No Formal Education	0.5		0.2

[a]From Sindlinger (85, p. 36).
[b]From Britt (6, p. 101).
[c]Data available listed as college, high school, grammar school.

high school and college students (61 percent) and the average level of education among the art film audience was a college degree.

The present study's sample was largely white (89 percent) with just a sprinkling of blacks (8 percent). No significant difference among attendance groups as to racial composition was found ($X^2 = 0.61$, $df = 2$, $p = .736$). Catholics comprised nearly half (44 percent) and Protestants a quarter (26 percent) of the audience. Nearly one-quarter (23 percent) expressed no religious preference. A significant difference among the attendance groups by religion was found ($X^2 = 9.81$, $df = 4$, $p = .044$, Cramer's $V = .12$); Frequents were more likely to report Catholicism as their religious preference. The distribution of religious affiliations reflects the population of the area in which the study was conducted.

The respondents were asked to report which political party they identified with and their usual stand on political issues. More than one-third (36 percent) classified themselves as Independents, 20 percent said they were Republicans, 24 percent said Democrats, and 19 percent "Other." No significant difference by attendance group was found ($X^2 = 1.15$, $df = 6$, $p = .979$). Half the sample (53 percent) said they took a middle-of-the-road posture on political issues, 18 percent reported themselves as conservative, and 29 percent said they were liberals. No significant difference by attendance group was found ($X^2 = 2.20$, $df = 4$, $p = .699$). Similar percentages for party affiliation and usual political stand were found among the cult film audience.

Previous research has indicated that the drive-in audience attends movies frequently. In addition to this sample's frequency of drive-in attendance, they were also asked to report how often they went to movies altogether (drive-ins and walk-ins combined) and how often they went to just walk-in theaters. Identical eight-point response scales ranging from "never or almost never" to "more than four times a month" were provided. Attendance at walk-in theaters for the sample as a whole averaged once a month. Total movie attendance for the entire sample averaged twice a month.[2] These findings suggest that respondents in the present sample were, indeed, heavy moviegoers. The Opinion Research Corporation has reported that persons attending movies at least once a month constitute only 27 percent of the U.S. public over 12 years of age, and these same individuals account for 87 percent of all movie admissions (cited in 40, p. 32A). Thus, regardless of how movie attendance was measured, the present sample falls into an elite frequency of moviegoing group. The cult film audience, too, had an average movie attendance of twice a month (not counting attendance at the cult movie) while the art film patrons averaged one film a month (not counting attendance at their repertory theater).

---

[2]Note that the reliability of the respondents' answers to their frequency of movie attendance is demonstrated by the findings from these three questions: Attendance at drive-ins averaged once a month, walk-in attendance was once a month, and total movie attendance was twice a month.

Differences among attendance groups as to their frequency of total moviegoing were significant ($p < .001$). The mean rank for Infrequents was 199.48 while for Occasionals and Frequents the ranks were 334.91 and 459.13 respectively; the Mann-Whitney *U*-test revealed that the differences in total movie attendance between all three groups were significant. For attendance at just walk-in theaters the differences in frequency of attendance among audience aggregates were also significant ($p = .011$). As was the case for frequency of total moviegoing, the rank scores increased in a linear fashion from Infrequents to Frequents; post hoc analysis indicated that only Frequents and Occasionals differed significantly on walk-in attendance. These findings indicate that individuals in the Frequent drive-in category not only attend drive-ins more often than others, but are heavier moviegoers in general.

The sample's consumption of three other media was also measured. For the sample as a whole, daily television viewing averaged nearly two to three hours a day, newspaper reading averaged almost four times a week, and number of magazines read averaged 2.5 a month. No difference among attendance groups was found for newspaper reading ($p = .533$) although the ranks for the three groups decreased in a linear fashion from Infrequents to Frequents. Significant differences were found for magazine reading ($p = .041$) and television viewing ($p = .039$). Ranks for televiewing increased linearly from Infrequents to Frequents; just the reverse pattern was true for magazine reading. Post hoc analysis on these two variables showed that only the differences between Infrequents and Frequents were significant regarding their consumption of television and magazines. Thus, heavy drive-in goers appear to be more attracted to moving image media while the lighter drive-in goers consume more print media. Both the cult and art film audiences averaged one to two hours a day of televiewing. The art film audience were heavier newspaper (six times a week) and magazine (four a month) consumers than both the cult film and drive-in audiences.

A series of questions was asked concerning the respondents attendance behavior and decision-making process for their moviegoing on the evening they were interviewed. These questions were designed as context-specific rather than context-free, a methodologically preferable approach since respondents' answers can be assumed to be more accurate, and hence valid, when asked to recall information about a specific film situation rather than drive-in moviegoing in general.

First the respondents were asked if they had planned to go to the drive-in on the evening they were interviewed or if their attendance was a "spur-of-the moment" decision. The sample divided nearly equally on this question; 51 percent said their attendance was a spur-of-the-moment decision and 49 percent said they had planned to attend. Although no significant difference by attendance group was found ($X^2 = 1.03$, $df = 2$, $p = .598$), a higher (and identical) percentage of Frequents and Occasionals reported having planned to attend than Infrequents (50.9 to 46.7 percent respectively). This may be indicative of a certain degree of habitual behavior among a modest segment of the drive-in audience. Higher percentages of planned attendance than those found for the drive-in audience were found among both the cult film (76 percent) and art film (92 percent) audiences. A follow-up question asked if the respondents had decided to see the particular movie playing before deciding when to go see it, or if they first decided to go to the movies and then selected a film. Again the sample divided nearly evenly in their response: 58 percent indicated they picked the movie first and 42 percent said they decided to go to the movies before selecting a particular film. No significant difference among attendance groups was found ($X^2 = 0.08$, $df = 2$, $p = .958$); the percentages within the six-cell cross-tabulation were virtually identical.

The responses to these two questions indicate that about half the sample went to the drive-in on the spur of the moment and half the sample decided on moviegoing before selecting the specific film. At least for some individuals, drive-in attendance occurs regardless of interest in what film is being shown. Further, cross-tabulation of the responses to these two questions supports what would be intuitively expected: Respondents who planned their attendance were more likely to have decided to see a particular picture first. Conversely, respondents who reported attending on the spur of the moment were more likely to have decided to go to the movies before selecting a particular film.

The respondents were asked to recall where or from whom they learned about the movie they were attending. Table 6 presents the responses to this question. More than half the respondents used the newspaper as their source of information; word-of-mouth accounted for almost one-fifth of the responses, and television 8 percent. No significant difference among attendance groups was found. A follow-up question asked where or from whom the respondents learned specific information (e.g., time and location) necessary for them to attend the film. Again no significant difference among groups was found ($X^2 = 16.59$, $df =$

Table 6
Source of Information About the Film Attended[a]

	% Infrequents (n = 257)	**% Occasionals (n = 229)**	**% Frequents (n = 116)**	**% Total (n = 602)**
Newspaper	58.4	50.7	53.4	54.5
Friends	19.5	17.9	17.2	18.4
Television	7.4	10.5	6.0	8.3
Other	5.1	7.0	10.3	6.8
Marquee	3.5	6.1	8.6	5.5
Don't recall	2.7	3.1	2.6	2.8
Radio	1.9	1.3	1.7	1.7
Previews	0.4	2.6	0.0	1.2
Magazine	1.2	0.9	0.0	0.8

[a]$X^2 = 19.84$, $df = 16$, $p = .228$.

16, $p = .412$). Reliance on newspapers increased (to 67.5 percent) while word-of-mouth and television decreased (to 11.5 and 2.2 percent respectively). Among cult film patrons personal contacts were the primary source of information (83 percent) about the film and for more specific information the respondents relied equally on newspapers (44 percent) or personal contact (44 percent). For the art film audience, most (88 percent) of the sample learned about the films they attended from the schedule brochure published by the art film theater. In short, newspapers were the predominant source for providing the drive-in respondents with information about the film as well as specific information about show time and theater.

Two questions probed the respondents' reasons for drive-in attendance. Responses to a question on the respondents' most important reason for going to drive-ins are presented in Table 7. Altogether 14 different types of responses

Table 7
Most Important Reason for Drive-In Attendance[a]

	% Infrequents ($n = 227$)	% Occasionals ($n = 217$)	% Frequents ($n = 114$)	% Total ($n = 558$)
Less expensive than walk-ins	17.2	18.0	20.2	18.1
Most comfortable than walk-ins	13.2	17.1	24.6	17.0
Privacy	14.5	20.3	8.8	15.6
Can have fun (e.g., party, drink, and smoke)	13.2	18.0	15.8	15.6
To be outdoors	8.8	6.5	8.8	7.9
To see the movie	8.8	6.0	7.9	7.5
Convenience (e.g., can take the baby)	5.7	5.5	4.4	5.4
Entertainment	3.5	1.4	1.8	2.3
Casual; don't have to dress-up	2.2	2.8	1.8	2.3
To get out of the house	2.6	1.8	1.8	2.2
Change of pace; a different movie experience	3.1	0.9	1.8	2.0
Nothing else to do	3.1	0.9	1.8	2.0
Quieter than walk-ins	2.6	0.0	0.9	1.3
Romance; to "make-out"	1.3	0.9	0.0	0.9

[a] $X^2 = 33.07$, $df = 26$, $p = .160$.

Table 8
Reason for Drive-In Attendance on the Evening Interviewed[a]

	% Infrequents (n = 238)	% Occasionals (n = 218)	% Frequents (n = 110)	% Total (n = 566)
For the movie playing	57.1	57.3	61.8	58.1
Closest drive-in	16.4	16.5	12.7	15.7
Nothing else to do	3.8	6.9	3.6	4.9
Other	5.9	2.8	6.4	4.8
To have fun (party)	2.5	4.6	7.3	4.2
Change of pace	3.4	2.3	2.7	2.8
"Not my choice"	4.6	1.8	0.9	2.8
Less expensive than walk-ins	2.1	4.1	0.9	2.7
To be outdoors	2.1	1.8	1.8	1.9
To relax	2.1	1.8	1.8	1.9

[a]$X^2 = 19.75$, $df = 18$, $p = .347$.

were reported. Overall no significant difference among attendance groups was found. Four reasons accounted for two-thirds of the responses. Drive-ins were perceived with nearly equal frequency among the three sample groups as being less expensive than walk-in theaters to attend. The privacy offered by drive-ins (i.e., the car as a "private booth") was also noted by, especially, Infrequents and Occasionals as a key factor in motivating attendance. The comfort of one's automobile was emphasized to a greater extent among Frequents than Infrequents, with Occasionals falling in-between. The opportunity to "party," the fourth of the top four reasons for drive-in attendance, was cited with nearly equal frequency among all three groups. The sixth most frequently cited reason for attendance was to see the movie being screened; all three groups reported this in nearly equal percentages. The apparent low salience of this reason for attendance offers support for the conclusions drawn earlier from the two questions on planning attendance and temporal ordering of decisions (i.e., deciding to go to the movies and then selecting a film or vice versa).

While the data presented in Table 7 offer general reasons for drive-in attendance, Table 8 presents the respondents' reasons for attendance on the evening they were interviewed. Although, again, no significant difference among attendance groups was found, an interesting rearranging of reasons for attendance may be noted. Whereas the movie being shown accounted for only 7.5 percent of the reasons for attendance at the drive-in in general, fully 58 percent of the respondents reported this as their reason for going to the drive-in on the evening they were interviewed. One explanation for this large difference may be that when asked about motives for drive-in attendance in general, the respondents reported perceived *advantages* of the form of exhibition (as compared to walk-ins), while their response to the context-specific question more accurately reflected the actual salient behavioral incentives. The reasons for drive-in attendance found in the present study parallel, at least in part, those found in earlier research concerning reasons for drive-in *preference*. Sindlinger reported (without numeric values) six reasons for drive-in preference in 1955: can take the children, don't have to dress, cooler outside, can talk and smoke, better for a date, and more comfortable (85, p. 17). Two years later the ORC reported the following reasons (and percentages) for preferring drive-ins for their sample of 5,021 persons 15 years of age or older: more comfortable and don't have to dress to go (9 percent each), better with children (8 percent), more privacy (5 percent), can smoke, drink, eat (5 percent), and better ventilation (4 percent) (73, p. 107).

A second important reason for attendance on the evening interviewed was the proximity of the theater. Fifteen percent reported this as their reason for attendance, suggesting, perhaps, some degree of overlap between a desire to see the film playing coupled with the ease, or convenience, of attendance. The remaining reasons for attendance each accounted for 5 percent or fewer of the responses. Cult film attendance was largely motivated by the social nature of the film audience ambience. Art film attendance was motivated by desire to see old "cinema classics" and recently made films that had not received wide distribution and exhibition.

Are there differences among the three attendance groups for the type of film exhibited? Overall five types of films were shown on the different evenings when interviews were conducted: comedy, horror, drama, crime drama, and "soft pornography" (R-rated films with sexual themes). Results of the cross-tabulation of the data was significant ($X^2 = 17.20$, $df = 8$, $p = .028$, Cramer's $V = .12$). Comedies were attended with virtual identical frequency across groups. Infrequents were more likely to be present at "soft porn" and drama, Occasionals at horror, and Frequents at crime drama pictures.

Finally, a set of three questions was posed concerning the respondents actual or expected purchase of snacks and whether they had brought snacks with them. A number of reports, dating from the 1950s, have indicated that drive-ins earn as much as 20 to 50 percent of their income from sales at the concession stand. Further, drive-in refreshment stands were reported to have earned as much as four times that earned by hardtop theaters (see 16, p. 151; 34, pp. 66–67; 62, p. 401). Only 5 percent of the sample reported that they had purchased something from the snack bar at the time when interviewed. No significant difference among attendance groups was found ($X^2 = 0.15$, $df = 2$, $p = .928$). However, since the interviews were conducted up until the beginning of the first film, the respondents may not have had time to get to the concession stand. Consequently, they were also asked if they expected to purchase something at the snack bar. More than one quarter (29 percent) of the sample indicated they did expect to buy snacks, 59 percent said they did not expect to buy snacks, and 12 percent chose the "not sure" response option. No significant difference ("not sure" responses were omitted) in response by attendance group was found ($X^2 = 1.20$, $df = 2$, p

= .549). Lastly, the respondents were asked if they had brought any food or drinks with them. More than three-quarters (78 percent) of the sample indicated they had brought refreshments with them. No significant difference in response among attendance groups was found. Casual observation of the drive-in patrons found many fully equipped with picnic coolers and lawn chairs. And, although a systematic count was not kept, vans and pickup trucks were popular vehicles at the drive-in; often they were backed into the parking spaces and chairs arranged in and around the vehicle.

CONCLUSIONS

Over the course of a half century, the U.S. drive-in has grown from a novelty to a prospering form of exhibition and, now, a declining industry. The popularity of the drive-in was such that it transcended the domestic border. Its popularity was also such that it engendered various technological innovations, helped create an outlet for the exploitation movies of such film producers as New World Pictures, and aroused the ire of indoor exhibitors, film distributors, moralists, and local legislators.

According to the results of the present audience study, the drive-in audience has changed since Britt reported his research in 1960. The present sample differs in terms of occupation, education, and number of children. Moreover, the present study has shown that the size of the attendance unit as well as its relationship composition has been altered. The attendance unit has become smaller and the family is no longer the dominant attendance relationship unit.

What this study suggests about attendance at drive-ins in general is that it is motivated by the low cost, the comfort and privacy afforded by one's car, and the opportunity to socialize. For many, the motion picture being screened, it seems, serves as merely a backdrop and the drive-in lot a convenient meeting place. Attendance was as likely to have been spontaneous as it was to have been planned for this sample. The Frequent drive-in patron tends to be somewhat older, to have completed fewer years of formal education, is more likely to have a less prestigious job, and goes to the movies (including walk-ins) more often than Occasional or Infrequent drive-in patrons. All three drive-in groups identified here were similar on such dimensions as sex, race, political party preference, usual political stand, planning of drive-in attendance, and the decision process used for drive-in attendance.

Based on the data gathered in the present field study, the forecast for drive-ins is not optimistic. While more than half (55 percent) of the present sample reported they went to drive-ins (as compared to walk-ins) half the time or more, the size of the attendance unit has diminished since the 1950s, thereby lowering revenues on a per-person admission basis. The refreshment stand is apparently not as popular among patrons as it once was since many bring their own food and beverages. And the number of patrons attending as a family unit comprises less than one-fifth of the total audience. Thus, while the Newspaper Advertising Bureau found that among individuals with young children their desire to go to the movies more often was high, this desire did not translate to actual behavior for drive-in attendance among the present sample—despite the fact that drive-ins may offer the most convenient and least restraining movie ambience for parents.

Contemporary film audience research has focused on three contexts thus far: the cult film, the art film, and the drive-in theater. Further research on the contexts of moviegoing needs to be directed at the audience for various film genres such as the horror, science fiction, sneak preview, and X-rated film. Additionally, research attention is needed on such audience contexts as the various forms of film exhibition including the suburban multiplex and theaters located at shopping malls. Analysis of audiences by type of film distribution (e.g., first- and subsequent-run) would also be useful in gaining a full understanding of the audience for motion pictures. Finally, it should be noted that the empirical case study, such as the one reported here, offers abundant data on a particular situation. Although this is advantageous in developing insight on the phenomenon, it also serves as a clear limitation. The external validity—especially the population validity—of case studies can always (and correctly) be called into question. Hence, there is a clear need for replication of case study research in addition to expanding the research focus on various film audience contexts.

REFERENCES

1. Auerbach, Alexander. "Despite the Christmas-Season Chill, Circuit Heads Remain Optimistic About the Future of the Theatre." *Boxoffice* 118, April 1982, pp. 22–25.
2. Austin, Bruce A. "Portrait of a Cult Film Audience: *The Rocky Horror Picture Show.*" *Journal of Communication* 31 (2), Spring 1981, pp. 43–54.
3. Austin, Bruce A. "The Motion Picture Audience: A Neglected Aspect of Research." In *The Film Audience: An International Bibliography of Research with Annotations and an Essay.* Metuchen, NJ: Scarecrow Press, 1983.
4. Austin, Bruce A. "Portrait of an Art Film Audience." *Journal of Communication* 34 (1), Winter 1984.
5. Best, Katharine and Katharine Hillyer. "Movies Under the Stars." *Cue,* June 19, 1948, pp. 18–19.
6. Britt, Steuart Henderson. "What is the Nature of the Drive-In Theater Audience?" *Media/scope* 4, June 1960, pp. 100–102, 104.
7. "Camden's Drive-In Theater." *Literary Digest* 116, July 22, 1933, p. 19.
8. "Canada Briefs." *Business Week,* October 17, 1953, p. 146.
9. "The Colossal Drive-In." *Newsweek,* July 22, 1957, pp. 85–87.
10. Conant, Michael. *Antitrust in the Motion Picture Industry.* Berkeley: University of California Press, 1960.
11. Council of Motion Picture Organizations. *Special COMPO Report, November 1954.* In National Association of Theatre Owners file, Department of Archives and Manuscripts, Brigham Young University, Box 9, Folder 9. (Hereinafter cited as NATO Archives.)
12. Cullman, Marguerite W. "Double Feature—Movies and Moonlight." *New York Times Magazine,* October 1, 1950, pp. 22, 68–69, 72.

13. DeChiera, Frank. *Foreign Language Film Exhibition and Distribution in Australia.* North Ryde, Australia: Australian Film and Television School, 1980.
14. "Denmark's First Drive-In Cinema." *The Illustrated London News,* July 22, 1961, p. 126.
15. "Diversified Land Use Will Spur Drive-In Boom." *Independent Film Journal* 73, February 18, 1974, p. 21.
16. Downs, Anthony. "Drive-Ins Have Arrived." *Journal of Property Management* 18, March 1953, pp. 149–162.
17. "Drive-In Battles Berlin, Conn. Closure to Suppress Sexplicity." *Variety,* February 3, 1982, p. 31.
18. "Drive-In Broadcast Sound Systems." *Boxoffice* 118, March 1982, pp. 54–55.
19. "Drive-In Cine." *New York Times Magazine,* September 29, 1957, p. 32.
20. "Drive-In Containment Screen Seen as Key to Big Energy Savings." *Independent Film Journal* 74, November 13, 1974, p. 24.
21. "Drive-In Film Business Burns Up the Prairies." *Life,* September 24, 1951, pp. 104–106, 108.
22. "The Drive-In Lie-In." *Newsweek,* July 8, 1963, p. 78.
23. "Drive-In Movie Holds Four Hundred Cars." *Popular Mechanics* 60, September 1933, p. 326.
24. "Drive-In Shows Booming; Famous Players to Add 7." *Financial Post* 43, December 10, 1949, pp. 1, 3.
25. "Drive-In Theater." *Business Week,* August 5, 1933, p. 19.
26. "Drive-In Theaters: Happy but Griping." *Business Week,* May 9, 1953, pp. 129, 131.
27. "Drive-In with a 'Balcony'." *Business Week,* June 30, 1951, p. 70.
28. "Drive-Ins." *Time,* July 14, 1941, p. 66.
29. "Drive-Ins are Experiencing a 'Renaissance' Across U.S." *Boxoffice* 113, July 17, 1978, p. E-1.
30. "Drive-Ins Steal the Show." *Business Week,* August 5, 1953, p. 114.
31. Durant, John. "The Movies Take to the Pastures." *Saturday Evening Post* 223, October 14, 1950, pp. 21–22, 85, 89–90.
32. "Exhibs Evaluate Cinema Radio Sound Installations." *Independent Film Journal* 74, October 2, 1974, p. 48.
33. "The Family 'Drives In.'" *New York Times Magazine,* June 26, 1955, p. 16.
34. Flaherty, W. "Drive-In Theatres." *British Kinematography* 23, September 1953, pp. 66–72.
35. "Fly-In Theatre." *Science Digest* 24, September 1948, p. 94.
36. Fox, William Price. "The Drive-In." *Esquire* 84, December 1975, pp. 156–157, 223–224.
37. Francis, Tony. "Improving Drive-In Picture and Sound." *Boxoffice* 118, March 1982, p. 56.
38. "German Drive-Ins Boom." *Variety,* July 27, 1977. p. 39.
39. Gertner, Richard (Ed.). *International Motion Picture Almanac 1977.* New York: Quigley Publishing Co., 1977.
40. Gertner, Richard (Ed.). *Motion Picture Almanac 1981.* New York: Quigley Publishing Co., 1981.
41. Gertner, Richard (Ed.). *Motion Picture Almanac 1982.* New York: Quigley Publishing Co., 1982.
42. Giles, Dennis. "The Drive-In Economy: 1946–1981." Paper presented at the Ohio University Film Conference, April 1982, Athens, OH.
43. Giles, Dennis. "The Outdoor Economy: A Study of the Contemporary Drive-In." *Journal of the University Film and Video Association* 35 (2), Spring 1983, pp. 66–76.
44. Ginsberg, Steven. "Drive-Ins Rate Firstrun; Hardtop Sites Re-Valued." *Variety,* April 26, 1978, p. 23.
45. Ginsberg, Steven. "Indoor Sites Forced to 8 Wks; Protest Drive-Ins 'Half-Runs.'" *Variety,* July 5, 1978, pp. 7, 27.
46. Grant, Lee. "Selig: Can Movie House Be Saved?" *Los Angeles Times,* September 26, 1981, Part II, p. 4.

47. "Growth of Drive-Ins." *Commonweal* 65, November 16, 1956, p. 166.
48. Handel, Leo A. *Hollywood Looks at Its Audience*. Urbana: University of Illinois Press, 1950.
49. Hine, Al. "The Drive-Ins." *Holiday,* July 1952, pp. 6–10.
50. "Hollywood Learns How to Live with TV." *Business Week,* August 9, 1952, pp. 46–48.
51. Horton, Andrew. "Turning On and Tuning Out at the Drive-In: An American Phenomenon Survives and Thrives." *Journal of Popular Film* 5 (3 and 4), 1976, pp. 233–244.
52. Hungerford, Chris. "A Survey of Los Angeles Theater Attendance of Two Motion Pictures Which Were Advertised on Television." Unpublished M.A. thesis, University of Southern California, 1955.
53. Jobes, Gertrude. *Motion Picture Empire*. Hamden, CT: Archon Books, 1966.
54. Jowett, Garth. *Film: The Democratic Art*. Boston, MA: Little, Brown and Co., 1976.
55. Jowett, Garth and James M. Linton. *Movies as Mass Communication*. Beverly Hills, CA: Sage Publications, 1980.
56. Kocian, Billy. "Costs, Redtape, Public Opposition Keep German Drive-Ins Few." *Variety,* October 20, 1976, p. 150.
57. "Land Values, Short Year, Single Screen All Hamper Drive-Ins." *Variety,* April 7, 1982, p. 29.
58. Langway, Lynn with Susan Agrest. "The Disappearing Drive-In." *Newsweek,* August 9, 1982, p. 65.
59. Lond, Harley W. "Drive-In Operations: Still in the Game." *Boxoffice* 118, March 1982, pp. 53, 55.
60. *Los Angeles Times. A Look at Southern California Movie-Going*. Los Angeles: *Los Angeles Times,* 1972.
61. Luther, Rodney. "Marketing Aspects of Drive-In Theaters." *Journal of Marketing* 15, July 1950, pp. 41–47.
62. Luther, Rodney. "Drive-In Theaters: Rags to Riches in Five Years." *Hollywood Quarterly* 5, Summer 1951, pp. 401–411.
63. "Marketing Briefs." *Business Week,* October 10, 1953, p. 56.
64. Mayer, Michael F. *The Film Industries,* 2d ed. New York: Hastings House, 1978.
65. "Million-Dollar Drive-In Offers Films, Fun and Food." *Popular Science* 171, September 1957, pp. 118–121.
66. "Moon-Washed." *New Yorker,* October 1, 1949, pp. 20–21.
67. Morton Research Corporation. *The Movie Entertainment Industry: An Economic, Marketing, and Financial Study of the Motion Picture and Movie Theater Market*. Merrick, NY: Morton Research Corp., October 1976.
68. "Movie Theater Lets Cars Drive Right In." *Popular Science* 123, August 1933, p. 19.
69. "Must Shield Ozoners Showing X Pictures." *Boxoffice* 104, February 11, 1974, p. E-1.
70. National Association of Theatre Owners. *Encyclopedia of Exhibition 1976*. New York: National Association of Theatre Owners, 1976.
71. "NATO Screen ($3 Ft.) Should Improve Technology, But DST Remains Foe of Drive-In Ops." *Variety,* February 20, 1974, p. 4.
72. Newspaper Advertising Bureau. "Movie-Going in the United States and Canada." New York: Newspaper Advertising Bureau, October, 1981.
73. Opinion Research Corporation. *The Public Appraises Movies, December 1957*. In NATO Archives, Box 9, Folder 10.
74. Opinion Research Corporation. *The Public Appraises Movies: Highlights of a Survey Conducted in June and July 1957*. In NATO Archives, Box 9, Folder 10.
75. "Outdoor Technology Upcoming; Could Yield Film Biz Plus." *Variety,* May 29, 1974, pp. 4, 23.
76. "Ozoners." *Time*, April 26, 1948, p. 96.
77. "Ozoners in Bay State Closing; Can't Spurn Land-Value Offers." *Variety,* June 28, 1978, p. 7.

78. Paletz, David and Michael Noonan. "The Exhibitors." *Film Quarterly* 19, Winter 1965–1966, pp. 14–40.
79. Plotkin, Harris M. "Protolite Screen: Drive-In Breakthrough?" *Boxoffice* 119, March 1983, pp. 64–65.
80. "Production Briefs." *Business Week,* August 22, 1953, p. 52.
81. Pulman, R. E. "Drive-In Theatre Operation." *British Kinematography* 32 (4), April 1958, pp. 92–106.
82. Randall, Richard S. *Censorship of the Movies.* Madison: University of Wisconsin Press, 1968.
83. "Sees Cinema Radio Boom; Predicts Drive-In Resurgence." *Independent Film Journal* 75, January 22, 1975, p. 21.
84. "Selig Nixes Drive-In Doomcriers: L.A. Ozoner Biz Hit Peak in '82." *Variety,* June 22, 1983, p. 23.
85. Sindlinger and Company, Inc. *A Study and Analysis of Theatre Screen Advertising, March 1, 1955.* In NATO Archives, Box 8, Folder 15.
86. Sindlinger and Company, Inc. *An Analysis of the Motion Picture Industry 1946–1953, Volume 1.* In NATO Archives, Box 9, Folder 8.
87. "So. Africa Drive-Ins Shift to Flat Fee Per Vehicle to Fight TV Competition." *Variety,* March 9, 1977, p. 38.
88. Stanley, Robert. *The Celluloid Empire.* New York: Hastings House, 1978.
89. Sterling, Christopher H. and Timothy R. Haight. *The Mass Media: Aspen Institute Guide to Communication Industry Trends.* New York: Praeger Publishers, 1978.
90. Taylor, Frank J. "Big Boom in Outdoor Movies." *Saturday Evening Post* 229, September 15, 1956, pp. 31, 100–102.
91. Theatre Owners of America. *TOA Business Builders. Ticket-Selling Ideas for Drive-In Theatre Showmen! A Manual for Promotion and Exploitation.* 1957 (approximately). In NATO Archives, Box 11, Folder 5.
92. Thomas, Dana L. "Flicker of Hope? Things May Be Looking Up for the Movie Theatres." *Barron's* 38, June 23, 1958, pp. 3, 17–19.
93. Thompson, Toby. "The Twilight of the Drive-In." *American Film* 8, July-August 1983, pp. 44–49.
94. Thorp, Margaret Farrand. *America at the Movies.* New Haven: Yale University Press, 1939.
95. Tusher, Will. "Drive-Ins Lure to Young Weds." *Variety,* September 30, 1981, pp. 5, 40.
96. Tusher, Will. "Land Value Up; Ozoners Down; Tenser's Market Now in Multis; He's Dubious About Upper Ages." *Variety,* December 2, 1981, pp. 3, 32.
97. "Twice as Many Drive-In Theaters?" *Business Week,* January 1, 1949, pp. 44–45.
98. UNESCO. *World Communications: Press, Radio, Film.* Paris: UNESCO, 1951.
99. "Unshielded Ozoner Cues X-Rated Arrests." *Variety,* July 20, 1983, p. 24.
100. "W. German Cinemas Dip to 3,072; Drive-Ins Big, With 20 Now Operating." *Variety,* August 23, 1978, p. 51.
101. Wolfe, Tom. *The Kandy-Kolored Tangerine-Flake Streamline Baby.* New York: Pocket Books, 1965.

6
A Study of the Effects In-Home Entertainment Alternatives Have on Film Attendance

Wenmouth Williams, Jr. and Mitchell E. Shapiro

The size of the film audience has generally declined over the past 83 years. De Fleur and Ball-Rokeach document the diffusion of film as a mass medium in terms of average weekly attendance per household from 1900 to 1977. Their data indicate that film attendance increased from 1900 to approximately 1945; audience attendance declined rapidly through 1970. From 1970 to 1977, film attendance was relatively stable, with a slight increase in the late 1970s (1).

Data collected from the *Motion Picture Almanac* support these conclusions. In fact, film attendance was at its highest in 1978, with over 1.2 billion admissions. However, attendance has decreased since this time with just over one billion admissions in 1980 (3,4,5).

Other evidence of a declining audience is suggested by public expenditures for recreational uses since 1941. The largest percentage of recreational dollars devoted to film attendance occurred in 1943; 25 percent was for the movies. The most current data, collected for 1976, find that only 4.12 percent of the money spent on recreation was allocated for the movies. A similar decline in total expenditures for spectator and amusement activities has also occurred (3,4,5).

These data surely document a decline of the film audience. What have not received sufficient attention are the reasons for this decline. De Fleur and Ball-Rokeach point to economic conditions brought on by competition with television as one reason. Interestingly, the temporary resurgence of film attendance in the late 1970s seems to correspond to a concomitant decrease in the number of television sets per household at this time (1). The conclusion from these data is that technological innovations, such as television in the 1950s, affects the use of the popular mass media. For example, some media critics attempt to explain slight decreases in the viewing of prime time television in terms of the competition from other video services offered through cable television. The point is that when new technologies are introduced, and they are accepted by the American public, existing forms of the media that are in direct competition must either find new needs to satisfy, as radio did in the 1950s when faced with competition from television, or be eliminated.

Prognostications concerning the demise of the film industry as we know it today have already been made. De Fleur and Ball-Rokeach predict that today's movie theater will disappear (1). The primary reason for this prediction is competition from other visual media such as television, cable television, direct broadcast systems, etc. Polon suggests that the most important competition for theatrical films is the home communication center. These centers, according to Polon, will allow consumers to access films by interconnecting computers with videocassette recorders and other sophisticated recording devices. Such competition will increase as alternate delivery systems, such as satellite to home technology, allow the recording of movies, esoteric entertainment, etc. The film industry will continue to decline unless it spends more money on research and development (8).

Jowett and Linton suggest that the real problem for the film industry is that technological innovations such as home video recorders will further fragment the film audience. The result will be films produced for the in-home delivery systems such as video recorders, or the simultaneous release of theater and home versions. Regardless, the theatrical film audience should continue to decline in the near future. As these technologies approach the theatrical film in visual sophistication, such as high-definition, large-screen television receivers, competition for the film audience will increase (6).

A recent study by the Newspaper Advertising Bureau, however, failed to support the predictions discussed above. The NAB found that although younger film attenders, the largest group in the film audience, were most likely to desire an in-home delivery system such as a video recorder, they were still likely to view movies in theaters. The NAB concluded that the younger film audience will enjoy films both in the theater and at home (7). Unfortunately, the data used to make these conclusions were based on asking respondents if they plan to buy a videocassette player in the future. These data do not support the conclusion that typical frequent film attenders will not decrease or even eliminate visits to the theater. Further, a plan to purchase items such as videocassettes is not valid evidence that such purchases will occur in the near or distant future. Therefore, although these data are interesting, they do not show the actual impact of in-home delivery systems, nor other entertainment alternatives on film attendance.

The inescapable conclusion from the preceding discussion is that the decline in film attendance will continue in the face of competition with existing and future visual technologies. The impact of in-home delivery systems and the interconnection of other home entertainment media will have potentially dramatic effects on film attendance. Unfortunately for those interested in quantifiable evidence, these predictions, although strongly grounded in film attendance and video purchasing data, do not establish a causal link between the use of in-home entertainment alternatives and film attendance. The purpose of this study was to attempt to establish such a link.

METHOD

Data for this study were originally collected for a study on politics and the mass media in 1982 (9). The present study is a secondary analysis of these data.

Procedure

A telephone survey was conducted with residents of Normal/Bloomington, Illinois concerning their use of in-home delivery systems and related media use behaviors. Telephone numbers were randomly generated to control for unlisted numbers and all interviews were conducted by trained interviewers. Four hundred eleven residents were initially contacted, with a total sample of 326. The completion ratio, computed by dividing the number of completed interviews by the total number of completions and refusals, was 79 percent.

Independent Variables

The independent variables used in the present study to determine the effects in-home technology has had on film attendance were divided into four categories: (a) demographic, (b) media use, (c) technology, and (d) innovativeness variables.

Demographic Variables. Four demographic variables have been identified as crucial to predicting film attendance. Probably the most important of these variables is age. According to many studies, the film audience is comprised primarily of younger viewers (7, 10). Age was measured in the present study as an interval variable with the youngest respondent at least 18 years old.

The second demographic variable used in the present study was income. According to data reported in the *Motion Picture Almanac,* the most frequent film-goers earn over $15,000 a year (1977 data), the highest category included in the report (4). Income was measured on an interval scale in this study.

Education has also been an important demographic variable. Data reported by Squire suggest that the more educated are more likely to be frequent attenders of theatrical performances than those less educated (10). Education was also measured on an interval appearing scale in this study.

The final demographic variable, the number of children in the household, has long been an important determinant of film attendance. Again, Squire found married couples with children under the age of 18 to attend films more frequently than married couples without children. However, adults who are not married are much more likely to attend films than their married counterparts (10). In the present study, respondents were asked if they had children living at home. If they answered yes, a value of one ("1") was recorded. Adults with no children living at home received a value of zero ("0"). The responses were then treated as a dummy variable in the analysis.

Media Use Variables. The selection of media use variables included in the present study was based on past research. Studies have found that such activities tend to be interactive, i.e., people high in one area of media use also tend to be heavy users of other media (11). The behaviors included in this study were: television viewing, magazine and daily newspaper reading, and radio listening.

Probably the most important of these behaviors is television viewing. De Fleur and Ball-Rokeach suggest that one primary reason for the decline in film attendance is the increased viewing of television (1). The actual number of hours viewed during the average day was recorded for each respondent. The total number of hours spent listening to the radio per day and the number of television network news programs viewed per week were also recorded.

Two media behaviors measuring use of printed material were also included in this analysis. Newspaper reading was measured in two ways. First, respondents were asked how many issues of the daily newspaper they read during the average week. Then, they were asked to estimate the actual time they spent reading the newspaper on an average day. The number of magazines read during an average month was also determined.

Technology Variables. Jowett and Linton and others suggest that the in-home delivery systems are most likely to negatively affect film attendance (1, 6). Respondents in the present study were asked if they owned one of the following "innovative" entertainment alternatives that could be classified as an in-home delivery system: a home computer, a home electronic games package, cable television, and subscription television channels. Responses were recorded as either a "yes" or a "no." Then, they were asked how much time per week they spent watching subscription channels and if these channels provided a useful method of entertainment. Ownership or subscription to the entertainment alternatives was measured as a dummy variable. (A score of one was assigned for every entertainment alternative owned or used by each respondent.) The total amount of time spent watching subscription channels was recorded on an interval scale. Finally, although not a technology question per se, respondents were also asked if films provided a useful means of entertainment. Responses were recorded on a Likert scale for this item.

Innovativeness. No research to date has uncovered a relationship between innovativeness and film attendance. However, if technological advances are to have an initial impact on film attendance, then early users of this technology might easily be classified as innovators. In the present study, innovation was measured on a scale developed by Hunt, Joseph and Cook (2). Basically, the scale operationalizes innovation as a personality trait measuring the likelihood to be innovative in the future. Ten items, with sufficient validity and reliability, comprised the unidimensional scale (2).

Dependent Variable

The dependent variable was measured on an interval scale. Respondents were asked the number of times they attend the movies a month. This number was then converted to the number of times they attended a year to eliminate fractions for the infrequent film attender.

RESULTS

The demographics of the sample were representative of the general population from which it was drawn. The average age was 36 years. The median education level was having at least some college education; 34 percent had graduated from high school. The median income was either under $15,000 or over $30,000 a year. Thirty-six percent of the respondents had at least one child living at home at the time of the survey. Fifty-five percent of the sample was female.

The impact of in-home technology on film attendance was determined by a stepwise, multiple regression analysis. Items in the four categories of independent variables were independently regressed on the dependent variable, annual film attendance. Prior to determining the causal linkages between the technology and film attendance, the internal validity of the innovativeness scale was determined.

Innovativeness Analysis

The 10 items designed to measure innovativeness were subjected to a factor analysis with varimax rotation. Criteria for selecting factors were a minimum eigenvalue of 1.00 and at least two items that met the loading criterion of ±.40. The data presented in Table 1 display the results of this analysis.

Table 1
Factor Analysis of the 10 Innovativeness Items

	Observation	Challenged
I am generally cautious about accepting new ideas.	.30	−.04
I rarely trust new ideas until I can see whether the vast majority of people around me accept them.	.60[a]	.08
I am aware that I am usually one of the last people in my group to accept something new.	.46[a]	.20
I am reluctant about adopting new ways of doing things until I see them working.	.52[a]	.16
I find it stimulating to be original in my thinking and behavior.	.04	.30
I tend to feel that the old way of living and doing things is the best way.	.56[a]	.07
I am challenged by ambiguities and unsolved problems.	.38	.05
I must see other people using new innovations before I will consider them.	.18	.11
I am challenged by unanswered questions.	.09	.71[a]
I often find myself skeptical of new ideas.	.12	.76[a]

[a]Met loading criterion of ± .40.

Table 2
Regression Analysis Predicting Film Attendance[a]

Variables	Beta	F	Significance
Age	−.22	7.47	.007
Children	−.21	8.09	.005
Magazines	.16	5.65	.019
Films Useful	−.16	5.06	.026
Cable Television	−.13	3.71	.050

[a]*Note:* The F value for the entire equation was 3.34, $R^2 = .24$.

According to Hurt, et al., the 10 items represent a unidimensional measure of innovativeness. In fact, they found two dimensions, but discounted the second one because it consisted of just the items with reverse wording. Almost identical results were obtained in the present study. The first factor, labeled "observation," consisted of four items that indicated respondents were interested in observing an innovation before adopting it. The second factor, consisting of two items, represents a dimension measuring the challenging nature of innovations. Despite the suggestion by Hurt, et al. that this factor structure be treated as unidimensional, two separate scales were constructed for each dimension. Scales were calculated by adding standardized values created by multiplying the factor score coefficient times the difference between each of the 10 variables and its respective mean, then dividing this number by the appropriate standard deviation.

Regression Analysis

The results of the regression analysis are displayed in Table 2. The final equation, significant at .05, consisted of five variables. In order of their predictive ability, these variables were: age, having children in residence, magazines read a month, perception of film as a useful form of entertainment, and subscription to cable television.

Negative beta weights indicate an inverse relationship between the independent and dependent variables. Therefore, the most frequent film attenders were: younger, without children at home, likely to read magazines, likely to find films useful for entertainment, and not cable television subscribers.

DISCUSSION

The results of the regression analysis support traditional research concerning the predominant audience for theatrical films and suggests that in-home technology has and probably will continue to have a detrimental impact on film attendance in the future.

First, the results indicate some validity of the data analyzed in the present study. Much research has found that the most frequent film attender is younger than those who do not frequent the theater (7, 10). Squire also suggests that families with children are somewhat more likely to attend the theater, with single adults much more likely to view films than their married counterparts (10). The results of the present study contradicted those of previous research because adults without children were more likely to attend films. Unfortunately, the married respondents could not be separated from the single adults in this analysis.

The inclusion of perception of films as useful sources of entertainment is actually an internal validity assessment of the data. Logically, respondents who view films most frequently should also find them a most suitable form of entertainment. This assumption was confirmed.

Magazine reading was also included in the regression equation. Unfortunately, no attempt was made to determine which magazines frequent film attenders read. These results suggest that some media use behaviors are interactive. However, the failure to find a relationship between the other media use behaviors considered in this study do not support the generally accepted notion that television viewing negatively affects film attendance. This finding suggests that these media behaviors satisfy very different needs. Evidence for this conclusion can be found in the study conducted by the Newspaper Advertising Bureau. They found that respondents indicating a desire to purchase home recorders also were frequent film attenders. These data, considered with the results of the present study, suggest that broadcast television no longer poses the threat to film attendance indicated by the data collected by De Fleur and Ball-Rokeach. The impact has already occurred.

The real competition for the leisure time spent viewing theatrical films is the in-home delivery systems. The inclusion of cable television in the regression equation, indicating that the most frequent film attenders *did not* subscribe to cable television, suggests that some needs once satisfied by attending films are now satisfied by programs viewed on cable television. However, the exact nature of this satisfaction should be a topic for future research.

The failure to find a relationship between the other technological innovations and film attendance can be explained by their diffusion in society. Cable penetration in the market considered in the present study is 78 percent. Subscription cable channels were received by 45 percent of the sample. Further, the average number of hours a week spent viewing subscription programs was only 7.75. This finding departs significantly from the weekly average time spent watching television of 18 hours for respondents in this study.

Ownership of the other in-home delivery systems also shows their relative newness. Only 9 percent owned home video recorders, 20 percent owned home game packages and 6 percent owned home computers. The results of this study suggest that once these alternative entertainment options are as diffused as cable television subscriptions, they too will negatively affect film attendance. Then the dire predictions made by De Fleur and Ball-Rokeach should be realized. The demise of the theatrically exhibited motion picture, as we know it today, is inevitable unless the film industry, especially exhibitors, becomes more interested in and competitive with the home technology.

Naturally, future research should also be concerned with these effects. De Fleur and Ball-Rokeach suggest that future studies consider how use of various mass media declines. They contend that most past studies have shown how the media have diffused throughout society. Studies on the proliferation of various in-home delivery systems have predominantly been concerned with acceptance by American society. Little research has attempted to explain how the various established media in direct competition with innovative forms have declined. Research such as the present report is a step in this direction. Future studies should continue to document how film attendance has declined and offer reasons for this decline.

REFERENCES

1. De Fleur, Melvin L. and Sandra Ball-Rokeach. *Theories of Mass Communication* (4th ed.). New York: Longman, 1982.
2. Hurt, H. Thomas, Katherine Joseph and Chester D. Cook. ''Scales for the Measurement of Innovativeness.'' *Human Communication Research* 4(1), Fall 1977, pp. 58–65.
3. *International Motion Picture Almanac*. New York: Quigley Publishing, 1982.
4. *International Motion Picture Almanac*. New York: Quigley Publishing, 1981.
5. *International Motion Picture Almanac*. New York: Quigley Publishing, 1979.
6. Jowett, Garth and James M. Linton. *Movies as Mass Communication*. Beverly Hills, CA: Sage Publications, 1980.
7. Newspaper Advertising Bureau. ''Movie-Going in the United States and Canada.'' New York: Newspaper Advertising Bureau, 1981.
8. Polon, Martin. ''Future Technologies in Motion Pictures.'' In Jason E. Squire (Ed.). *The Movie Business Book*. Englewood Cliffs, NJ: Prentice-Hall, Inc., 1983.
9. Shapiro, Mitchell E. and Wenmouth Williams, Jr. ''Agenda Setting in the 1982 Illinois Gubernatorial Campaign.'' Paper presented at the Central States Speech Association, April, 1983, Lincoln, Nebraska.
10. Squire, Jason E. ''Industry Economic Review and Audience Profile.'' In Jason E. Squire (Ed.). *The Movie Business Book*. Englewood Cliffs, NJ: Prentice-Hall, Inc., 1983.
11. Williams, Wenmouth and William D. Semlak. ''The Validation of Factored Gratifications and Avoidances and their Relationship to Political Effects.'' Paper presented at the Eastern Communication Association, March 1982, Hartford, Connecticut.

7

Hollywood, New Technologies and International Banking: A Formula for Financial Success

Janet Wasko

> In a sense, Hollywood is a small town that owns the world. Everyone pays attention to everything that goes on here. (17)

One would hardly expect modesty from the publisher of *Variety*. Still, Syd Silverman's exaggerated remarks deserve at least some attention in light of the changes taking place in the world of information and entertainment. How are new media technologies influencing the American film industry's export business?

Hollywood's past domination of international film markets and its strength in the worldwide export of television programming have been well-documented by European and American scholars over the years (7, 8, 14, 15, 16, 19). Today we need to inquire as to new technologies and how they may threaten Hollywood's leading position in international film and television markets.

Silverman explained Hollywood's position in a speech to the Los Angeles World Affairs Council:

> The energy and flexibility of the production industry here is remarkable. Television didn't destroy Hollywood, it gave it a bigger market. Now the potential of cable and paycable may offer opportunity for even greater growth. Despite all the ups and downs, feuds and disputes, Hollywood will survive and thrive—because it delivers what people pay for. No one ever bought a ticket to watch technology. The people in Hollywood who make the crucial decisions know that *content* will determine the entertainment choices of the public, regardless of the means of distribution. (17)

With the introduction of new video technologies, the means of distribution for Hollywood products definitely is expanding. It was estimated that by the end of 1983, there would be over 40 million homes with video recorders in 63 countries. In one of Hollywood's favorite markets, Western Europe, it is expected that there will be 120 million homes receiving cable and satellite services by early 1990. Seventy-five percent of these homes will watch premium film channels. Thus, some European observers agree with Silverman's assessment of program supply. CIT Research Executive, Patrick Whitten, in London commented: "it is programming, not channel capacity, which is the new scarce resource" (18).

What about other production resources, especially in Western Europe? Patrice Flichy has observed:

> Just as Hollywood is discovering new markets, the greater part of European audiovisual media are not likely to create their own program industry, and if they cannot be supplied by existing producers, they will appeal to other sources abroad, essentially to Hollywood. (5)

In light of these remarks, this article sorts out the reasons why Hollywood may continue to dominate international film and television markets, especially in Western Europe, and examines in some detail Hollywood's vital relationships with international financial institutions.

HOLLYWOOD'S CONTINUING STRENGTH

One of Hollywood's inestimable advantages is its home market. The U.S. box office generates enough revenue to recoup initial production investments, test risky products or marketing strategies, and develop specialized products for "minority" audiences. The U.S. also represents a more or less closed market through a form of "de facto protectionism." Attempts to penetrate the U.S. film market continue to fail, as illustrated by EMI's American Film Distribution effort, which lasted two years, but finally buckled. (EMI now distributes its films in the U.S. via Universal.)

The U.S., most importantly, already provides a huge home market for new technologies. The number of video recorders in the U.S. to date is almost 9 million, which only represents 10 percent of the total U.S. households. Cable systems in the U.S. offer additional opportunities for expansion and experimentation, both for television programming and feature films.

A second aspect of Hollywood's domination is its international distribution system which remains strong, effective, and profitable. American and non-American media products are distributed through alliances with large cinema chains and television companies abroad. As noted recently by the European Economic Community, these activities are sometimes carried on through monopolistic practices, including block-booking, price fixing, etc. The international strength of the majors is due in some part to the joint efforts of "competing" American corporations and their active, powerful trade association, the Motion Picture Association of America (M.P.A.A.) (see 7).

It has been estimated that Hollywood collects nearly 50 percent of the worldwide box office for feature films. Although the dependence on foreign revenue has declined recently to 30 percent of the total annual revenues for the industry, and while some European countries manage to *keep* 50 percent of their domestic box office in any given year, still, all in all, a handful of U.S. based corporations control the major share of European film markets.

Thus, Hollywood remains strong with an established distribution system, experience and expertise in international sales, and a well-defined commitment to international marketing.

Diversification is another one of Hollywood's strong points. The operations of the majors have long included television, which is especially important when considering new forms of media technology. Thus, Hollywood is already prepared with new marketing strategies, which include new release patterns sometimes featuring video and pay TV distribution following, or at the same time as, theatrical release, but prior to network and syndicated television sales. Also, there are enhanced merchandising schemes promising "very clean" profits from licensing TV and film characters, such as E.T. or Mr. T., and the manufacture and distribution of games, T-shirts, cookie jars, and the underwear of these especially "toyetic" characters. According to one Hollywood executive, the Miss Piggy phenomenon has especially revitalized the Hollywood merchandising wizards (1). These anxious corporate marketing executives now urge writers and producers to include marketable characters in their feature film and television scripts. This merely reminds us again that the Hollywood majors who dominate feature film and television are diversified entertainment conglomerates or part of large multinational organizations, and not dependent on only one line of business for survival. Ironically, thanks to the antitrust action resulting in the Paramount decrees in the 1950s, the majors no longer are dependent on theatrical film exhibition or the declining—perhaps dying—institution called CINEMA. (More on this point later.)

Diversification strategies—especially the successful adaptation to television—have meant that the Hollywood majors are not only ready to supply "software" for new media technology, but also are participating in the technological development and implementation of "hardware." Both activities involve new alliances with each other *and,* importantly, with other non-entertainment multinational companies. Examples include Warner Communications' alliance with American Express in the area of cable and MCA's involvement with Phillips and IBM to manufacture a videodisc system.

The general political and economic climate in the U.S. is another factor contributing to the strength of major Hollywood corporations. New media technologies are developing within the private sector in a climate of government deregulation, with attempts to revitalize the domestic market system, as well as to regain international political, economic, and military leadership. While denationalization and commercialization trends in Europe are proceeding rapidly, but with much debate and discussion (see 12), broadcast deregulation is proceeding in the U.S. with much less resistance (see 22,23). Thus, the major corporations are left with wide latitude to develop markets as they please.

Although there certainly have been strong links between Hollywood and Washington in the past, it seems that there is a special relationship with the present administration. President Reagan's recent involvement in the tentative decision on syndicated television programming is evidence of the close ties between Hollywood and the White House.

Yet another element in Hollywood's international success has been pointed out by Andrew Filson in a study for the Commission of the European Communities on distribution of films in community countries:

> The success of the American film industry is based on its financial strength, which enables them to survive periods of bad management. They were pioneers in the film business and established an early leadership which they have maintained in the face of all challengers. Success now breeds success, for the box office winners of today are providing and attracting the finance for producing the winners of tomorrow. (3)

Whereas European audio/visual production is generally in a weak or stagnating state, the Hollywood majors (for the most part) are in excellent financial health. This has prompted a flurry of takeover bids, management and ownership shifts, and has provided important advantages for moving into new markets and new media activities which require increased capital investments and expenditures. Meanwhile, the majors are able to continue financing American and non-American media production, attracting talent both in the U.S. and abroad, as well as promoting films and other media activities through substantial advertising budgets.

The majors' financial strength is not only represented by surplus profits from the successful seventies, as Filson notes, but the ability of successful companies to *attract* capital when needed or desired. Thus, the development and maintenance of continuing and close ties with the financial community—especially commercial banks—both domestically and internationally, becomes an important factor in assessing Hollywood's international strength.

INTERNATIONAL BANKING AND HOLLYWOOD

As with other multinational corporations, American-based media conglomerates depend upon and are involved with financial institutions in a variety of ways. Elsewhere I have documented the history of this relationship between the American motion picture industry and banks (21). The conclusions of that study are relevant here, as banks are found to support the majors' diversification and international activities. Since the transitional period in the 1950s, those banks involved with the major film corporations have encouraged and participated in the ongoing diversification process described previously.

Today, Hollywood bankers praise "splendidly diversified" companies such as MCA and Twentieth Century-Fox. The "new Hollywood" executives who make the day-to-day decisions involved in running these various activities are also commended. Indeed, the legal and financial backgrounds of many of these managers not only suit their banking "partners," but also may contribute to the more rapid acceptance of new technology than was the case with past Hollywood moguls. In addition, many Hollywood executives today have already had experience in television programming, thus making them ready and able to tackle new TV technologies.

It might be noted here that those banks dealing with the American film majors have also diversified their own activities, generally offering a variety of services, but also, expanding their relationships with media industries. Since the fifties, Hollywood banks have developed important relationships with the television industry, as an important component of their entertainment divisions or special industries groups.

Internationalization has been encouraged by movie bankers. As noted by Bank of America president, Jess W. Tapp, in commemorating the bank's 50 year involvement with Hollywood in the mid-fifties: "Hollywood's boundaries are the world's, selling the American way of life and also selling some of our products" (21). This point of view set the stage for the Bank of America's enhanced international services for the American film industry in the 1960s through the 1970s.

More recently, Wells Fargo banker John Fisher has predicted increased growth for the American entertainment industry—"an industry with the ability to bring back many American dollars spent abroad" (4). Investment banker Herbert Allen boasted that selling software is even better than the oil business (21).

Banks have also become increasingly international. Especially since the late 1960s, U.S. banks have experienced dramatic international expansion. Only a few statistics need be cited here. In 1960, only eight American banks had overseas branches, while by 1977, there were 730 foreign branches with 1,600 subsidiaries and affiliates abroad. During the same year, 50 percent of the income from seven New York "money center" banks was derived from foreign operations.

Western European and Japanese banks have expanded as well, as international financing and banking have grown with international trade, and especially with the growth of multinational production and investment since the 1960s. But, U.S. international banks remain especially important, handling one-half of all worldwide lending (which totaled over $174 billion in 1974). Again, this activity is concentrated with a few of the largest U.S. banking institutions (20).

The internationalization of banking is important in several ways. First, the dependency and alliances between multinational electronic and media conglomerates and the questions of control inherent in these relationships must be considered. In a recent study of international information and finance, Dutch researcher Cees Hamelink concluded that there is an increasing "convergence of interests between these two sectors, with a 'financial-information-industrial complex' as well as a significant degree of financial control in [the] transnational information industry." Hamelink concludes that this convergence is probably greater for the information sector than for other industries (10).

There is still another key component that has yet to be mentioned. International banks have been and continue to be the prime customers as well as initiators of new electronic and computerized information technology systems through their use of data processing, electronic funds transfer systems, and other computerized financial services. They also employ some of the most sophisticated information and communication systems, which utilize all forms of telecommunications, telex, telephone, cable, satellites, videotex, etc. Such systems as Citibanks' GLOBECOM, SWIFT, EUREX, and others, link banks worldwide. (The complex, yet crucial, issues involved in these developments for the international monetary system, as well as for national economies, are somewhat beyond the scope of this paper. Our concern is the interaction of the Hollywood majors and these banks abroad.)

The small community of banks used by and affiliated with the Hollywood majors include some of these large and important international banking institutions. Perhaps this is not too surprising, given the American film industry's international focus. Exploring this relationship, however, is not an easy task. The problems of gathering information and data are compounded by four. As usual, there are the problems of dealing with the film industry in the U.S. and the traditionally secretive and cautious banking business, where veils of secrecy are shrouded with cries of "customer confidentiality." Confronting both of these institutions at an international level results in even less disclosure of information and even more cautious discussion of affairs and affiliations. In addition, access to those involved can become too costly and totally beyond the means of most researchers. However, based on a few interviews with Hollywood's commercial bankers at their London offices, it has been possible to gather some interesting data on these relationships.

London might be said to serve loosely as headquarters in Europe for Hollywood activities. Most all of the Hollywood banks have recognized branches in London. London also becomes important with the majors' entrenchment in the U.K. and London's role as a key European money center in general.

Although there are individual differences between different banks and corporations, generally the primary American banks serving the Hollywood majors in the U.S. support the corporate activities of these companies abroad. As with other international banks, the large, multinational corporate customers are favored.

Although many of these services are more or less routine, particularly relevant are the advice and services related to diversification and investments abroad by American media conglomerates. Hollywood's London bankers are able to "keep an eye out" for merger possibilities, as well as "watching over" foreign investments.

Related to this activity is the servicing involved with the majors' international production schedule. Production funds and accounts, money transfers, etc., are often handled for films and television series produced abroad by American majors, or their "dependent-independent" producers, or for those foreign producers affiliated with the American distribution corporations.

There are American banks involved with individual picture financing or project loans, as well as becoming involved with financing packages arranged internationally in a number of ways. Yet, this point must be carefully qualified. First, only a few banks participate in this type of lending, which requires a good deal of time and specialized expertise, as compared with other forms of financing. As in the U.S., few banks are interested in developing this expertise. During the last few years, the First National Bank of Chicago has been actively involved in "project loans" for film production. The Bank of America has been in the past. No doubt, other banks will be in the future.

One other important point must be added. None of these banks will even consider *any* film financing project without the involvement of one of the major American distributors. "One cannot make an investment decision that is dependent on the whims of the general public," as one international banker has noted (9). (There goes the myth of a consumer-controlled market.) Thus, "internationally marketable films" are preferred over local products for these film bankers.

It might also be noted that the Hollywood banks in London are involved with what's left of the British film industry. The First National Bank of Boston and First Chicago maintain close relations with EMI, Rank, ITC, and Sir Lew Grade—again, *corporate* clients with *international* orientations.

As far as actual distribution business, in the U.K. at least, the American majors utilize the services of the national banks, with their local banking networks for collection and payment of box office profits, and their expertise in domestic banking matters.

In general, then, the international relationships of the American majors and their key banks abroad are extensions of their relations in the U.S. Foreign activities most often pertain to *operational* services, while corporate lending and *allocative* decision-making—even involving international activities—remain, for both bank and corporation, within a national framework.

An illustration of this general principle is provided by the comments of a banker at the London branch of First National Bank of Boston. He noted that though one might find a foreign production over budget, his job is only to advise Boston. The pressure on the producer, if any, will come from Boston, and most likely, to one of the executives at the American major involved. In fact, First Boston's London film man claimed to know little of current corporate lending restrictions and covenants applicable to the major corporations he deals with in London.

It might also be suggested that these internationally extended relationships further intensify an already-concentrated structure of control over resource and capital allocations for a good deal of the American culture industries and their cultural exports around the world. This situation has implications for the production and distribution of cultural goods, both in the U.S. and Europe.

First, it offers no relief from the American majors' domination of the European commercial film market. Hollywood's international bankers and many others defend the majors' position, noting that they take the risks and invest the funds, and thus, their profits are well deserved. Banks, of course, ultimately share these profits.

Furthermore, there is not much relief in store for those other forms of cinema that are not commercial, whether in the U.S. or in Europe. Local and/or indigenous, truly independent, avantgarde, or politically unfashionable filmmaking is less possible without the support or backing of ''rich uncles''—whether private or public. For instance, Uncle Sam has lately become less and less responsive to the needs of the creative arts, generally, which makes it increasingly difficult to obtain funds for independent cinema and video production. In addition, the subsidies and aid systems for European cinema are either inadequate or currently in a state of flux, with the possibility of cutbacks constantly looming on the horizon.

Private financing sources, including film financing companies and various private investors, are not reliable or adequate sources for funding films, either. And, as we have seen, the usual suppliers for the private sector (banking institutions) have restricted their lending to the safe and reliable, mainly the majors. Although there is some bank lending by European banks, and even specialized film financing institutions, there are still significant problems gathering adequate production funds without an American major involved.

Despite numerous proposals within the European film community for the establishment of co-distribution and co-financing consortiums, there has been no actual implementation of these plans, despite continuous cries of crises from many quarters. Indeed, some of these cries have turned into agonized moans, predicting the death of the European cinema altogether. But perhaps this is inevitable, since cinema, at least in its present form of theatrical exhibition, could become the next cultural dinosaur, according to some predictions. As Nicholas Garnham has observed:

> The specificity of cinema lies, not in its technology of reproduction but in its institutionalisation as a form of mass distribution. That form must be seen as transitional within a wide historical perspective. (6)

Certainly this may not even be considered as such a great loss in the long run to the Hollywood majors, who are no longer burdened with investments in exhibition, and with their ever-growing involvement in new media technologies. Their activities are encouraged and supported by the international bankers involved, who are also intimately involved in the use and development of some of the same new technology.

What about the promises of greater diversity and choice in cultural goods, plus the enhanced public participation and access possible as a result of new technologies? Certainly the potential is there for more personal control over media replay (via videocassettes, discs, etc.), as well as the expansion of the number of channels offered for diverse and minority interests (via cable and satellites). However, these promises may remain only utopian dreams or slick sales gimmicks, as new media technologies develop generally within the private sphere under marketplace principles. And, as we have seen, this trend is supported and encouraged by the international financial community.

One of the most significant limitations in these developments has been pointed out by Graham Murdock:

> By making access to the "new" television commodities conditional upon ability to pay, the price system reinforces the already powerful connections between economic and cultural advantage and further widens the gap between the information rich and the information poor.
> This gap has already grown significantly in recent years as the deepening economic recession has already produced a large claimant class who are living on or below the official poverty line and therefore are unable to translate their full needs for information and entertainment into effective demands. (13)

CONCLUSION

The MacBride Commission Report on Communications observed that the transnationalization of production, *financing,* and marketing of communications serves as a barrier to democratization of communications (11). It might be added that the concentration of ownership and control over communication resources, both at the national and international levels, impedes the potential for democratic communication as well. And if we are to break down these barriers we must also be aware of and understand more fully than we do now, as communications and film scholars, whether in the U.S. or in Europe, the actual political and economic framework within which new media technologies are evolving. The continuing close and complex relations between international banks and communications conglomerates must not be neglected in our analysis.

REFERENCES

1. Borden, Lester J. "Merchandising and Distribution Techniques of Programmes." Paper presented at the New Dimensions in Television Conference, March 26, 1981, Venice, Italy.
2. Degand, Claude. "The U.S. Film Industry, 1969–79." Commission on Culture and Education, Council of Europe Conference, December 1979, Strasbourg, France.
3. Filson, Andrew. "The Distribution of Films Produced in the Countries of the Community." Council of Europe Conference, April 28–30, 1980, Strasbourg, France.
4. Fisher, John G. "Screen and Tube Financing in the Inflated Years Abroad." *Variety,* January 9, 1980, p. 80.
5. Flichy, Patrice. *Les Industries de l'Imaginaire*. Paris: Institut National de l'Audio-visuel, 1980.
6. Garnham, Nicholas. "The Economics of the U.S. Motion Picture Industry." Study for the Commission of the European Communities, Council of Europe Conference, April 1980, Strasbourg, France.
7. Guback, Thomas H. *The International Film Industry: Western Europe and America Since 1945*. Bloomington, IN: Indiana University Press, 1969.
8. Guback, Thomas and Tapio Varis. *Transnational Communication and Cultural Industries*. UNESCO Reports and Papers on Mass Communication No. 92. Paris, 1983.
9. Hollinger, Hy. "O'Sea Pic Sales Pioneers Eye Altered Biz." *Variety,* October 26, 1983, pp. 7, 366.
10. Hamelink, Cees. *Finance and Information*. Norwood, NJ: Ablex Publishers, 1982.
11. Macbride, Sean, et al. *Many Voices, One World: Communications and Society, Today and Tomorrow*. London: Kogan Page, 1980.
12. Mosco, Vincent and Janet Wasko. *The Critical Communications Review-Volume II: Changing Patterns of Communications Control*. Norwood, NJ: Ablex Publishing, 1984.
13. Murdock, Graham. "Programming: Needs and Answers." Paper presented at the New Dimensions in Television Conference, March 28, 1981, Venice, Italy.
14. Nordenstreng, Kaarle and Varis Tapio. *Television Traffic—A One-Way Street?* UNESCO Reports and Papers on Mass Communication No. 70. Paris, 1974.
15. Pendakur, Manjunath. "Cultural Dependency in Canada's Feature Film Industry." *Journal of Communication* 31 (1), Winter 1981, pp. 48–57.
16. Schiller, Herbert I. *Mass Communications and American Empire*. Boston: Beacon Press, 1971.
17. Silverman Syd. "Entertainment in the Satellite Era." *Variety,* October 26, 1983, pp. 12–13.
18. "Suitable Program Packaging Crucial to DBS' Success." *Variety,* October 19, 1983, p. 70.
19. Tunstall, Jeremy. *The Media Are American: Anglo-American Media in the World*. New York: Columbia University Press, 1977.
20. U.S. Congress. House of Representatives, Committee on Banking, Currency and Housing. *Financial Institutions and the Nation's Economy,* Book II, Part 4. Washington: Government Printing Office, 1976.
21. Wasko, Janet. *Movies and Money: Financing the American Film Industry*. Norwood, NJ: Ablex Publishers, 1982.
22. Wasko, Janet. "New Methods of Analyzing Media Concentration." In Vincent Mosco, ed., *Policy Research in Telecommunications*. Norwood, NJ: Ablex Publishers, in press.
23. Wasko, Janet. "The Role of Political Economy in the Information Age." In Mary Mander, ed., *Communications in Transition*. New York: Praeger, 1983.

8
Non-Market Factors in the International Distribution of American Films*

Thomas Guback

Motion pictures made in the United States customarily account for less than a tenth of the world's annual production of feature-length theatrical films. Yet no one can deny that American films capture a share of global box-office receipts greater than that received by any other nationality, and that they also have the largest share of global screen time. Moreover, the companies producing and distributing these pictures dominate their own home market to such an extent that foreign films rarely receive broad theatrical release in the United States. Consequently, earnings of foreign films have been extremely modest given the wealth of the market, as well as compared to the money garnered by American films abroad. Similarly, American commercial television virtually is closed to feature motion pictures and programs made overseas.

The foreign market, which contributes close to half of the theatrical revenue earned by the major U.S. companies, obviously has great importance for the American industry. The development and stabilization of this market, therefore, warrants attention. The foreign policy of the U.S. film industry is necessarily a broad subject that could be examined relative to particular countries or time periods. This essay, though, is concerned mainly with aspects of industry–government relations. It treats as well the operations and functions of the trade association established by the Hollywood majors to assist them in foreign markets: the Motion Picture Export Association of America. It is not the purpose of the essay to provide a comprehensive account, or even the highlights, of the Association's 40-year history, but rather to indicate its place in the industry's foreign policy, and to identify the lines of intersection that have drawn business and state together.

The preeminent position of American companies and American films has been achieved principally at the expense of competitors abroad. Domination by American pictures has meant that industries overseas have had to struggle to find and maintain a place in their own home markets, and often this has led to stunted and financially weak production in countries around the globe. Such conditions, in turn, negatively affect the ability of these industries to expand and thrive. When they have difficulties in their own home markets, then they have even less chance in other countries.

With perhaps minor qualifications, depending upon the country considered, this general description applies to western industrialized nations as well as to the Third World. The inability of Canada, for example, to develop a theatrical film production industry cannot be understood without reference to the exportation of American films to that country, the political role played by American distribution companies, and the American ownership of the largest theater circuit (see 2, 21). Only through Canadian government intervention in the marketplace, by providing tax incentives and loans to production, has a limited amount of filmmaking been stimulated. Developing countries, often with fewer economic resources, face a less optimistic future.

The ability of American companies to achieve this global market dominance has been explained in several ways. It is attributed frequently to the world wars, which devastated or weakened film production in most industrialized countries, while leaving U.S. production unscathed, if not stronger. After the First World War, the United States changed from being a net importer of film to a net exporter. The Second World War served to consolidate that status. The great size of the domestic American market also has been mentioned as a significant element, allowing the industry to recover a substantial portion of its costs at home—an advantage not enjoyed by film industries elsewhere. The inherently expansive nature of capitalism in general, when worked out in the film industry in particular, also cannot be overlooked as a basic factor. All these explanations must be taken into account, of course, because they identify ingredients that have contributed in important ways to American superiority.

Public pronouncements from the American industry frequently declare that its success overseas or at home is due entirely to the natural operation of supply and demand in the marketplace. Jack Valenti, president of the Motion Picture Export Association, told a Senate subcommittee in 1977:

> One of our assets is that the American film market is totally free. Swedish film, Indian film, Soviet film, or Italian film, has the same access to this market as American film, and that is the way it ought to be. The public ought to decide. That is one reason why the American film is the most wanted export abroad. While governments may fulminate against American films, foreign audiences love them. We dominate world screens—not because of armies, bayonets, or nuclear bombs, but because what we are exhibiting on foreign screens the people of those countries want to see. . . . In a strange way, though, American film sometimes so dominates in a country that this causes envy, distaste, and sometimes rebuttal in various forms

by foreign governments. This is not because of our power but because the public prefers to see these films over the local product.[1] (25, pp. 211–212)

Whenever the market is free from governmental restraints, this argument goes, consumers consistently have chosen American pictures from among the many alternatives. According to this view, what we see as American domination is nothing less than unfettered public preference expressed on a global scale. A corollary of this line of reasoning is that American interests should be absolved from any responsibility or blame for the feeble conditions of their competitors abroad.

The problem with *all* these explanations is that they rely on causal forces largely external to the American film industry, and apart from its own volition and institutional practices. The explanations imply that this industry has been merely the passive recipient of the good fortune of historical circumstances and economic laws. Its preeminent position is assumed to flow from factors over which it has had little, if any, control.

Such thinking totally ignores the policies developed by the American industry itself to capture and maintain markets and to obstruct foreign competitors (see 6). It also overlooks the often mutually profitable alliances between American production-distribution companies and elements among the foreign bourgeoisie who favor and support the interests of international capital at the expense of their domestic capital. Similarly, such reasoning refuses to recognize the intricate and extensive set of relations between the industry and the American government that have contributed to the growth of this dominance.

The latter point requires at least brief elaboration because a prevalent assumption of dominant ideology, as it has emerged in western liberalism, is that private (individual) interest and government interest are antithetical, if not entirely hostile. Private interest seeks liberty as a condition for its fulfillment, whereas government interest is innately restrictive, and therefore inherently suspect. Grafted onto this assumption about the dichotomous nature of private and state interest is a view positing the state as a somewhat less antagonistic entity, at least in politically democratic societies. This pluralist position contends that state action is nothing but the result of a largely impartial umpire selecting among alternate policies proposed by differing but basically coequal groups in society.

In contrast to those views stand two others that see the state as neither hostile nor necessarily neutral toward dominant interests (see 5). Both situate the state within the context of a liberal democratic society that is *also* a capitalist society in which conflicting and unequal classes exist. The instrumentalist posi-

[1]Mr. Valenti seems to ignore that governments abroad hardly act independently of their business sectors' demands, and that the "rebuttal . . . by foreign governments" is nothing other than the official reaction provoked by the threatened condition of foreign film industries, especially the production and distribution segments.

tion (see 15) conceives the state as an entity through which the capitalist ruling class exercises its will. In this way, the state, which itself may have little scope for independent action, advances the interests of capital by developing and enacting appropriate policies. The activator is the capitalist class that controls state apparatus through influence, election, appointment, and by placing its own members in crucial posts. A more complex arrangement is proposed by the structuralist position (see 1, 22), which contends that the state possesses a considerable degree of autonomy. The state acts, of course, to serve and accommodate the interests of capital in general, but also pursues policies to support its own needs. The latter may conflict with immediate requirements of particular economic sectors, as may advancement of the broad interests of capital. The state functions somewhat independently, sorting and adjusting conflicting demands from various capitalist spheres, but ultimately seeks to preserve and perpetuate the system as a whole.

As the evidence will demonstrate, the state hardly has been an impartial bystander when the interests of the film industry have been concerned. Indeed, the foreign policies of the state and the industry have been mutually supportive. Aspects of the instrumentalist and structuralist positions aptly explain this reality in ways that other perspectives simply cannot handle. Although the foreign activity of the film industry obviously has not been the highest priority item on the state's agenda, an alliance has been created that serves the interests of the state, the industry, and capital in general. While the film industry is part of the economic infrastructure, as are its products when they are construed only as commodities, these same products also are part of the superstructure because of their ideological function.

INDUSTRY–STATE COOPERATION

In the decades up to 1945, the American motion picture industry developed from an ingrown collection of small, diverse production and distribution companies into a tiny group of vertically integrated giants that dominated America and every other film market to which they had access. They brought foreign competitors to their knees, and film production industries abroad, even in the largest countries, were able to survive only with government assistance of one sort or another. When World War II began, American companies were receiving at least 35 to 40 percent of their theatrical revenue from overseas (excluding Canada) even though they faced a bewildering array of trade barriers in some of these countries.

During the 1920s and 1930s, as overseas trade became more significant, the Motion Picture Producers and Distributors of America Inc. expanded its Foreign Department, which spoke for MPPDA members and represented their interests in film trade negotiations abroad. The Department also had a few offices overseas with small staffs. In addition, it established and maintained close relations with the Department of State and American embassies, cooperation that was important for the expanding commercial interests of these companies.

In view of the industry's success in creating a thriving foreign business, why did it organize the Motion Picture Export Association of America in 1945?

For one thing, the major companies throughout the 1930s had been the target of government and private legal suits for restraint of trade in the domestic market. Government attorneys, studying collusive tactics of major companies at home, hardly could have failed to observe parallels between domestic and foreign operations, especially agreements among MPPDA companies operating overseas. American antitrust law, although applying chiefly to the American market, also declared to be illegal contracts restraining trade with foreign nations. In this respect, the MPPDA and its members might have feared that their foreign activities could be subject to prosecution under antitrust law. They sought protection for their behavior and found it in the Webb-Pomerene Export Trade Act of 1918, which gave a legal shield to anticompetitive activity abroad, provided it took place within a formally chartered export trade association. Agreements among competitors concerning their foreign trade, when worked out within such an association, would be immune to domestic challenge from the antitrust law.

Other concerns, stemming from World War II, also prompted the companies to establish an export association. It was clear that in continental Europe, and in some markets elsewhere, massive devastation had disrupted economies, and this naturally affected the film business. Cinemas were destroyed, civilians had little disposable income, and needs infinitely more pressing than Hollywood films commanded available economic resources. In many countries, local production demanded continued government protection and assistance. It was a struggle, not just against American films, but to recreate a national film industry in the face of material hardships and capital shortages. Protective legislation, enacted in many countries in the 1920s and 1930s, had been overturned during the war, but there was every likelihood that such measures would be resurrected when peace came. To American companies, this posed an exceptional threat in Europe, the largest foreign market.

A diminished market in postwar western Europe, due to stunted economies and commercial protectionism, would decrease companies' revenue relative to their overhead expenses, making it more difficult for each company to maintain its own distribution network. Similarly, unbridled competition among the companies, each scrambling for a big slice of a diminished pie, certainly would be a bloody battle that they wanted to avoid.

It was evident to the American companies that they had to develop a plan to structure the postwar world cinematic market to benefit their own commercial interests. What this entailed was revealed in March 1944 by the head of the Motion Picture Section of the government's War Production Board:

> I was gratified to learn that certain arrangements have already been made by the State Department in furtherance of the free and unhampered distribution of American films. . . .
>
> But this is only one phase of the program which the industry should press for the removal of embargoes and other barriers to the free distribution of our films. The need exists for a permanent, well-organized industry committee, capable of dealing with national and international problems, particularly in relation to the peace conference and post-war conditions.
>
> Unless the industry lays the groundwork in advance for presenting its case it will miss a golden opportunity. The proper committee or agency should be set up now to begin preparing a program. . . .
>
> Without a properly organized committee to keep the United States Government and all its agencies, as well as foreign nations, thoroughly conversant with the needs and requirements and problems of the industry, there is little hope that the motion-picture producers of the country will be given proper consideration at the peace table or in the domestic affairs of foreign nations with regard to consumer goods produced in the United States. (9, pp. 2878, 2879).

These material considerations certainly were commanding practical reasons why an export association could function with great effectiveness, but there were important ideological concerns as well that must not be underestimated (see 7). Particularly in western Europe, the end of Nazi control would create a somewhat fluid political climate that could offer the Left an opportunity to win popular support and to come to political power, or to exert substantial influence through coalition governments. The possibility of a strong swing to a democratic Left in the European capitalist countries was regarded with serious concern by the United States, which mounted an intensive campaign, planned long before the war ended, to thwart such a political tendency. Beside diplomatic and economic pressure, all means of official and private communications were enlisted in this propaganda program, and obviously American films had their role to play. The need was to get the American message around the world, openly through the United States Information Agency (U.S.I.A.), the Voice of America, etc., and unobtrusively through the seemingly innocent quality of motion pictures. For this reason, distribution of films was encouraged actively by the American government, in addition to their traditional place in international commerce.

Ushering in the era of American hegemony, this communications offensive was formalized in a new doctrine—the free flow of information—that became a cornerstone of American foreign policy. Stripped of rhetoric, it meant unhindered access by America's media to the world's markets, and this was to be accomplished with the full support of the government. In this case, there was total convergence of industry and state policy. As the annual report of the MPPDA, released in March 1945, declared:

> Our State Department has announced an enlightened policy that places our government firmly behind the principle of unhampered transit for all mediums [*sic*] of

> expression, including press, motion pictures, cables, and radio. . . . Our industry . . . continues to need, and is grateful for receiving, understanding and support by all the governmental agencies concerned with the export of American films to the world market. (16)

The Motion Picture Export Association of America (MPEA) was established under terms of the Webb-Pomerene Act and incorporated in Delaware on June 5, 1945. Columbia, Loew's, Paramount, RKO, Twentieth Century-Fox, United Artists, Universal, and Warner were the founding companies. On October 1, the MPEA announced that its members had elected Eric Johnston president of the association; two weeks earlier, he had succeeded Will Hays as head of the MPPDA. (On December 12, the MPPDA changed its name to Motion Picture Association of America.)

The Certificate of Incorporation declared that the MPEA was established to "engage solely in export trade to foreign nations," and "in connection with such export trade," the association was empowered "to do any and all things necessary or incidental thereto." By the end of 1945, members of the MPEA had granted it an exclusive license, for a limited but renewable period of time, to distribute their films to theaters in the Netherlands. Soon, additional contracts were arranged between the members and the MPEA allowing it to distribute their films in Germany, Austria, Yugoslavia, Hungary, Rumania, Bulgaria, Poland, Czechoslovakia, the Soviet Union, the Netherlands East Indies, Japan, and Korea. Elsewhere, companies distributed their own films.

The initial MPEA licenses to distribute films in 13 countries were due to expire at various times throughout 1949, so MPEA members agreed to extend the association's joint distribution operation for at least two years. Gradually, as political and economic stability returned to these territories, the individual MPEA members resumed physical distribution of their own films. By the beginning of 1952, the companies were releasing their own pictures in the Netherlands, Germany, Japan, Korea, and the Netherlands East Indies; Austria was added to the list in August 1952. Except for Yugoslavia, countries in the Soviet bloc stopped importing American pictures toward the end of 1948. The MPEA continued to export directly to Yugoslavia, and received revenue from it through 1956. By 1957, however, the MPEA itself no longer distributed pictures of its members, and all foreign releasing was handled by companies themselves (19).

As the MPEA closed its distribution operations, it seemed that the principal overt purpose for the Association's being no longer existed. It would have appeared that the MPEA had played its important role to reestablish the market for American films in certain countries, and that it could be dissolved. But since its founding, it was clear that its activities were much more extensive than joint distribution, and that its life was far from ended.

In 1953, all international activities of the MPAA were formally transferred to the Motion Picture Export Association. The MPEA announced its duties: expanding overseas markets by reducing foreign government restraints on American films through direct negotiation "and other appropriate means", expediting the remittance of foreign earnings, developing markets abroad for American films, serving as a central liaison for the dozens of American film boards throughout the world, collecting and disseminating information to members about market conditions, dealing with tax problems and wage negotiations in foreign territories, and representing members before the Department of State and other government bodies (17). Other foreign functions, whose legality was ratified by the MPEA's incorporation under the Webb-Pomerene Act, were: dividing business among members, fixing minimum and/or maximum prices for members' films, implementing boycotts, and promoting uniformity in film booking practices (4).

The concrete application of these powers has left a history demonstrating the extent to which the MPEA created healthy operating conditions abroad for its members. It would be incorrect, though, to believe that the success of American films and companies overseas was due entirely to this trade association. The role played by the American government has been exceptionally important, and were it not for this state intervention, American pictures would not have achieved such a secure position. Government assistance was especially crucial in the postwar years when political, economic, and commercial policies were being reformulated by foreign countries. This support was frequently reiterated, as when Willard Thorp, Assistant Secretary for Economic Affairs, Department of State, wrote to Eric Johnston in June 1948: "I should like to reassure you of our intention to cooperate fully with you and your associates in the motion picture industry." Thorp said the department was planning "the permanent assignment of a fully competent officer to motion picture work" (23).

While one need not recite the entire catalog of forms this cooperation took, it is instructive to identify a few examples.

In March 1946, William Clayton, Assistant Secretary of State, wrote to Eric Johnston:

> The Department is sympathetically aware of the problems involved and I believe that it is doing everything possible in the circumstances to assist the American industry. It is in daily touch with industry representatives in New York and meets fortnightly in Washington with [Carl] Milliken, the secretary of the Motion Picture Association and manager of its foreign department, for a discussion of problems throughout the world, and it keeps your offices in New York fully and promptly informed of developments. (3)

Clayton explained that the American industry's problems in Spain were being handled by the American ambassador to that country. In order to bring pressure, the Department of State had been using its power for "shutting Spain off from the raw film for their productions." According to Clayton:

> In due time, the Spanish supplies of raw film dried up and the [Spanish] Government requested the [American] Embassy's good offices in bringing about a conference with the American trade representatives with a view to relieving the existing situation. The implication, of course, was that the Department would be willing to have resumed the raw film shipments in return for the cancellation of the film restrictions [on American companies].
>
> The American ban on raw film shipments to Spain continues and it is doubted that Spain can obtain needed supplies from any other country for a good while to come (3).

The Spanish experience was not isolated or unique. Shipments of raw film stock also were used as instruments of policy to reward and punish countries in Latin America during the early 1940s.

The Department of State and its embassy staffs often played crucial roles assisting the MPEA to deal with commercial restrictions overseas and to arrange film trade treaties. In Spain during 1951, the MPEA was able to hammer out a satisfactory trade agreement, thanks to the help of Ambassador Stanton Griffis, an investment banker and, since 1935, a member of Paramount's board of directors. The minutes of an MPEA board meeting on June 7, 1951, reveal that the Association's vice president, John McCarthy, who had recently returned from Spain, "paid tribute to the excellent support he got in his negotiations with the Spanish Government from Ambassador Griffis" (18). A year earlier, when he was ambassador to Argentina, Griffis helped MPEA interests in that country.

In these instances, as in others, commercial trade matters were elevated to a governmental level, and American film interests were able to benefit from inside information and access to high ranking diplomatic personnel. Indeed, it was never entirely clear whether ambassadors were talking for the film industry, the American government, or both. This was especially the case when Eric Johnston was sent on overseas diplomacy missions by President Eisenhower.

Credit extended to many foreign countries by the United States government became an important multi-use policy instrument, permitting—if not persuading—them to import American films, and allowing the earnings to be exported, even during a period of severe dollar shortages. This Marshall Plan economic aid became the lever used by the United States to force countries to rescind trade barriers of various sorts, some of which applied to motion pictures. In 1946, for example, when the American $1.4 billion loan to France was being negotiated, the agenda included discussion of restrictions on American films in that country (3). The resulting Blum–Byrnes Agreement, signed in May of that year, consisted of four texts, one of which dealt exclusively with films and liberalized the exhibition of dubbed American pictures in France. That motion pictures were singled out in this way, from among all commodities in international trade, underlined their ideological importance for the United States, especially at that time.

Also in 1946, President Truman signed a bill authorizing a $3.75 billion credit for the United Kingdom. Film matters figured in discussions for that loan, too, and the demands of the American companies received special consideration. William Clayton confided to Eric Johnston that

> the [State] Department took unusual action on behalf of the American industry during the recent loan negotiations with Britain by requesting the British negotiators for assurances that there would be no interruption in the free flow of film-dollar remittances to the United States. (3)

Two years later, Johnston wrote about the loan's impact on American film business and was able to say that "the motion picture industry received in dollars from Britain about 4% of the entire British loan" (11).

Although France and the United Kingdom were major markets, small countries were not overlooked. In Denmark, the representative of an American company informed his European manager that he had learned about a possible reduction in the Danish government's allowance of currency for the importation of American films during 1949. "I of course maintained," the representative wrote, "that on account of Denmark's improved economical [*sic*] situation, especially with regard to the Marshall [Plan] help, we had taken it for granted that we would be given better conditions next year." Having received this information from the field, the MPEA explained the problem in an October 8, 1948 letter to the Department of State, and solicited its support.

> It is hoped that with the assistance of the Department and the Embassy in Copenhagen this year a more satisfactory result can be obtained for 1949. . . . [W]e shall appreciate the Department's forwarding appropriate instructions to the Embassy in Copenhagen to assist our people in negotiations for the film import year 1949. (14)

Naturally, American film companies have acted on their own behalf, independently of the official support they have received from the United States government. The MPEA can bring to bear a variety of other pressures to neutralize foreign opposition, and sometimes this can be achieved through American companies' formal membership in foreign industry trade association. On the other hand, less formal avenues of influence can be used effectively to counter resistance. The minutes of meetings of the MPEA board of directors (June 7 and September 21, 1951) reveal that when it was facing difficulties in Germany, the MPEA launched a campaign to manipulate public opinion:

> The Chairman [John McCarthy] suggested that it might be desirable to send a public relations man to Germany for a short time to work there in conjunction with Mr. Spiegel [MPEA representative in Europe] with the object of getting together with certain German community groups which were presently showing a pronounced anti-American bias. (18)

Three and a half months later:

> The Chairman [McCarthy] reported that he had temporarily engaged Mr. Gronich to perform certain public relations functions with German groups such as religious and educational bodies in order to clear away presently existing misunderstandings regarding American pictures, and that Mr. Gronich has already obtained considerable success. (18)

Similarly, the MPEA's *Interim Report on Television* (20) disclosed the Association's plan to preserve its position in Mexico:

> [T]he hearings on regulations to implement the new Mexican TV Film Law, have led to energetic campaigns by the local unions to 'protect' native artists and technicians. Salvador Carrillo, leader of the Syndicate of film industry workers, has sought energetically to secure a Government prohibition against the import of all foreign television film. They and other local industry executives have testified at the Government hearings against the 'invasion by 30 foreign companies with their television series.' A drive was instituted by the Actors' Union to celebrate the 150th Anniversary of Mexican independence by eliminating all but Mexican-produced TV programs from the air this year [1960] during the month of September. Another move which would prove injurious to American film companies is the attempt, also fostered by the unions, to ban subtitled features from Mexican television. In combatting all of these proposals, MPEAA has enlisted the aid of advertising agencies and clients, the television stations and others whose influence can be exerted in behalf of preserving a free market. . . . So far, none of these strongly nationalistic and anti-U.S. movements have succeeded, but continuing efforts will be required to thwart them. (20, pp. 5–6)

Mexico was not the only country in which the MPEA was able to influence national policy on television. The same MPEA *Report* explained how an MPEA representative worked to obtain advantageous trading conditions:

> In Germany, where the new commercial network is scheduled to begin operations in January of 1961, Mr. [Leo] Hochstetter has been in constant touch with the executives of Deutschland Fernesehen [*sic*] and Freies Fernsehen GmbH, the operating company for the upcoming network and the basic program contractor, respectively. Just as, some 18 months ago, MPEA [in] Frankfurt was largely responsible for eliminating a proposed ruling that would have banned American features older than two and a half years from German television, Mr. Hochstetter has been working toward liberalized trading conditions for the new German network. A principal objective is an increase in the planned proportion of film to live programming during the early stages of operation. Precedents set at the beginning are likely to influence programming patterns for years to come. (20, p. 8)

Concerning the theatrical market, it is probable that the Federal Republic of Germany never established a quota on the importation of American films because of diplomatic and economic pressure from the United States. In July 1949, Eric Johnston wrote to Dean Acheson, secretary of state: "I urge our Government to take the strongest possible stand against the imposition of a film quota in Germany.'' Johnston declared that a ''film quota would be a negation of America's national policies and traditions'' (12).

In nations whose currencies could not be converted readily into dollars in the postwar period, the MPEA companies were confronted continuously with the problem of how to retrieve their films' earnings that were accumulating there. Threats to stop exportation naturally worried American government officials, who saw this as an impediment to the international communication program. As a solution, the Informational Media Guaranty (IMG) plan, devised in 1948 under the Economic Cooperation Administration, authorized the American government to pay the companies in dollars for certain currencies they earned abroad with their films. This thinly disguised subsidy stimulated the companies to continue exportation to soft currency countries, and permitted their pictures to circulate with the rank of ambassador. From the start of the IMG program until mid-1966, American film companies received close to $16 million under the currency conversion provisions.

Although remittance problems were solved by the 1960s, persistent trade restrictions and tax difficulties have plagued MPEA members. Their demands for free trade and free markets, consequently, have continued to enlist the support of the U.S. government. MPEA president Valenti enumerated foreign commercial barriers to film trade when he spoke to the U.S. Senate's Foreign Relations Committee in 1977, but he was simply updating the list that his predecessor, Eric Johnston, had presented to the Department of State three decades earlier. Similarly, MPEA briefings of foreign service officers continue, as does the presentation to other government agencies of lists of the industry's trade woes around the globe. Valenti has pointed out, of course, that the MPEA tries to operate by itself, but he also has had to admit:

> There are occasions . . . when we need the strength and support of the U.S. Government, not for any special favors but for the kind of assistance we believe it is proper for the Government to provide to all American industries doing business overseas. . . .
>
> The State Department has generally supported us whenever we have turned to it to lend a hand on a hard and delicate problem created by a foreign government. . . .
>
> Many times our ambassadors have accompanied me to conferences with heads of state and with leading cabinet officials to express the concern of the United States in a successful outcome (25, pp. 214, 215).

Aside from this kind of pressure to manipulate the policies of foreign countries, the MPEA companies frequently belong to trade associations overseas. By financial contributions to these groups, and in the votes they have by virtue of being members, the American companies can influence motion picture policy as it pertains to rental rates, taxation, quotas, import restrictions, etc. Moreover, film trade treaties between the MPEA and foreign countries can bind the MPEA's competitors to positions of neutrality. For example, Appendix G to the 1959–1962 film agreement between the MPEA and Italy, signed by Eric Johnston and ANICA's Eitel Monaco, bound Italian film authorities "to take all steps necessary with the . . . Italian government to ensure that . . . there will be no alterations in the Italian film legislation which would unfavorably affect . . . the activities of the member companies of the MPEAA operating in Italy." Moreover, the Italian film industry, through ANICA, pledged to "abstain . . . from demanding legislative or ministerial measures which could in any way represent restrictions against or new burdens on the importation, dubbing or distribution of films belonging to the MPEAA member companies" (10).

The major film markets around the world do not have quotas on the importation of American films, although this would seem to be a logical way in which nations could afford some protection in a cultural industry of immense importance. A principal reason for the absence of quotas is the General Agreement on Tariffs and Trade (GATT), which was drawn up in 1948 by the industrialized nations to stimulate all forms of commerce. During preparatory meetings in Geneva in 1947, the American delegation, according to an MPAA internal document (8), was "working vigorously to secure agreement" for the inclusion of a provision in GATT under which "all film restrictions would be removed except quotas on playing time for domestically produced motion pictures." The MPEA's representative in Paris, Frank McCarthy, who had been an assistant secretary of state in 1945, was "working closely with the American delegation in Geneva" in order to secure the measure's approval.

Thanks to extensive cooperation between MPAA-MPEA officials and the American government, the provision became GATT's Article IV, which recognizes a screen quota as the only legitimate trade restriction a country may use to protect its domestic film industry. Article IV also decrees that a screen quota can be subject to negotiation in the same manner as a tariff, thus allowing it to be a bargaining issue in film trade treaties. In the early 1960s, the MPEA also worked with the Department of State to try to have inserted in GATT a provision eliminating international restrictions on TV program trade, but a GATT working party assigned to this task could not reach agreement.

High level diplomatic maneuvering to reduce trade barriers to American films, through a multinational instrument such as GATT, is not an atypical case. Similar policy has been developed by the Organization for Economic Cooperation and Development (OECD), which, in 1961, succeeded the Organization for European Economic Cooperation. Although the OECD's program is basically informative and persuasive in nature, its recommendations on what are called "invisible transactions"—which include trade in film and TV programs—seek to stimulate international commerce in such commodities by relaxing restrictions. In reality, these rules are serious impediments to any member country that wishes to change the balance between imported and locally-produced theatrical films and television productions.

CAPTURING THE INTERNATIONAL MARKET

The industry has developed rhetoric on several levels to rationalize and justify its expansion into foreign markets. Until the beginning of World War II, the industry relied chiefly on the free trade banner and often argued that the exhibition abroad of American films stimulated a demand for American consumer goods in those countries. On this basis, American film companies felt they deserved help, not just for their own sake, but also because they contributed to American commercial growth. Moreover, in the postwar period and through the late 1960s, the industry frequently justified its export program on the ground that its films spread democracy and contributed to world freedom. Motion pictures had their place in the nation's international communication program, and helped to perpetuate American prestige and hegemony abroad. More recently, America's serious international trade deficits have provided a third rationalization for the exportation of Hollywood's motion pictures and television programs. Due to their substantial earnings abroad, they make a positive contribution to America's balance of payments. Consequently, the argument goes, the United States government should actively encourage their continued exportation, and work vigorously to persuade other governments to abolish restrictions on the importation and exhibition of films and television programs.

Since the 1920s, the American motion picture industry has had an active program for international expansion, and as the evidence shows, this often required the assistance of the American government. In this alliance, the state, far from being neutral or hostile toward business, has used its power to advance the interests of the private sector. It would be wrong to assume as a matter of course that state and industry necessarily are two separate entities. Indeed, as a close reading of the material reveals, the state shares the ideological commitments of the private sector and fosters its activities. Moreover, in particular instances, the line between state and industry vanishes, and their individual and separate interests are no longer discernible. It is not a case of the state being captured by private interests, or the state achieving its own goals through manipulation of the private sector. A clearer understanding of the relation is possible if it is seen as a coalescence. At many historical moments, the intersection of state and industry provides strong support for the instrumentalist position, although at some others, there is confirmation of a structuralist view. But it is clear that neither explains adequately the broad range of relations, while even together they also fail to describe the complexity of the industry–state interlock. Obviously, further inspection needs to develop an additional theoretical position to account for what has been happening—a position that more aptly accounts for the variety of relations, as they have worked out between the film industry and the federal government.

It simply is impossible to attribute the preeminence of American companies and their films entirely to exogenous forces, such as the automatic operation of economic laws. In the same way, it would be naive to believe that this dominant position, as it exists in the 1980s, is the direct result of decades of free choice exercised by peoples around the world. International trade, involving billions of dollars of investments and receipts, can hardly be left to chance. The market must be controlled as much as possible, and uncertain elements must be reduced or eliminated. This demands tactics and strategy that, when successfully implemented, attenuate risk and skew the market to one's advantage. Consumers, of course, are at liberty to select from what is on the market. But the shape of this market, including its range of alternatives, is the result of conscious efforts to structure it and keep competitors in their place.

American films and American companies are dominant, not because of the natural operation of marketplace forces, but because the marketplace has been made to operate in their favor. It has been not only a case of competition between big and small, but also between those with and those without the power to write the rules in order to win. America's success, therefore, has been built on others' failure—but their failure may have little to do with the intrinsic qualities of their products.

American films dominate the markets of Europe, and other areas as well. But how do films from those countries fare in the United States? The evidence is in play-off patterns and receipts. The American industry's answer is the standard free trade argument. Although it has been reiterated often, probably its most concise expression was in a letter by Gerald Mayer, the managing director of the MPAA's International Division, who wrote in 1947 to the Department of State's Office of International Trade Policy: "if foreign films are not as successful in this country as American films, this is the result of the operation of the law of supply and demand in a free market rather than of any restrictive industry practices" (13). Mr. Mayer obviously overlooked that the major American film companies, members of the MPAA and the MPEA, had just been convicted by a United States District Court of repeated violations of the Sherman Antitrust Act, and had been found guilty of a variety of anti-competitive practices such as price fixing, block booking, and conspiracy to restrain trade in the distribution and exhibition of motion pictures (see 24).

It is not so much a question whether officials of the MPAA and the MPEA actually believe the rhetoric of a free market. Part of their job is to make other people believe it. The other part of their job is to make sure the market operates in their favor.

REFERENCES

1. Althusser, Louis. *For Marx*. New York: Random House, 1970.
2. Berton, Pierre. *Hollywood's Canada*. Toronto: McClelland and Stewart Ltd., 1975.
3. Clayton, William. Assistant secretary, Department of State. Letter to Eric Johnston, President,

Motion Picture Association of America, March 25, 1946. Department of State file 840.4061 MP/3-25-46.

4. Federal Trade Commission. *Webb-Pomerene Associations: A 50-Year Review,* June 1967; and *Webb-Pomerene Associations: Ten Years Later,* November 1968.
5. Gold, David, Clarence Lo, and Erik Wright. ''Recent Developments in Marxist Theories of the Capitalist State.'' *Monthly Review* 27 (5), October 1975, and 27 (6), November 1975.
6. Guback, Thomas. *The International Film Industry.* Bloomington: Indiana University Press, 1969.
7. Guback, Thomas. ''Hollywood's International Market.'' In Tino Balio (Ed.) *The American Film Industry.* Madison: University of Wisconsin Press, 1976, pp. 387–409.
8. Harmon, Francis. Vice president, Motion Picture Association of America. Memorandum to presidents and foreign managers of MPAA member companies, August 20, 1947.
9. Hopper, Harold. Chief, Motion Picture Section, War Production Board. Quoted by Senator Sheridan Downey. *Congressional Record—Senate.* March 22, 1944, pp. 2878, 2879.
10. *Italo-American Film Agreement.* September 1, 1959 to August 31, 1962. Appendix G.
11. Johnston, Eric. President, Motion Picture Association of America. Letter to Gradwell Sears, United Artists Corporation, May 21, 1948.
12. Johnston, Eric. President, Motion Picture Association of America. Letter to Dean Acheson, Secretary of State, July 31, 1949. Department of State file 862.4061 MP/7-1349.
13. Mayer, Gerald. Managing director, International Division, Motion Picture Association of America. Letter to Clair Wilcox, Office of International Trade Policy, Department of State, March 28, 1947. Department of State file 841.4061 MP/3-2847.
14. McCarthy, John. Managing director, Motion Picture Export Association. Memorandum to representatives of member companies, October 21, 1948. This memo quotes the October 1, 1948 letter from S. A. Henriksen, Paramount Films, Copenhagen, to John Nathan, Continental manager, Paramount Films, Paris, as well as the MPEA's letter of October 8, 1948 to Merrill Gay, Division of Commercial Policy, Department of State.
15. Miliband, Ralph. *The State in Capitalist Society.* London: Quartet Books, 1973.
16. Motion Picture Producers and Distributors of America. *Twenty-Third Annual Report,* March 26, 1945.
17. Motion Picture Export Association. *1953 Annual Report* and *1954 Annual Report.*
18. Motion Picture Export Association. Minutes of a Special Meeting of the Board of Directors.
19. Motion Picture Export Association of America. Annual submissions for 1956 and 1957 to the Federal Trade Commission.
20. Motion Picture Export Association of America. *Interim Report on Television,* October 21, 1960.
21. Pendakur, Manjunath. *Canadian Feature Film Industry: Monopoly and Competition.* Ph.D. dissertation. Simon Fraser University, 1979.
22. Poulantzas, Nicos. *State, Power, and Socialism.* London: New Left Books, 1978.
23. Thorp, Willard. Assistant Secretary, Department of State. Letter to Eric Johnston, President, Motion Picture Association of America, June 8, 1948. Department of State file 811.4061 MP6-848.
24. *United States v. Paramount Pictures Inc. et al.* 66 F. Supp. 323 (June 11, 1946) and 70 F. Supp. 53 (December 31, 1946 and February 3, 1947).
25. Valenti, Jack. President, Motion Picture Export Association of America. Testimony in: *International Communications and Information,* hearings before the Subcommittee on International Operations, Committee on Foreign Relations, United States Senate, 95th Congress, 1st Session, 1977. Washington, DC: Government Printing Office, 1977.

9

Film Advertising, the Film Industry, and the Pin-up: The Industry's Accommodations to Social Forces in the 1940s

Mary Beth Haralovich

During World War II, pocket-sized editions of fan magazines such as *Modern Screen* and *Screen Romances* were chosen for distribution to GIs. The Special Services branch of the U.S. Army printed these magazines in a government issue size containing no advertising. Their purpose was to satiate the

> appetite (of khaki-clad film fans in the United States forces overseas) for news of Hollywood and its product and people—principally the ladies.

These GI fan magazines were different from the domestic variety:

> The home office publicity departments are asked . . . to contribute special copy and pictures. Pin-up girls are in special demand for the military edition. (19)

The pin-up was not the exclusive property of the GI during the 1940s; the pin-up or its variations was an extensive part of American cultural life. Writing in *Life* in 1947, Winthrop Sargeant discussed "The Cult of the Love Goddess in America" pointing to the scope of the pin-up in American culture: "In the field of advertising she is the supreme symbol of mankind's desire for comfort and luxury." Sargeant went on to list the variety of commodities sold by their association with the pin-up arguing that "Americans subscribe with unquestioning faith to her incessant litany that sex is the most important thing in the world" (55).

Sargeant recognized the importance of Hollywood in the dissemination of the pin-up and the complicity of the Motion Picture Association of America (MPAA)[1] and the Production Code Administration (PCA):

---

[1]In 1946 the Motion Picture Producers and Distributors of America—MPPDA—changed its name to the Motion Picture Association of America—MPAA. In this article, the terms MPPDA and MPAA will be used when historically correct.

> The industrial machinery which communicates this interesting way of life to America's faithful moviegoers is vast and complex. . . .
> The Johnston Office, which controls the taboos of the goddess' cinematic ceremonies, devotes a great deal of its energies to censoring the letter of her true sexual nature while letting her spirit triumph without limit (55).

Sargeant credits the film industry with promulgating the pin-up in American culture and recognizes the "vast and complex" industrial machinery which guided her manifestations.[1]

The 1940s pin-up figure and its variations constituted a marked change from 1930s figures of women in film advertising which were generally more wholesome, more fully clad and less overtly sexual. Industry approval of the pin-up in film advertising required major adjustments in extant advertising policies and practices. The film industry was well aware of its mediating role between representations of women in its products and the audience it sought to attract. Industry policies on film advertising were altered as the industry's perceptions of its external conditions changed. The issue of how film advertising could subscribe to historically appropriate representations of women was negotiated on two levels: industrial perceptions of the social forces within which advertising was conducted and the necessity of internal guarantees that film advertising would meet the needs of the industry by harmonizing with those perceptions.

In the arguments and discussions in the mid-1930s which led to the adoption of the Advertising Code, there were two motifs which stressed the industry's awareness of its mediating role. One was the necessity of self-regulation in an industry which is dependent upon broad-based public acceptance for its existence and the other was the means by which self-censorship could be accomplished. Will Hays, President of the MPPDA, summarized the situation in 1933:

> The industry cannot and should not tolerate the individual practices of any producer which threaten to destroy public support for the whole industry. . . . Large portions of the public would desert motion picture entertainment and the industry would be stunted by lack of public support. (21)

In order to accomplish industry-wide self-regulation of advertising it was necessary for the disparate branches of the industry to cooperate through the auspices of the MPPDA's Production Code Administration. An Advertising Advisory Council was established to pass judgment on all forms of film advertising prior to their distribution.

The self-regulatory machinery which oversaw film advertising was established during a period when threats of federal censorship, public disaffection, and the oligopoly potential of the National Recovery Act necessitated a uniform interpretation and compliance with the Advertising Code. The 1930s shift from sensationalized advertising to relatively desexualized representations in advertising finds its context both within the film industry and in greater historical events.

The 1930s were characterized by a strong tendency toward standardizing the advertising product under guidelines established by the MPPDA and its Advertising Advisory Council.

Just as understanding this consolidation of industry advertising policies required attention to the multiplicity of factors leading to the adoption of the Advertising Code, its subsequent erosion in the 1940s is also the result of a complex congruence of positions. The policy changes which resulted in the second diachronic shift of film advertising during the studio period, the return to a variation of the sensationalized representations of women such as those in evidence prior to the Advertising Code, emerged from an intersection of factors similar to those of the 1930s: the industry's advertising practices, the internal hierarchy of the industry which negotiated changes in policies, and the external conditions the industry perceived as important to its policies.

The late 1930s and 1940s were characterized by challenges to the MPPDA through the established structure of advertising self-regulation. It is significant that wholesale anarchy did not occur. Instead, those opposed to the provisions of the Advertising Code worked within its machinery to challenge its definition of norms of good taste. By the late 1930s, tensions existed between the need to harmonize with a significantly different sense of appropriate representations of women from that of the mid-1930s and the restrictions which the Advertising Code had put on film advertising. This conflict was not one of public antagonism versus industry practices. It was, instead, within the film industry. Film advertising personnel, faced with the exploitative photography characteristic of the widely popular candid-camera magazines such as *Life* and *Look,* were unable to publish the pin-up stills which were popular with the public.

Having established the Advertising Code during a period when the film industry became convinced of the need for self-protection from external censorship, film advertising was now faced with competition from free-lance and magazine photographers whose work (especially cheesecake stills and the pin-up) was both popular and not subject to review by censoring bodies like the MPPDA. The emphasis of industrial and social conditions now turned to the necessity of adjusting extant policies on film advertising. Some branches of the film industry worked from within to confront the Advertising Code yet they concurrently maintained the centralized structure of self-regulation of advertising developed in the mid-1930s.

In addition, a single person caused national attention to be placed on the restrictions established by the MPPDA through the Advertising Code. Due to his personal peculiarities and his financial independence, Howard Hughes was able to challenge the right of the MPPDA/MPAA to impose standards of good taste on film advertising. While the events surrounding the advertising of *The Outlaw* are certainly unique, the tenor of the Hughes lawsuit points to the concerns of independent producers about their relationship with the MPPDA/MPAA. At the same time that Hughes disputed the Advertising Code, the antitrust suit which would become *United States* v. *Paramount, et. al.* in 1948 was progressing. The industry required a broad base of support before it would substantially alter its restraints on film advertising. The desires of one recalcitrant member, although fundamentally speaking for the position of independents within the industry, were couched in representations of sexuality which were inappropriate to the industry's position in that historical context.

What follows is a historical explanation of the 1940s shift in film advertising to the display of female sexuality through a representational practice commonly known as the pin-up. As will be seen, the pin-up did not become a standard figure in film advertising solely on the basis of her ability to boost the morale of America's soldiers. Evidence from trade journals of the period indicates a complex situation which eventually led to loosening the restrictions of the Advertising Code thus allowing Hollywood to participate in the cultural phenomenon of the pin-up.

These discussions point to particular moments of tension about the industry's advertising policies and to the interest groups who had something at stake in the way film advertising was conducted. They help in understanding how the industrial hierarchy negotiated, internally and externally, with many disparate groups. In addition, the ways in which these tensions were resolved point to the broad cultural context of the film industry's advertising policies and practices. As will be seen, ideologies surrounding the representation of woman were but one of the factors which allowed the pin-up figure to dominate film advertising in the 1940s.

The historical conditions which fostered adjustments in the industry's advertising policies and practices can be located within the internal hierarchy of the studio system taken in its relationship with other American cultural institutions. This historical explanation of the pin-up tries to understand how the film industry functioned both internally and in relation to its notions of dominant culture. The conclusions generated bring with them further questions on historiography, especially about the construction of cultural explanations for film industry representational practices.

RESISTANCE TO THE ADVERTISING CODE

The MPPDA and the Advertising Code Administration were aware that the industry was no longer willing to comply with the provisions of the Advertising Code. Although they tried to maintain the norms of good taste established in the 1930s, it rapidly became evident that popular attitudes about representations of sexuality had changed markedly. Among the first to recognize this change were studio still photographers. Stills are the primary material of visual advertising. They are the basis of poster art and newspaper and magazine advertisements. Table 1 presents percentages of stills and still-related materials either rejected or returned for revision by the Advertising Advisory Council (AAC).

Table 1
% of Rejected or Revised Stills or Still-Related Materials: 1934–1948[a]

Year	Stills	Advertisements	Posters
1934	2.1	3.0	1.5
1935	0.9	2.8	3.0
1936	0.7	2.2	1.8
1937	0.6	3.9	1.0
1938	0.3	2.3	0.6
1939	0.8	1.6	1.6
1940	1.2	2.9	2.2
1941	1.9	4.2	2.3
1942	1.3	3.1	2.3
1943	0.8	2.7	3.4
1944	0.8	2.5	4.4
1945	0.6	3.6	4.7
1946	0.7	4.2	1.6
1947	0.5	3.7	2.0
1948	2.1	3.4	2.5

[a]*Source:* MPAA (39).

Taken individually, each of these three categories of film advertising exhibits a different trend. While the early 1940s was a period of dramatic rejection of stills, they returned to levels similar to the pre-1940 lows by the mid-1940s. Advertisements and posters remained at a fairly high level of rejection throughout the 1940s although posters dipped to a pre-1940 low in 1946.

Despite the fact that these figures indicate that stills were less subject to rejection or revision than advertisements and posters, there are several factors which can account for these relatively low numbers. First, stills were produced in much greater quantities than advertisements or posters. For example, in 1940 there were nine times as many stills produced as advertisements and 49 times as many stills as posters. Similarly, in 1941 there were more than eight times as many stills produced as advertisements and 56 times as many stills as posters (30). Second, stills were much cheaper to produce than either advertisements or posters since photographs require much less labor than either advertisements or posters.

The MPPDA met with severe challenges to its prescriptions of good taste in film advertising in the 1940s as the data, taken collectively, indicates. In fact, the MPPDA itself reported that the AAC "increased watchfulness . . . during the past year (1940) in the administration of the Advertising Code." The reason cited was the "many new types of advertising ideas" which attempted to increase domestic box office due to the loss of the European market with the beginning of World War II in 1939 (42).

Despite the fact that advertising in 1940 required increased vigilance by the AAC, the MPPDA was also happy to report that most of the rejected material was "brought into conformity with the tenets of the Advertising Code" (42). If this were the case, there would have been no dramatic differences in representations of sexuality in film posters in the 1930s and the 1940s. Despite this and subsequent claims by the MPPDA, the AAC must have simply and quietly changed its standards of objectionable material in order to meet the demands for a different emphasis in advertising.

A change in the AAC's standards of good taste is probable because the Advertising Code was so vague that flexibility in its interpretation was likely. Furthermore, the guidelines followed by the AAC were succinctly stated by J. J. McCarthy, director of the AAC, in 1933: "If we feel that the material is improper or objectionable, it is rejected" (37). The 12 tenets of the Advertising Code upon which the AAC operated were:

1. We subscribe to the Code of Business Ethics of the International Advertising Association, based on 'truth, honesty and integrity'.
2. Good taste shall be the guiding rule of motion picture advertising.
3. Illustrations and text in advertising shall faithfully represent the pictures themselves.
4. No false or misleading statements shall be issued directly or implied by type arrangements or by distorted quotations.
5. No text or illustration shall ridicule or tend to ridicule any religious faith; no illustration of a character in clerical garb shall be shown in any but a respectful manner.
6. The history, institutions and nationals of all countries shall be represented with fairness.
7. Profanity and vulgarity shall be avoided.
8. Pictorial and copy treatment of officers of the law shall not be of such a nature as to undermine their authority.
9. Specific details of crime, inciting imitation, shall not be used.
10. Motion picture advertisers shall bear in mind the provision of the Production Code that the use of liquor in American life shall be restricted to the necessities of characterizations and plot.
11. Nudity with meretricious purpose, and salacious postures, shall not be used.
12. Court actions relating to censoring of pictures, or other censorship disputes, are not to be capitalized in advertising. (78)

Anyone who has compared an ad or poster with the film being advertised knows that tenets 3 and 4 were obviously neither very well heeded nor enforced. As will be seen, in the 1940s tenets 2, 7, and 11 were implicitly the issues with which the industry's hierarchy was concerned.

With so little specified by the Advertising Code or the AAC, it would have been easy for the AAC to quietly shift its standards of good taste in advertising. Thus, the MPPDA could report success in its Advertising Code at the same time that it acquiesced to changing advertising practices by the studios. In its Annual Report on 1941, the MPPDA used a typical tactic to stress industry cooperation while also mentioning the increase in rejections. In 1941, the report gloated that "no completed (press) books had to be rejected." Two paragraphs later it stated that rejected or revised advertisements numbered 4.25 percent. This discrepancy is not discussed in the Report (43).

It was not until the Annual Report covering 1944 that the MPPDA admitted the severity of the challenge to its prescriptions. Prior to that year, the MPPDA consistently reported on the effectiveness of the AAC. In 1942 there was a "high degree of compliance" with "only two violations . . . the first violation of the sort since 1933." 1943 saw "no major derelictions." But in 1944, it became apparent that the MPPDA had been battling with the studios throughout the early 1940s. The 1944 Annual Report declared that "all branches of the industry have continued a sustained vigilence against the pressure for 'letting down' so evident in wartime" (44, 45, 46). The percentages in Table 1 belie this vote of confidence in the studios' attitude toward the MPPDA. Advertisements rejected were lower from the previous year by only 0.2 percent and posters rose an entire percentage point.

Similarly, in 1945 rejected or revised advertisements rose 1.1 percent over 1944 and posters rose 0.3 percent. Yet the MPPDA Annual Report for 1945 states:

> All companies gave uniformly good cooperation in making revisions necessary to meet the requirements of the Code. As a result there were no serious public protests during the year over any motion picture advertising or displays. The moral content of film advertising continues to meet the requirements of the Code. (38)

Using the MPPDA Annual Reports as evidence is difficult. The discrepancy between the MPPDA's insistence that its self-regulation program is working and the change in the representation of sexuality in posters in the 1940s is compounded by the MPPDA's refusal to explicitly acknowledge changing standards. In its Report on 1944, the "motion picture industry maintaining . . . its position" (46) can be interpreted to mean its position *since* 1940, the year that the challenge to the AAC began in earnest.

This reluctance of the MPPDA to admit defeat also points to the success of the MPPDA as a self-governing body. The studios' participation in the MPPDA guaranteed freedom from external censorship and the preservation of the structure of vertical integration. It is safe to assume that the cultural context of the United States during the 1940s required changes in advertising and that the MPPDA had to work to ensure the perpetuation of the film industry at the box office by adjusting its interpretation of the Advertising Code.

Changes in advertising practices were subsumed by the AAC through loosening standards of good taste. To maintain the "sound morals" pertinent to the 1930s period of public outcry would negate the necessity of the film industry changing with the times. Also, the MPPDA was composed of representatives of the film industry. If it were to operate in their best interest, then it would have to recognize what advertising personnel already knew: that the pressures of candid-camera magazines had contributed to changes in its advertising practices.

The MPPDA Annual Reports for 1938 and 1939 did express a concern about increasing rejections of still photographs, putting the blame on the "candid camera craze" (40, 41). In addition, Joseph Breen (director of the Production Code Administration) and James Doolittle (still photographer and co-founder of IATSE Local 659, studio still photographers) complained about the influence of these magazines on still photographers (11, 15). The climate of self-censorship of advertising had changed markedly from that of the previous decade.

In the 1930s, self-regulation meant protection from federal censorship and calming public concerns about morals in advertising. The MPPDA's Advertising Code and Advertising Advisory Council were necessary for self-protection. In the 1940s, there is no evidence of similar threats of censorship. If there were, there is no doubt that the studios would have "self-regulated" and the MPPDA Annual Reports would not contain high instances of rejections and revisions in advertising.

Further evidence of the MPPDA's participation with the film industry on changing advertising practices lies in the potential control the AAC had in the distribution of films. As a condition of the Production Code's Seal of Approval all advertising had to be submitted to the AAC. If a studio attempted to release a film whose advertising was deemed objectionable or if a studio made changes in advertising approved by the AAC, then the Seal of Approval was nullified (57). This power of the AAC was never levied against any of the major studios. It was not until Howard Hughes flagrantly abused advertising practices with *The Outlaw* that the MPPDA took the unique step of withdrawing its Seal of Approval (76).

CANDID-CAMERA MAGAZINES: SETTING THE STAGE FOR THE PIN-UP

> A new brutally frank era developed—an era in which an audience of 25,000,000 people the world around, thoroughly 'movie-wise', demanded more than formula pictures—stills as well as motion pictures.
> The sponsors of *Life, Look, Pic, Click* and newspaper editors realized this. They changed their perspective, lifted their sights and magazines which started out hoping for 250,000 circulation suddenly found a demand for 2,500,000 copies. That was no accident. The public mind had changed. Sponsors of motion pictures never thought to analyze the situation; few realized that these popular pictorial magazines were catering to exactly the same clientele motion pictures cater to (Johnston, 30).

On November 23, 1936, Henry Luce's *Life* appeared on the newsstands and the candid-camera craze began. In January 1937, *Look* appeared, followed the same year by *Pic*, and by *Click* in early 1938 (50). These four magazines are the ones Doolittle complained about: ''If they have 'raised their sights' it was only to get them far enough above the mud to keep clear of the law. Magazines and newspapers have no Hays office—yet!'' (15). What he objected to was the type of photojournalism practiced by these magazines.

According to Theodore Peterson, *Life* ''emphasized news, the arts, the cultural, the scientific, albeit with sex for seasoning.'' *Look* ''dwelt on personalities and animals, food and fashions, photo-quizzes and photo-mysteries, the spectacular and thrilling.'' *Pic* was a monthly ''heavily laden with photographs of young women not far removed from nudity'' and *Click*'s ''themes of sex and shock'' managed to get it blacklisted by the Catholic church and banned by the Canadian government (50). Four months after *Life* first hit the newsstands, its circulation rose to 1,080,000. Ten months after *Look* first appeared, its circulation was 1,700,000. Their circulation steadily increased to make them the top two mass circulation magazines (81). Since these magazines had combined circulations in the millions, Johnston, Director of Publicity for Walter Wanger Productions, was correct in positing their importance to the film industry.

In February 1939, Johnston argued strongly for a change in the attitude of still photographers toward the candid-camera magazines and the audience for these magazines. His argument was based on two observations important to the film industry. First, the style of the photographs published by the magazines was new by ''eliminat(ing) static, posey art'' and ''demand(ing) pictures that moved and lived and had feeling'' (30). Johnston's concern was that the film industry's still photographers were not meeting the requirements for publication in these mass circulation magazines.

His second observation drives his point home. The industry's still photographers were not the only photographers working in the studios:

> Syndicates, magazines and newspapers are covering Hollywood today—not just studios. The studio's job is to employ stills to sell motion pictures; the magazine, newspaper and syndicate photographers are charged only with making interesting, natural pictures of people who are news. What is ahead rests with how quickly publicity men and stillmen realize they must think like editors. . . . It takes a pretty smart picture to sell theatre tickets today. The editor doesn't care for publicity—as such—but, he will trade a good break for art that helps him sell his paper. (30)

In order for studio still photographers to compete with staff photographers from the candid-camera magazines, Johnston argued that they must realize who their audience is. This audience included the editors of the magazines and newspapers who decided what kinds of stills to print.

This article by Johnston began a series of articles in *International Photographer* (hereafter *IP*), the trade journal of still photographers, which discussed the problems of Hollywood still photographers with regard to candid-camera magazines. A debate between Johnston and Doolittle led the controversy. While Doolittle, in March 1939, argued against adopting the sensational policies of candid-camera magazines, Johnston countered in July that if still photographers "do not keep pace with the times the product they are intended to sell suffers" (15, 31).

Hollywood's still photographers were faced with a serious problem in 1939. Their access to mass circulation magazines was barred by the Advertising Code:

> The job of merchandising personalities—and particularly the many facets of feminine allure—has been accomplished under a variety of hindrances, censorships and other limitations never encountered by the widely exploited photographic wizards in other fields. (19)

These hindrances and censorships included the working relationship of still photographers with other personnel. The Johnston–Doolittle articles cited lack of cooperation on nearly every level of film production. Johnston argued that still photographers were so ill-considered that they began to question their own importance in the film industry (30).

While Johnston called for public forums for the display and discussion of studio still photography in order to "encourage still art, to train and help stillmen", Doolittle responded with a pessimistic picture of the state of still photography in the industry. Stars were permitted approval of their stills:

> Haven't you seen them rip off the corners of thousands of prints simply because a teeny-weeny shadow crossed the Luxefied, Factorized cheek?

Films themselves did not cooperate: "have you ever stopped to observe how comparatively little action or novelty there is in the run of even exceptional productions?" Long-shots are full of scenery which cause the players to be lost in the shot and close-ups are "stills wired for sound." For a still photographer to rearrange lighting on a set meant that "the Local would have another member on the 'available' list!" And to require that a director, star and film staff cooperate with the "artist of the still camera" was a virtual impossibility (15, 30).

IP's readers responded to the Johnston–Doolittle discussion. In July 1939 the trade journal began a series of articles on the specifics of still photography including "oustanding newsworthy shots by studio photographers." By 1941, the Academy of Motion Picture Arts and Sciences (AMPAS) sponsored the First Annual Exhibition of the Hollywood Studios' Still Photography Show complete with prizes for the best stills in a number of categories (23, 31, 59).

The purposes of these Annual Exhibitions spoke to the concerns raised by Johnston and Doolittle. The work of the studio photographer was uncredited. The exhibitions would place the names of the photographers in view for both the public and the industry to see. The photographers could learn technique and heighten their skills by looking at the work of other photographers. The competition would make the still photographer a "better pictorial reporter" (8).

Yet competition from candid-camera magazines in the work of studio still photographers remained fierce. In 1941, Warner Brothers sponsored a contest just for magazine photographers. The winners included photographers from fan magazines (Fawcett Publications, *Screen Guide,* and *Hollywood Pictorial*) as well as mass circulation picture magazines (*Click*) (79).

Even the AMPAS-sponsored still shows were not immune from the candid-camera controversy. The 1941 and 1942 shows were judged by editors from magazines such as *Life* and *Look,* representatives from each news photo syndicate and newspaper art editors from across the country. Some still photographers objected to this type of panel of judges "claiming they were art *editors* and not *artists*." The result was a realignment of the judges for the show in 1943. These judges were selected by still photographers representing every studio and two were chosen by studio publicity directors. The five judges composed a panel of "expert technical judgement of pure art" to please the still photographers and "what editors of art think" to please AMPAS. In addition, a third appraisal was made by the people who attended the Exhibition: viewers were asked to name the most popular still of the show (1, 8).

The competition between studio still photographers and those from external magazines and newspapers was strong. It seems that both the Academy and *IP* were bent on convincing recalcitrant still photographers that their best interests lay in pleasing magazine and newspaper editors. Johnston, the organizer of the 1943 still show and chair of the Public Relations Institute of AMPAS, insisted that

> all still photographers are in reality pictorial reporters whose work must please art editors as well as artists, theatre operators and the public. (8)

Undoubtedly some of this concern emanated from the fact that magazines, newspapers, and syndicates assigned photographers to cover the film industry. While studios had the right to bar any offending journalist/photographer from the lot, it is obvious that magazine and newspaper coverage of studio activities was important in publicizing the film industry. The necessity of keeping the institution in the public eye required studio still photographers to meet the challenge of their mass circulation-affiliated counterparts. This challenge was based on the editorial policies of candid-camera magazines.

That candid-camera magazines were crucial to the craft of the still photographers is shown by the emphasis *IP* put on the style of photography published by *Look* magazine. In 1944 and again in 1947, *IP* published a series of articles by Earl Theisen (a photo-reporter for *Look* and an associate editor of *IP*) (60–75). In this series, Theisen gave specific advice on how to construct stills which would be acceptable for publication in mass circulation magazines. His advice included the editorial guidelines of these magazines as well as dynamics of composition and techniques to achieve certain effects. In demonstrating which stills would be appropriate to magazines such as *Look,* Theisen devoted a great deal of space to advice on capturing the sexuality of women in stills. Thus, the intersection of candid-camera magazines with the pin-up figure was emphasized in *IP*.

In 1944 *IP* ran a series of eight articles ''on the formulations and problems of producing photographs for a national magazine.'' Theisen reported that Harlan Logan, editor of *Look,* wanted photographs to have ''five basic qualities in various degrees'' in order to warrant publication:

> (1) visual impact, (2) the photos must add to the reader's information, (3) motivation in that the reader will want to imitate what is seen in the photo, (4) must interest as many members of a family as possible, (5) the photo must have mass appeal. (60)

Theisen admitted that ''visual impact'' was a nebulous term ''difficult to put a finger on.'' Yet the significance of visual impact in studio stills was one crux of the *IP* debate of 1939 and the early 1940s. Studio still photographers had argued the merits of ''action'' in stills in opposition to posed or ''stagey'' stills (30). To capture the interest of mass circulation magazine editors and readers, visual impact was a quality to be attained.

A still which ''adds to information'' contains information without much recourse to a caption. For instance, a still could show a celebrity in his or her home, thereby giving information on what the person is like at home, so ''the reader may know more about him and the way he lives.'' ''Motivation'' in stills stresses playing on the desire of the viewer to imitate and identify with the person in the still so that the viewer ''will remember it longer and be influenced by it'' (60). The emphases in these two categories of magazine editorial approval are focused on the desire of the viewer to partake of and imitate the life of celebrities. Needless to say, Hollywood's institutional emphasis on the star system could benefit from the publication of such stills.

The last two of the ''five basic qualities'' are geared toward the mass appeal of stills and the mass audience of the magazines. To ''interest as many members of the family as possible'' means, according to Theisen, that a photographer ''must 'feel' human relationships, be enough of a psychologist to capture the intangible things that add interest.'' More specifically, this means that the photograph should be about ''human situations in which anybody could project'' her or himself. An example of this ''human situation'' is the fashion photograph:

> in connection with a fashion story the models must be clean-cut and wholesome so that the male reader would like to know them better and so there could be awakened some wishful thinking. The average male interest is lessened in proportion to any posiness or high fashion note introduced in a fashion story.

While Theisen assumes a gender relationship between fashion stills and women readers, he argues that the male reader "is less interested in cold, aloof, impersonal fashion models than he would be in the more real" (60). To achieve the "more real" is relatively simple to attain. The female model need only be posed in such a way as to correspond to a pin-up figure.

In his second article, on lighting, Theisen discussed how lighting is "the carrier of his idea" for photo-reporters:

> If I am photoing a glamour girl, her face must bounce out of the photo and must be relatively free of skin texture or lines; for this the sidelight is projected to the background. . . . Backlighting . . . may be used for halos in the accepted notion of abstract beauty. (61)

What Theisen was arguing for was not incompatible with the work of Hollywood still photographers. While few studio photographers constructed the high style portraits for which George Hurrell was famous, Theisen emphasized the distinction between glamour photos and those of a more accessible "real" person.

Theisen's subsequent articles on composition, camera angle, timing and picture action and shooting in continuity continued to integrate technique, mass appeal, and the centrality of the female body to maintaining reader interest. Composition "may not dominate or interfere." The main idea of the still must "be centrally located so that the eye is not required to travel too far." The importance of composition leading the eye through the photograph "is particularly so in bathing suit shots where patterns and suit details prohibit the study of the figure." Costumes should be chosen so as to not "prohibit the study of the figure" and camera angles could help slenderize women and make men more forceful or friendly (62). Similarly, in tips on timing a gust of wind can capture a woman's skirt blowing around her hips (63). Theisen also specified the role of "Sex" in establishing reader interest: "Pretty girls, legs, always get man interest and if the fashions are novel and good, women become interested, too" (64).

Theisen's discourse on photojournalist technique integrates the display of female sexuality with the mass audience of the candid-camera magazines. In order for studio still photographers to break into these magazines, they must be able to at least intimate the availability of female sexuality for the male readers in combination with the identification of female readers. While Theisen's examples are not particularly sensational in their reference to the exhibition of the female body, what is of interest is the tendency to specify female sexuality as a marketing strategy, an aspect of *IP* which did not occur in such detail until the 1940s.

In 1947 Theisen published the second series of eight articles in *IP*. These were called ''Photographic Glossary'' and were intended to reduce any confusion about the terminology used with regard to stills. In this series, Theisen became much more specific about defining types of sex appeal. This indicates the increasing interest of *IP* on the use of female sexuality as a marketing strategy for the film industry. By the time this series appeared, the pin-up was already firmly established in American culture.

In the first article of this 1947 series, Theisen articulated 22 ''Types of Pictures'' of which six are of interest to this study: poster, portrait, glamour, sex art, home art, and leg art. These indicate the range of still photographs and point to the differences between stills used in pressbooks and those more suitable for mass circulation magazines:

> POSTER, bold, full, simple composition and lighting. Not always intended to be a good likeness, but designed to illustrate or sell, and to capture reader's attention from a distance. Widely used in motion picture illustration. (68)

Similarly, the portrait and the glamour still are more formally constructed than the mass circulation still which emphasizes the ''natural'' aspects of composition and technique:

> PORTRAIT, formally posed, intended to give flattering likeness. Lighting effects used to enhance pleasing illustration. Posing not always natural but intended to support composition; not too much novelty in camera angle.
>
> GLAMOUR, in concept an abstraction of sex or beauty using novelty lighting and posing. Eye appeal gained by striking effects and use of semi-opaque shadows, soft highlights to impose on reader imagination. Suggests idea impersonally by formal manner of subject (68).

These three types of stills—poster, portrait, glamour—are a fundamental aspect of film industry advertising and exploitation focusing on the idealized glamour and perfection of the female star(let).

Sex art, home art, and leg art, in contrast, emphasize the female star(let) outside of the confines of the formal institution. Theisen described all three:

> SEX ART, any picture where sex interest becomes dominant in the picture theme; gained by lighting, informal pose and manner of subject. Subjectively personal for reader titillation; preferably not obvious but casual and not necessarily in the leg art category. Lighting soft and pose natural to play on imagination.
>
> HOME ART, intended to show character of subject in home surroundings. Photographic treatment records and reports with realism; natural lighting and settings serve as a backdrop for the subject. Primary purpose is illustration of way of life and habits rather than character delineation.
>
> LEG ART, play clothes or bathing suit pictures made to satisfy interest in model's figure, fashion detail, or activities. Preferably action is not stilted but natural and

> the model wholesome with the photographic effects pleasing. The note of the picture and its action disguises the obviousness of sex. Cheesecake lacks this. (68)

In subsequent articles in his 1947 series, Theisen went into more detail on obtaining the proper display of the female body. In an illustrated essay on lighting, Theisen indicated how sunlight ''highlights direct attention to model's conformation'' leading to a ''sex picture.'' With synchro-sunlight the attention of the reader is not hindered by ''dense shadows.'' Low sun ''produces a soft or 'warm' light suitable for fashion or sex photography.'' High sun ''keynotes wholesomeness in pretty girl photographs.'' Legs can be emphasized using ''tone and contrast ranges . . . to force the reader attention to predetermined areas in the picture content . . . and force the eye to look at the more important things first'' (69).

In his article on ''Composition,'' Theisen detailed how the reader's eye can be forced to travel the female body by the use of the L-shape, the curve, the S-shape, and the balanced composition (70). Similarly, ''Camera Viewpoint'' uses disembodied legs to indicate the speed with which the eye travels in left-handed or right-handed pictures (71).

Theisen also returns to his point in the 1944 series on the necessity of integrating male and female interest in stills. In the ''Situation Picture''

> the picture or ''interest accent'' exists as a result of the actual or suggested dealings between models. . . . A female fashion picture is given a situation when a male is added to the photograph. (72)

In order to ensure the proper degree of female sexuality in stills, Theisen included a series of instructions to be given to the female body to ensure the desired effect. To ''Sit Flat'' with ''an even distribution of weight on both buttocks'' is to ''give the illusion of more slender hips.'' To say ''Palms Up'' is

> to accentuate the note of femininity to the hands. Masculine hands seldom are posed this way. . . . It (also can) draw attention to the model's legs.

To ''Arch the Back''

> means sit up straight and pull in the stomach so the conformation and chest line are accentuated; has the additional connotation that the breasts are lifted. . . . ''On Your Toes'' directs the model to stand on her toes to lengthen the legs and improve the ankle line. When seated the same idea is expressed with the phrase 'Point Your Toes'. (74)

Theisen summed up his arguments on the display of the female body in stills in his illustrated article on ''Sex in Pictures: Effect of Model Action on Sex.'' In addition to identifying a range of sexuality from the ''classic madonna pose'' to ''negligee art'' and ''show girl art'', Theisen also warned that ''over-sex'' can be offensive. He established distinctions among ''wholesome'' sex, ''exotic or glamourous'' sex, and ''floosey'' sex using the key words ''seemingly natural'' to make the difference between offensive and acceptable stills of female sexuality. He argued that

> of the many elements in a picture, sex is considered to be of major importance in capturing reader interest . . . yet to have value in the picture it must be in good taste and preferably so subtly presented that the reader seldom recognizes the quality without critical study. (73)

By 1947, the notion of ''subtly presented'' sex appeal in pictures of women was a far cry from what the AAC would have approved in the mid-1930s.

Theisen's designation of paradigms for obtaining ''natural'' sexuality in the poses of female models is given legitimacy by his association with *Look*. Candid-camera magazines placed studio still photographers in competition with other still photographers with respect to the visual representation of female sexuality. While Theisen argues for fundamental differences between poster art and stills appropriate for publication in mass circulation magazines, it is apparent that the overall tone of sexuality had been intensified.

Taking their cue from candid-camera magazine editorial policies, the AAC rose to the occasion. The infamous still of Rita Hayworth clad in a skimpy slip kneeling on an unmade bed (''in attractive deshabille'' as *Life* described her) was first published in *Life* in 1941 (56). This still was exempt from the film industry's Advertising Code because it was shot by Bob Landry, a *Life* photographer. It was not until 1946 that the AAC approved the still for use by Columbia in its advertising (28).

That same year the integration of the Hollywood pin-up into American culture reached its patriotic zenith with the A-bomb testing at Bikini Atoll:

> For us of movieland a special concern obtains about the blast at Bikini for the reason that the fourth atomic bomb was named and duly christened 'Gilda' and that it bore, according to lagoon-side report, a picture of Miss Rita Hayworth in a low-cut gown.
>
> Here is high recognition of the art of the screen even in the face of the crack of doom. Man tinkers with the desperate facts of the cosmos, and remembers the movies. In the face of the cosmos and the outlying infinities, standing in the valley of Now between the dim peaks of the two eternities, past and ahead, the mind, even the military mind, turns to the 'mountains of Nebraska'. It is fit.
>
> . . . And so 'Gilda' with its blow-up girl has been strewn to interstellar space. (6)

While the pin-up figure of Rita Hayworth could be officially approved by the film industry, *Life* magazine (''the best girl picture ever taken'') (56) and the U.S. government, Howard Hughes pushed representations of women beyond the point of social acceptance.

THE OUTLAW: HOWARD HUGHES' CHALLENGE TO SELF-REGULATION

> It should not be supposed that the present PCA program has been placidly accepted by the whole industry. Some of the independent producers have complained of favoritism. Their position of dependence upon the members of the association for distribution facilities and outlets for their films has, however, kept them from making unpleasant public accusations—that is, always excepting Mr. Howard Hughes. (27)
>
> The advertising now in controversy in substance consists of pictures, cuts, and lithographs of the lady Rio, featuring more of her breasts, legs and positions than the saga of Billy the Kid. (26)

On May 23, 1941, *The Outlaw* was granted the Production Code's Seal of Approval after considerable difficulty and months of negotiation. After repeated screenings and the deletion of footage, the certificate of approval was issued (26). Despite the fact that *The Outlaw* was ready for exhibition in 1941, Hughes chose not to premiere the film until February 5, 1943. In between, he hired Russell Birdwell to publicize the film (12). Despite the fact that the film was not yet released, Jane Russell garnered incredible publicity in a wide range of publications through Birdwell's work:

> A survey taken by a trade paper during a random three-week period in 1941 showed 532 papers put out 4256 pages on Miss Russell and 448 Sunday papers published 2016 columns about her. Her picture appeared on the covers of eleven national magazines and she was awarded spreads in 196 pages in said magazines. *Esquire* ran a double-page truck in color of Miss Russell. Circulation leaped 186,000 copies. . . . The Fawcett Publishing Company, with five magazines, ran a picture of Miss Russell on the cover of one publication or another every month. Even the staid *Ladies' Home Journal* came through with a full page of Russell in color.

Jane Russell was ''the only star to become a star before being seen in a picture'' (24).

During a four-year period, Hughes paid Birdwell more than $250,000 to publicize *The Outlaw*. The film's San Francisco premiere netted more attention for the advertising than for the film. The premiere was conducted ''under circumstances and conditions without parallel in recent showmanship.'' A 24-sheet billboard consisted of a ''full length picture of Miss Russell, half recumbent and equivalently revealed in a sultry moment on a mound of hay'' with the copy: ''The picture that couldn't be stopped'' (80).

Initially, the advertising campaign was successful. The combination of text and image

> left it to the public to guess why (it couldn't be stopped), and who had tried to do the stopping, but the columnists filled in the chinks to the satisfaction of most. (80)

Birdwell went even further. He announced that Russell and Jack Beutel (Billy the Kid) would appear on stage after the premiere in what ''might consist of a scene or scenes removed from the picture for reasons also whispered'' (80). As the *New Yorker* put it in one of its four-part series on the life and works of Russell Birdwell: ''A press agent who worries about taste is as badly miscast as a soldier who faints at the sight of blood'' (29).

As might be expected, Hughes and Birdwell were blasted by the trade press. Red Kann's ''On the March'' column in the *Motion Picture Herald* took them to task for everything from too much sex to hampering the progress of the war. Hughes' roadshow of *The Outlaw* at the Geary in San Francisco commanded a $2.50 reserved seat price. Kann argued that in a time of price-fixing, Washington might be forced to make the roadshow forbidden. The transportation of 41 reviewers to San Francisco from Hollywood on two trains called to mind the fact that the Office of Defense Transportation discouraged unnecessary travel. Hotel space was hard to find but the Birdwell crew rested comfortably at the Mark Hopkins. Kann was delighted that the wartime ''dimout'' meant that the billboard could not be illuminated at night but bemoaned the fact ''that sex had not been rationed'' (33).

The publicity might have been good but the reviews were bad and Hughes withdrew the film for several years (12). In early 1946, Hughes re-released *The Outlaw*. The advertising which accompanied the film was so outrageous as to cause the MPAA to object to it as a ''violation of the industry's self-imposed standards of good taste.'' *Business Week* reported that Hughes was ''ordered to stand trial as a member of the MPAA,'' which meant that Hughes would be called before an MPAA board for violating the Advertising Code (25). However, Hughes resigned from the MPAA and obtained a temporary injunction restraining the MPAA from ''revoking the Seal of approval, and taking any action on the advertising of 'The Outlaw' '' (54). Hughes filed a six-million dollar damage suit against the MPAA (*Hughes Tool Co.* v. *Motion Picture Ass'n of America, Inc.*) before the United States District Court in New York on June 14, 1946, arguing three claims against the MPAA. First, the MPAA's threat to revoke the Seal of Approval for *The Outlaw* constituted a breach of his contract as a member of the MPAA. Second, Hughes argued that the MPAA was a monopoly which conspired to restrain trade. Third, Hughes considered the Production Code and the Advertising Code to be in violation of the First Amendment guarantee of free speech (26). The motion was denied but the terms of the denial point to the role of the MPAA as a monopoly with independent producers as members and to the role of the MPAA in mediating between the industry and the public in assessing good taste in film advertising.

The Contract

The MPAA threatened to revoke the film's Seal of Approval because Hughes advertised the film with material which had not been submitted to the

AAC for approval. The certificate was accompanied by the standard letter stating, in part:

> The attached certificate of approval is issued, upon the condition that its acceptance by you, binds you, as producer, and/or your distributor, and any and all other agents of yours, and your assigns, and successors, to the following terms and conditions. . . . That any and all advertising and publicity matter, including material for press books, still photographs, poster and lobby card designs, and trailers, used in any manner in connection with the advertising and exploitation of this picture, shall be submitted for approval to the Advertising Advisory Council of the Motion Picture Producers and Distributors of America, Inc., and that only such advertising or publicity material or trailers, approved by such Council shall be used in advertising and exploiting the picture hereby approved, (and) That, in addition to any other applicable penalties, the Production Code Administration reserves the right to void this Certificate, at any time hereafter, for any violation of the conditions set forth herein and/or of the violation of any of the rules and regulations promulgated by the Board of Directors of the Motion Picture Producers & Distributors of America, Inc.

Hughes Productions was a member in good standing of the MPPDA and therefore was "bound by (its) constitution, bylaws and regulations." Therefore, Hughes was bound to honor the terms of the certification (26).

Hughes charged the AAC with being partial because it did not tamper with the advertising for *Gilda,* produced by Columbia in 1946. Because Columbia was a major, the AAC chose not to interfere with its advertising campaign (27). While Hughes, in principle, might have been right, there was a big difference between the use of the sexuality of Rita Hayworth advertising *Gilda* and that of Jane Russell advertising *The Outlaw*.

The judge maintained that the MPAA had given Hughes a fair opportunity to revise the ads for *The Outlaw* and had operated the AAC in a "desire to cooperate" with Hughes. The AAC had asked Hughes to retouch the ads and provided him with an avenue for appeal. Hughes refused and appealed this rejection and several others to the president of the MPAA who sustained the rejection of some and overturned the rejection of others (26).

The MPAA, therefore, did not break the terms of the contract. Because they had approved some of the ads, they were functioning as stated in their regulations. Hughes broke the terms of the contract by exploiting the film with material which had not been approved and by using rejected material. For example:

> Late in April, 1946, it is alleged, and not denied, a sky-writing airplane wrote the words "The Outlaw" in the sky over Pasadena, and then made two enormous circles with a dot in the middle of each. (26)

Nor did Hughes submit the famous San Francisco billboard of the 1943 premiere to the AAC. Hughes therefore violated the contract:

> The court argued that the plaintiff "cannot have its cake and eat it too." If it wishes to retain the seal, it must be on the conditions that it adhere to the agreement under which it holds and has used it. (26)

While it is obvious that sexuality in film advertising during the 1940s was far different from that of the mid- to late-1930s, the Hughes case points to the extremes of representations of women which the MPAA could not allow.

The Monopoly

The court's decision on the MPAA as a monopoly was, in some ways, remarkable. Ignoring the MPAA's restraint of trade, the judge concentrated on the issue of maintaining moral standards:

> Concededly, one of the purposes for which defendant was organized was to establish and maintain the highest possible moral and artistic standards in motion picture production. That was in part in response to objections voiced in press and otherwise throughout the United States to the kind of pictures which appeared from time to time in the theatres, and to some of the advertisements used in the promotion of pictures. I shall not interfere with the carrying out of that purpose, particularly in favor of one whose sole object is a selfish one.

Hughes argued that the MPAA was a voluntary organization whose membership "comprise(s) more than 95 percent of the producers, distributors, and exhibitors in the industry." The MPAA exerted "rigid control over the supply of motion pictures, (and) has compelled more than 90 percent of the exhibiting theatres (to) refuse to exhibit pictures which do not have defendant's seal." Hughes attempted to establish the relationship between the Production Code and the vertical integration of the majors within the MPAA (26). This was not a new charge levied by independents (27).

Hughes lost this part of his case for two reasons. Despite the many theaters owned by MPAA affiliates, the court found that Hughes was in fact able to distribute his film and make money. The judge also ruled that the MPAA was a favorable monopoly. There was no evidence that any exhibitor refused or threatened to refuse to exhibit *The Outlaw* without the Seal of Approval. Even if such refusal had occurred, the judge ruled that the prohibition of exhibition or distribution of *The Outlaw* would not entitle Hughes to an injunction restraining the MPAA from prohibiting the exhibition or distribution of the film. The MPAA membership was bound by the regulations of the MPAA to not distribute films without the Seal of Approval (26).

Although Hughes argued that

> (MPAA) members entered into an agreement and conspiracy to hinder and suppress competition . . . to create a monopoly . . . by reason of the economic control centered in the seal,

the judge found that even if the MPAA were in violation of the Sherman Act, the violation was justified because of

> the proper purpose of the defendant to censor pictures which it may consider are not up to the highest possible moral and artistic standards. . . . If there is any restraint in such a proper purpose, it is a reasonable one.

Second, violations of the Sherman Act was not the immediate reason that Hughes was having trouble with the MPAA. Its advertising approval was the reason the case was brought to court so the Sherman Act could not be invoked in his defense (26).

Writing in the *Texas Law Review,* Milton Regan noted that the U.S. District Court found that the MPAA

> was not a monopoly of exhibition but instead the maintenance of a nationwide level of decency acceptable to the American public.

Because the MPAA became a monopoly "as an incident to some other purpose, it is valid." The monopoly structure of the MPAA was less significant to the outcome of the Hughes case than the function of the MPAA as protector of public morality (51).

First Amendment

Hughes argued that the MPAA violated his First Amendment right to freedom of speech for three reasons. The MPAA bans the "treatment of certain controversial topics"; it prohibits "certain advertising"; and it prohibits "mention of prior censorship" in advertising. Hughes lost on all three counts because his membership in the MPAA meant that the MPAA had the right to deny his advertisements. In addition, the court recognized the MPAA's responsibility to the public and the public recognition of the Seal of Approval:

> By the issuance of the seal, which is shown on every motion picture approved by it (MPAA), the public is led to understand that that picture has defendant's approval. (26)

Hughes lost the celebrated lawsuit but received no penalty. The court merely upheld the relationship between the MPAA and its members as defined by the regulations of the MPAA. It seems odd that the court made no reference to the antitrust lawsuit pending against the MPAA since 1938. After all, only two years after the Hughes decision, *United States* v. *Paramount, et al.* would be decided against the majors.

A second curious aspect of the Hughes case was the relationship between Hughes Productions and United Artists Corporation (UA). UA distributed *The*

Outlaw but was not implicated in the 1946 court case. In fact, the Distribution Agreement between Hughes and UA provided evidence for the MPAA. The contract required a Seal of Approval for the film (13, 26). Yet Hughes argued that withdrawing the Seal from *The Outlaw* would be a breach of his contract with UA. The court found that, at the time of the trial, UA was no longer a member of the MPAA and was therefore not bound to demand the Seal of Approval before accepting the Distribution Agreement (26). UA was, then, not functioning as a member of the organization.

At no time during the decision did the court discuss the relationship of UA and Hughes in advertising. Yet the Distribution Agreement indicates that, obviously, producer and distributor work closely on the advertising and promotion of films. According to the Hughes/UA Distribution Agreement, dated December 19, 1944, UA was to consult with Hughes Productions on advertising and publicity and

> follow wishes and instructions of the Producer in advertising and publicizing each . . . motion picture to the best of its ability.

In addition, advertising materials used in the United States were to be "subject to the final approval of the Producer." The question arises as to whether UA conducted the advertising in contention. It would seem possible because stills used in advertising and publicity were to be delivered to UA by Hughes (13).

UA and Hughes were unhappy in their partnership due to a continuing argument about the payment of censorship fees. According to the Distribution Agreement, UA and Hughes were to share expenses for censorship charges (13). That is, each party was responsible for a portion of legal fees required to have *The Outlaw* passed by censorship boards. In correspondence between UA and the Hughes Tool Company, UA argued that it would not recognize (i.e., be financially responsible for) "any censorship charges other than normal censorship fees for licenses." The Hughes Tool Co. rebutted that *The Outlaw* could not be exhibited in some places without recourse to the fees which UA opposed (10). How much of this conflict surrounded advertising and promotion is not clear. But the fact that UA was never mentioned in the court decision indicates that Hughes Tool Co. undertook the bulk of the advertising itself. Yet it is improbable that UA had no part in the distribution of the offensive material.

It should be noted that the ruling on this 1946 case pertained only to the temporary injunction which Hughes filed before the case was heard before the United States District Court in New York. Hughes also filed a Federal antitrust suit against the MPAA. This may account for the lack of mention of United Artists and the judge's reluctance to discuss the MPAA's violation of the Sherman Act. However, the outcome of the antitrust case was predicted by a Department of Justice spokesperson who commented:

> He (Hughes) would have a difficult time proving that an association which he joined for his own protection had formed a trust to hamper his business. (32)

It seems that Hughes' complaints against the MPAA might have been considered more legitimate but for the ludicrous circumstances surrounding *The Outlaw*.

In September 1946, the MPAA withdrew the Seal of Approval from *The Outlaw*. According to 1942 revisions in the Production Code, the film could be shown without liability to exhibitors if it were independently distributed (27, 76). Yet *Printers' Ink* reported that in reality the film would not be shown in 85 percent of American theaters (76).

The Outlaw controversy provoked considerable revisions in the Advertising Code. In general, "a keener eye" was kept on copy and stills before approval was granted. "More modesty" was demanded in terms of costuming of female stars. Equally important, public protests about the advertising for *The Outlaw* gave "renewed life to hitherto dormant groups seeking state and municipal censorship both of film and film advertising" (76).

Hughes had taken the MPAA full circle—back to the mid-1930s when threats of external censorship forced the industry to organize and institute the Production Code and the Advertising Code. In 1947 the MPAA revised the 1933 Advertising Code because

> incidents beyond our control precipitated new demands for further legal restrictions. (But) a single deviation from the requirements of decency and good taste can imperil the entire industry . . . this program will demonstrate anew the industry's militant and sincere purpose of making self-regulation effective in accordance with the democratic tradition. . . . But we mean to stand free of undemocratic restraints and propose to carry the doctrine of self-responsibility to every segment, every individual and to the outermost periphery of our art. (47)

The way the industry would do this was to make major revisions in the existing Advertising Code.

Prior to Howard Hughes' *The Outlaw*, the Advertising Code was merely to "bear in mind" the provisions of the Production Code. Now it was to be "guided by" the Production Code. The 1933 Advertising Code applied to press books, newspaper advertising, trailers, outdoor display, novelty distribution, and (vaguely) to "all other forms of advertising." Now it would also specifically apply to magazine and trade paper advertising, publicity material, posters, lobby displays, and radio copy (47). The extension of other kinds of advertising under the Advertising Code is also a moot point. The Hughes case and MPPDA Annual Reports demonstrated that all advertising already came under the aegis of the MPAA.

The changes in the Advertising Code which seem especially pertinent were some of the revisions of the original 12 provisions of the Advertising Code. The first was changed to read:

> We subscribe to a code of business ethics based upon truth, honesty and integrity. All motion picture advertising shall: (a) conform to fact, (b) scrupulously avoid all misrepresentation. (47)

This change was undoubtedly prompted by Hughes's advertisements for *The Outlaw* which claimed: ''Exactly as filmed—not a scene cut'' and which were determined to be both ''false and misleading'' by the court (26).

The eleventh provision was changed to:

> Nudity with meretricious purpose and salacious postures shall not be used; and clothed figures shall not be represented in such manner as to be offensive or contrary to good taste or morals.

Hughes' display of Jane Russell was the case in point. The twelfth provision was changed to:

> Court actions relating to censoring of pictures, or other censorship disputes, are not (to) be capitalized in advertising or publicity (47).

Hughes' original billboard for *The Outlaw* and its publicity campaign capitalized quite successfully on industry self-censorship.

By 1948, the MPAA was engaged in a months-long campaign to explain that the loopholes in the Advertising Code which allowed *The Outlaw* scandal were now closed. Charles Schlaiffer, advertising and publicity director of Twentieth Century-Fox and chair of an MPAA permanent public relations subcommittee of advertising and publicity directors, toured the U.S. to promote the Advertising Code (53) and to quell fears such as those expressed by the Allied States Association of Motion Picture Exhibitors:

> Those of us who lived through the outburst against moral laxity on the screen in the early thirties, and witnessed the skillful job done by Will Hays in putting out that fire, cannot help wondering why the situation was again allowed to get out of hand. (2)

Yet by 1948 other events occurred to render the MPAA's revised Advertising Code practically irrelevant. The *United States* v. *Paramount, et al.* decision forced the major studios to divorce and divest themselves of their theaters, partially breaking up the economic coercion of vertical integration. A post-war slump in movie attendance was accompanied by the mass availability of television. Writing in *Advertising Agency* in 1950, John Rehm echoed the concerns of some advertising personnel:

> Within recent months, newspapers seem to be carrying an increasing amount of copy decorated with bosomy gals, overstandard cheesecake and clinch close-ups,

> all amply larded with text suggestive of lurid sex episode in movies . . . the moguls of the movies are perhaps striving to lure potential theater patrons away from their TV sets with allusions to things to delight the eyes the video doesn't and dares not offer. (52)

As this history of the film industry's advertising practices and policies in the 1940s shows, changes in film advertising took place within a context of multiple industrial and cultural imperatives. The film industry was a multifaceted hierarchy in which the perceived needs of less powerful members were heeded (still photographers) or vigorously fought (Hughes' *The Outlaw*) according to whether those needs harmonized with socially acceptable representations of sexuality and other significant cultural institutions such as candid-camera magazines and courts of law.

HISTORICAL SPECIFICITY AND THE FILM INDUSTRY

This study originally began with one question: Why did representations of women in film posters from the studio period exhibit such marked changes in the mid-1930s and the 1940s? In order to answer this question, I looked first to the film industry to find the conflicts, controversies, and strategies upon which historical analysis of changes in representations of women could be based. This approach to determining historical specificity privileges the film industry as a primary determining agency for several reasons.

The process of "accounting for" or "explaining" the history of the film industry is the subject of debate in film study. Kristin Thompson has recently argued for film histories which focus on the discovery of "the most basic facts" of film history which are interpreted according to a "coherent theory or model." Thompson criticizes histories which rely on secondary sources, construct teleological narratives, or reformulate theories based on preexisting information (77). While empirical evidence is an invaluable tool in the documentation of film history, there are two issues about "basic facts" histories which need to be addressed. The first is the necessity of an awareness of how theories or models constrain the kinds of evidence gathered and their interpretation. The second is the problem of the truth-bearing status of documentation. These issues are interrelated because the ability of evidence to adequately "explain" is fundamentally informed by its position in the theoretical structure or model. I would therefore like to consider these issues together in a discussion of the kinds of documentation I found useful in offering explanations for changes in representations of women in film advertising during the studio period.

In *Historians' Fallacies,* David Fischer presents "seven rules of thumb" for selecting historical evidence. He argues first that there must be a "satisfactory relationship between the proposition to be proved and the material which is offered as proof'' (17). Appropriate documentation extends from the questions which initiated the search for evidence. Documentation also extends from the analytical categories which make up the model of historical relationships. In economic histories, the film industry can be analyzed in terms which show how economic considerations conditioned its operations and products. Thus, modes of production are related to economies of scale in the development of the studio system; product differentiation informs the cultivation of star personas (58, 36). The evidence called upon is truth-bearing, or valid, not only because it helps to explain film industry activities but also because it is integral to the application of the model.

The problem with summoning forth evidence which is both adequate and appropriate is particularly thorny when dealing with the area of the film industry and culture. The very concept of culture is slippery in its refusal to fit into a nicely hermetic model. In ''Representation and Cultural Production,'' Michele Barrett, Philip Corrigan, Annette Kuhn, and Janet Wolff go to great lengths to articulate relationships between material conditions and representation arguing, finally, that ''analysis has taken the ultimately futile path of theoreticism'' and exhorting culture critics to analyze ''meaning production in its historically specific conditions of existence'' (3).

The question is: What are these material (empirical) conditions to be? If the notion of culture production has been unapproachable except in abstract debates on theory, then how tentative must fact-based historical explanation of cultural phenomena be? If attention is devoted to getting the theory right, in its ability to account for all aspects of culture production and effects, then the historian's hands are tied when proffering evidence and explanations except those of the most tentative nature. The crucial issue here is that a framework of historical explanation requires attention to how producing institutions mediate between culture and culturally-appropriate representational practices.

To approach this problem of the film industry in culture, I stressed the operations of the film industry both in the gathering of evidence and in its interpretation, concluding that changes in representations of sexuality could be contextualized within the hierarchical structure of the film industry and the industry's recognition of cultural conditions with which it tried to harmonize. The primary types of documentation which I found to be useful were a random sample of Warner Brothers film posters and the public statements of various industry groups as they argued positions and presented controversies in trade journals. Each type of evidence has a different status as basic facts because each has a different kind of validity as evidence.

Warner Brothers film posters from 1930 to 1948 were randomly sampled in order to obtain an overview of film industry products across the span of the studio years. The implication of accuracy which accompanies this type of social science method would seem, at first, to be at odds with a film study-based cultural analysis. The theory behind the notion of accuracy of random numbers is that the table is "scientifically prepared" to eliminate researcher prejudice. Thus, the status of the posters chosen can be, in one way, understood to be representative of Warner Brothers posters for the period.[2]

But to take the sampling procedure out of the hands of theory and into the realm of science requires an awareness of the theory and positivist assumptions behind random samples. For the positivist, the basic facts of analysis are first of all empirically observable. In addition, this evidence is both epistemologically and ontologically privileged in its status as truth-bearing. To embrace these assumptions is to feel assured that numerical data and social science approaches produce accurate data but it is also to reify such empirical evidence (34).

Yet, from this random sample of film posters, I found that there were three distinct periods in the way the posters represented sexuality during the studio years. In the early 1930s, representations of women typically emphasized sensational aspects of sexuality in terms of clothing, body positions, and narrative enigmas about illicit love. In the mid-1930s there occurred a marked shift to representations which idealized women as romantic beings. They were more fully clothed, less erotic in the ways their bodies were positioned, and involved in stories which stress romantic love rather than sexual attraction. In the 1940s the posters returned to a variation of the early 1930s representations. The pin-up or cheesecake posture largely replaced the romantic woman; narrative enigmas typically returned to illicit love and a more highly-charged sexuality. While each period contained examples of both kinds of representations, in each period one type was clearly dominant.

Such empirical evidence, which reduces representations of women in film posters to percentages, is neither value-free nor simply true or false. What it provides is one kind of evidence of changes in representations of women over time and a clue as to where (in history) changes in the industry's appropriation of representations of women might exist. To engage an entity as large and as long-term as the film industry sometimes requires positivist methods if only to provide a basis from which cultural analysis can proceed. As Thompson has observed, "we need to re-examine the data relating to the most basic questions" of film history (77). Fischer exhorts historians to look for the "best relevant evidence"(17); sometimes this can only be empirical.

Also, there is lacking in film history accounts of the day-to-day working conditions of many aspects of the film industry. While we know that stars get up before dawn to prepare for shooting and that art directors and costume designers are asked to obtain appropriate period flair for a film, there is little known about

---

[2]For further information on the Warner Brothers poster analysis and on film advertising in the studio years, see Mary Beth Haralovich, "Mandates of Good Taste: The Self-Regulation of Film Advertising in the 1930s", *Wide Angle,* 6 (forthcoming 1984); "Advertising Heterosexuality." *Screen,* 23 (2), July/August 1982, pp. 50–60; and "Motion Picture Advertising: Industrial and Social Forces and Effects, 1930–1948." Ph.D. dissertation, University of Wisconsin–Madison, 1984.

how essential industry workers functioned within the context of the industry's structure and within history. The second type of documentation specific to the industry was that of the discussions of the participants in film industry policies found in trade journals. Robert Berkhofer, in his arguments for *A Behavioral Approach to Historical Analysis,* writes that "the essential task of the culture concept is to tell us something about the viewpoint of a group of actors." Berkhofer constructs his position around the concept of "temperocentrism" which has an important primary assumption, that there should be an acknowledged split between historical "actors" and the "observer" (the historian). The cultural historian should

> view the past according to the conceptual categories of its time and . . . see behavior in terms of that conceptualization instead of today's. (5)

Berkhofer's insistence on reconstituting the actors' perspectives in their own terms is problematic in that it may be impossible to fully place historical participants in concrete relationships to each other. First, a concerted action might have knowingly taken place as in the 1930s when the MPPDA and various branches of the industry agreed to an enforceable Advertising Code. Conversely, the relationship among actors might only be perceptible from the distance of the historian. The acquiescence of the MPPDA to the demands of still photographers in the 1940s is not "verifiable" from primary documentation but only by showing how the pin-up figure became the mainstay of the industry. Also, Berkhofer's demand for temperocentrism can cut off the play of important historical analytical interventions such as the application of Marxist economic theory to the studio system. Yet he is correct in insisting that the immediate perceptions of historical actors are important in reconstituting the way industry policies were formed.

Trade journals are a primary means of keeping the industry informed of important trends and controversies. While trade journals speak to and for particular interest groups and may not represent the entirety of those groups, they focus on discrete entities within a large industry all of whose work is important to the functioning of that industry. Also, trade journals articulate positions which focus on problems particular to their readership. Each journal's perceptions of these problems affirm both the position of the interest group within the industry's hierarchy and production structure and the solutions which can best (in its view) protect that interest group.

To validate the trade journals' representations of industry activities and attitudes would necessitate several considerations. The way in which editorial policy is established in connection with membership/readership would be interesting to pursue. Also, the degree to which readers considered that the journals provided a forum for the open discussion of relevant issues would help establish journals as reliable voices of the industry's sub-systems. In the absence of this type of research, it is still apparent that trade journals allowed the intersection of the disparate groups important to understanding how industry policies changed historically.

To intervene in the studio period is to attempt to cut a relatively narrow swathe through an industry which is characterized by two contradictory definitions. "Studio system" is a monolithic concept; at the same time it evokes a multi-faceted industry. The studio system was a particular mode of production common to all of the studios (58). Yet, it was also a multitude of discrete units with their own duties and projects (20, 36). To document policies which contributed to changes in film advertising requires attention to the way the industry worked as a single hierarchical entity as well as the way its individual branches and interest groups asserted their own concerns.

Secondly, it is necessary to consider mediating factors between the industry's production of cultural products and the ability of those products to harmonize within a historically-specific framework. The central question here is whether documentation indicates a context large enough to help demystify the role of the industry. Three analytical categories were useful in this regard. The first is the general mode of production of film advertising which changed to allow the pin-up to be part of film advertising. The second is the role of the internal workings of the industry's hierarchy in initiating and maintaining changes in advertising. To this point, the issues of mediation are concentrated on the industry itself as a primary means of understanding why its products took the form they took.

To break away from the constraints of industrial motivations in answering historical questions, a third factor, external conditions, was considered. By doing this, the sense of mediation was enlarged to include how the industry perceived itself in relationship to dominant culture. While no one would argue that the industry exists in a vacuum, it is important to look for those external conditions which the industry considered to be important in adjusting its policies. In order to perpetuate itself as an institution dependent upon broad-based public acceptance of its products (whether films or advertising), the industry appropriated specific external conditions at particular points in the history of the studio years. Rather than arguing for changes in representations of sexuality as *effects* of industry policies, it is important to consider a larger framework of the conditions within which certain representations of sexuality were deemed appropriate.

What emerges from this are some important generalizations about the institution of the Hollywood film industry. There is a sense of coherence in the film industry which is based on hierarchical interaction and the institutionalization of policies which should apply industry-wide. This coherence is maintained by the constant balancing of the perceived needs of the industry against those of its disparate sub-systems. This balancing is essential for the subsistence of the industry which maintains its institutional hierarchy by regulating its products internally and by adjusting its regulatory apparatus to conform to its perceptions of external conditions.

Thus, explanation serves not to establish general causal relationships between producers of culture and cultural effects. Instead, it explains what happened and the characteristics of the processes involved in culture production. Using Hollywood's film advertising policies and practices of the 1940s as a case in point, I will suggest the terms of a conceptual model for the analysis of the film industry in culture. This model emphasizes historical processes to help determine the ideologies which sustain the production of dominant culture.

THE FILM INDUSTRY AND SOCIAL CONDITIONS: A MODEL FOR ANALYSIS

To propose a model for the analysis of the film industry in history requires the sometimes precarious balancing of a multitude of factors which would be crucial to such a model. If the purpose of historical analysis is to draw conclusions and offer evidence about lived existence, then the analytical interventions which draw out the terms of this lived existence must be carefully poised one against the others. The problem inherent in reconstructing the position of the film industry in history is primarily that of determining the ''historically specific conditions of existence'' of its products (3).

In Pam Cook's recent discussion of feminist theory, she offers a critique of totalizing concepts of commodity production and of ideology. The fundamental question she addresses is how the

> commodity production argument reinforce(s) the status of images as objects rather than as part of the process of producing meanings which change with history.

While she offers no specific procedures to construct a history of process, Cook does present what she prefers as an analytical model based on the interrelationship of three factors: the historical place of the cultural product in the film industry; other related definitions of the product in society and in ideology; and analysis of the product itself based on the first two considerations. Cook argues for refocusing feminist analysis in terms of history because images of women in film

> cannot be discussed outside . . . their particular historical context, as many arguments about identification and stars tend to discuss the subject.

This particular historical context includes ''definitions of femininity offered by the film *and* in society at that time'' and includes its conditions of studio production (9).

The model I propose is one which takes into consideration Cook's goals but which expands upon the analytical procedures which Cook suggests. A model of the film industry in history should include five aspects of analysis: the film industry; other institutions which share the industry's ideological and cultural premises; the means by which these premises are made known; the cultural commodities themselves taken in the context of the first three; and, after having established this historical specificity, other critical interventions such as psychoanalysis and sociology. In this way, historical specificity can be foregrounded and the plurality of processes which constitute the film industry in history can begin to be identified.

This model admittedly privileges the film industry. I would argue with Cook that the film industry need not be reduced to simply playing out the conditions of capitalist production. While economic histories are valuable in understanding how the industry functioned within capitalist structures, industrial analysis can be placed in specific historical contexts and reveal a great deal about how the studio system operated in history with emphasis on how its many subsystems perceived themselves in relation to social forces.

Given this emphasis on the film industry's perceptions, the second level of analysis is that of other institutions which share or contradict the industry's perceptions of dominant culture. We saw how studio still photographers looked to the practices of candid-camera magazines despite the restrictions of the MPPDA on the display of the female body and how a court of law shared the film industry's perceptions about the degree of exploitation in certain representations of sexuality in the advertising for *The Outlaw*. Thus, attitudes about appropriate representations of female sexuality are shared by institutions which help the industry find its own definitions of femininity.

This third level of analysis, shared discourses, is linked to the means by which we can identify relevant ideologies. Its value lies not only in showing shared attitudes which contribute to a notion of dominant culture but also in the way that contradictory ideologies can be identified. Ideologies can be seen as not only working to reproduce conditions of capitalist production but also as the means by which contradictions are resolved in favor of stability or are manifestly in conflict with dominant culture. In her discussion of the fetish figure of the female star, Cook argues for the analysis of the potential conflicts between film industry representational practices and social reality:

> In the gap between the interest of subordinate groups and the interests of capital a power struggle takes place to decide how certain commodities should be used. The fetish figure of the female star can be seen as just such a commodity; capital invests in an image of woman which may, at certain historical moments, conflict with the place it allocates for women in society. Thus the image is potentially subversive of capital's interests and can be used against those interests. (9)

In the 1930s the containment of female sexuality was an issue shared by the MPPDA, the federal government in its legislative capacity, the concerns of public interest groups, and the *Motion Picture Herald*, an exhibitors' trade journal. In order to close the gap between appropriate representations of women and then-current industry advertising practices, the self-protective potential of an industry structure of self-regulation was called upon. Here, the terms of the National Recovery Act, the consolidation of capital power in Will Hays and the trepidation of exhibitors joined to seek security for the industry from external censorship by restructuring film advertising under the MPPDA's Advertising Code. There are, then, two interrelated motifs—one on representational practices and another on industrial hierarchy—which were called upon in order to disassemble the conflict between the industry's representations of women and the place these groups felt was allocated for women in society.

Like Cook's, this summary does not define society. Rather, I assume that the closeness of exhibitors to audience, the voices of organized public interest groups, and federal representatives are one means of suggesting that the representations of women in film advertising were at some variance with the way these groups conceived of women in society. Thus, Cook's general concepts of struggle and contradictions can be grounded in historical specificity.

Similarly, in the 1940s certain images of women were potentially subversive of the interests of the film industry. This conflict also had two interrelated motifs. Studio still photographers recognized that the implicit ban of the pin-up by the Advertising Code was subversive of their interests as workers in industry advertising and publicity. Drawing upon the popular acceptability of the pin-up manifested in mass circulation candid-camera magazines, still photographers mobilized around candid-camera magazine editorial policies on still photography. These policies were then brought into alignment with those of the Advertising Code as the industry's hierarchy acquiesced to the cultural validity of the pin-up. Thus, discussions of representational practices of women and how to ensure the industry's harmony with dominant culture worked to eradicate this conflict.

The Howard Hughes antitrust case on advertising *The Outlaw* points to the disparity between the interests of the industry and extreme representations of female sexuality through judicial determinations of appropriate representations of women. Hughes' notions of sexuality were clearly seen as subversive of both the industry and the place of women in society. The necessity of industrial self-regulation was validated by judicial ruling which argued in favor of the hierarchical structure despite its monopoly practices. Arguments on socially acceptable representations of women were called upon by both Hughes and the court as well as the MPAA—but in radically different terms. For Hughes, the fetish figure of Jane Russell was the means of asserting the independence of independent producers. For the court and the MPAA, it was a means of gauging the degree to which the MPAA would have authority over the interpretation of good taste in film advertising.

In this fourth level of analysis in the model, the researcher can consider the commodity status of images of women in light of the processes of both industrial conditions of existence and the relationship of women to society. Representations of women play different roles as ideologies of sexuality are integrated into other ideological discourses about institutional power, the coherence of groups within the industry, and representations appropriate to particular historical and social moments.

At this point, more theory-based analytical interventions such as psychoanalysis can be brought to bear upon these historical conditions of existence of cultural products. By plotting out ideologies in history and identifying the institutions with which they are associated, historical explanation can determine what happened at a particular point in time and under what social conditions. We can now ask what ramifications this has for ensuring dominant culture through subject positioning and how the specificity of that dominant culture can be seen to change historically. Sociological analysis on the varied appropriation of cultural meanings by a plurality of social groups can be addressed in terms which can expand on both the consensus and the contradictions of dominant culture.

As this study has shown, the film industry worked to accommodate its advertising practices to its perceptions of social forces. It is apparent that the industry had a strong sense of how its products could be adjusted in order to harmonize with what it considered to be the dominant attitudes of its mass audience. This raises two important questions about other aspects of social conditions which undoubtedly helped the industry to position its advertising appeals: how to expand the identification of dominant attitudes and how to recognize the plurality and heterogeneity of the industry's social context.

That the film industry adopted representational practices which would maximize its audience is true. Yet that audience was not, and is not, composed of homogenous and uniform traits. Sociological analysis such as that of Richard Dyer and T. E. Perkins on how stereotypes position discrete groups within and against dominant representational practices can help specify how cultural meanings may be appropriated differently by different groups (16, 49). Gorham Kindem's research on the industry's use of George Gallup's Audience Research Institute statistical surveys ultimately shows that the industry was looking for common denominators among its audience rather than disparity and heterogeneity (35). Yet the plurality of social attitudes and the differences that exist in history can be approached.

In terms of this study, we can ask how men and women might position themselves differently in relation to the 1940s emphasis in film advertising on the pin-up. Earl Theisen offered some answers to this question by his assumptions that male viewers were likely to be attracted to stills which presented women as objects of desire while female viewers would identify with the woman as object and seek to imitate her choice of clothing. Like John Berger's analysis of envy in advertising, Theisen subscribed to gender-specific patterns of identification (4, 60, 72).

Given the fact that the issue of sexual difference is important to changes in representations of sexuality in film advertising, what could this mean for historically-grounded theories of spectator identification? If, as Steve Neale has argued, posters try to appeal to all segments of the population (48), how does the censorship and exploitation of female sexuality reposition this appeal? Mary Ann Doane has argued that women can identify differently with different representations of women in films (14). These terms could be applied to the historical changes in representations of women in film advertising during the studio years. The broad range of representations of women in film posters which include the inaccessible movie queen glamour photo, the sexual availability of low-cut dresses and direct address, romantic young love, and forbidden exploitation of sexuality has implications for definitions of women in society and for theories of female subjectivity.

The issue of how the institution sustains itself in and for dominant culture can be usefully approached by placing ideologies and culture within a historically-specific framework which includes the ways that cultural institutions express multiple ideologies. A sense of the way multiple ideologies can help define culture is shared by Lucy Bland, Trisha McCabe, and Frank Mort. In their discussion of the ideologies evident in three government reports on sexuality, the authors argue that ideologies can be determined by "making connections with popularly-held assumptions and beliefs" (7). We have seen how the pin-up was an acceptable popular representation of women before the film industry integrated the pin-up into film advertising. This study can proceed by researching other forms of representation in other cultural products to determine how widespread the mid-1930s containment of female sexuality and its late-1930s and 1940s exploitation was. However, each cultural product must also be considered in its own specificity. The editorial policies of *Look* magazine, as articulated by Earl Theisen, indicate that specific displays of female sexuality were institutionalized by candid-camera magazines.

Also, Bland et. al. (7) argue that the proliferation of official statements about a particular subject indicates that the topic has a strength or position with which the institution must deal (7). Thus, repeated statements from the film industry on topics such as cooperation with the MPPDA's self-regulation offices in order to preserve the relative autonomy of the industry invests that issue with institutional importance. Such topics have ideological significance because they were important to the way women could be represented in film advertising. Conversely and equally important in this regard is determining what is unsaid by official statements. Issues which are avoided or cloaked in silence have significance. The fact that only Howard Hughes publicly reacted adversely to the hegemony of the MPPDA through its Advertising Advisory Council could indicate either a widespread complicity with the MPPDA or the inability of other studios and independents to function without the MPPDA's cooperation. Research into this area can expand our understanding of the ways the industry's hierarchy related to its individual rungs.

I have tried to initiate a rapprochement in the form of an analytical procedure which can recognize that the empirical evidence necessary to ''basic facts'' historical inquiry need not be fundamentally at odds with more theory-based approaches. In his essay on *Jaws,* Stephen Heath called for attention to three component parts of the cinematic institution: industry–machine–text. Heath's approach requires both a totalizing concept of how cinema works as well as specific attention to each of these parts:

> Each of the three areas can bring with it its own set of tasks and study procedures, but attention to their intersection is *constantly* important. (22)

According to Heath's suggested model, ''industry'' includes ''the conditions of film production and distribution''; ''text'' includes both cinematic specificity and its heterogeneity; and ''machine'' is ''cinema itself understood in its stock of constraints and definitions, its possibilities and points of determination'' (22). Taken together, the three areas articulate the ways that the industry produces texts according to the codes of cinema (especially classical Hollywood narration), unconscious processes, and ideologies. But ''industry'' also includes the fact that the industry was aware of its mediating role between its products and society. The industry's perceptions of how it could best accommodate itself to historically-specific social conditions has implications for grounding ''machine'' and ''text'' in historical specificity.

REFERENCES

1. ''Academy Still Show.'' *International Photographer* 13 (11), December 1943, pp. 16–18, 24, 30.
2. ''Allied Tells MPA: 'Reassure Public.' '' *Motion Picture Herald* 169 (7), November 15, 1947, p. 14.
3. Barrett, Michele, Phillip Corrigan, Annette Kuhn and Janet Wolff. ''Representation and Cultural Production.'' In Barrett, *et. al.* (Eds.) *Ideology and Culture Production,* New York: St. Martin's Press, 1979, pp. 9–24.
4. Berger, John. *Ways of Seeing.* New York: Viking Press, 1972.
5. Berkhofer, Robert. *A Behavioral Approach to Historical Analysis.* New York: MacMillan Publishing Co., Inc., 1969.
6. ''Bikini 'Pin-up.' '' *Motion Picture Herald* 164 (1), July 6, 1946, p. 7.
7. Bland, Lucy, Trisha McCabe, and Frank Mort. ''Sexuality and Reproduction: Three 'Official' Instances.'' In Michele Barrett, *et. al.* (Eds.) *Ideology and Culture Production.* New York: St. Martin's Press, 1979, pp. 78–111.
8. Boyce, Helen. ''Third Annual Still Show: An Interview with John LeRoy Johnston.'' *International Photographer* 15 (11), October 1943, pp. 5–6, 12.
9. Cook, Pam. ''Stars and Politics.'' *Star Signs.* London: British Film Institute, 1982, pp. 23–31.
10. Correspondence between Harry L. Gold, Hughes Productions, and Arthur L. Kelly, Executive Vice-President, United Artists Corporation. April 1948, United Artists Collection, Record Group 2, Series 3A, Producers Legal File 1933–1966, Hughes Tool Co., Manuscripts, Wisconsin Center for Film and Theatre Research, University of Wisconsin–Madison.

11. Cunningham, James P. "Issue Not for Code Administration But Hays, Breen Holds." *Motion Picture Herald* 127 (4), April 24, 1937, pp. 14–15.
12. Dietrich, Noah and Bob Thomas. *Howard: The Amazing Mr. Hughes*. Greenwich, CT: Fawcett Publications, Inc., 1972.
13. "Distribution Agreement, Hughes Tool Co. and United Artists Corporation: Schedule B." United Artists Collection, Record Group 2, Series 3A, Producers Legal File 1933–1966, Hughes Tool Co., Manuscripts, Wisconsin Center for Film and Theatre Research, University of Wisconsin–Madison.
14. Doane, Mary Ann. "Film and the Masquerade—Theorizing the Female Spectator." *Screen* 22 (3–4), September–October 1982, pp. 74–87.
15. Doolittle, James N. "They Mustn't Stand Still." *International Photographer* 11 (2), March 1939, pp. 16–18.
16. Dyer, Richard. "*A Star is Born* and the Construction of Authenticity." *Star Signs*. London: British Film Institute, 1982, pp. 13–22.
17. Fischer, David Hackett. *Historians' Fallacies*. New York: Harper and Row, 1970.
18. "G.I. Pin-ups." *Motion Picture Herald* 153 (2), October 9, 1943, p. 9.
19. Gib, "Credit Due Stillman." *International Photographer* 11 (10), November 1939, p. 8.
20. Gustafson, Robert. "The Buying of Ideas: Source Acquisition at Warner Brothers 1930–1949." Ph.D. dissertation, University of Wisconsin–Madison, 1983.
21. "Hays Offers Five-Plank Program to Solve Readjustment Problems." *Motion Picture Herald* 111 (12), April 1, 1933, p. 16.
22. Heath, Stephen. " 'Jaws', Ideology and Film Theory." *Film Reader* 2, January 1977, pp. 166–168.
23. "Hollywood Studios' Still Photography Show: A Few of the Winners." *International Photographer* 13 (3), May 1941, p. 6.
24. Hubler, Richard. "As I Remember Birdie." *The Screen Writer* 3 (4), September 1947, pp. 13–15.
25. "Hughes Rebels." *Business Week,* May 4, 1946, p. 20.
26. Hughes Tool Co. v. Motion Picture Ass'n of America, Inc. 66 F.S. 1006. N.Y. D.C. 1946.
27. Inglis, Ruth. "Need for Voluntary Self-Regulation." *Annals of the American Academy of Political and Social Science* 254, November 1947, pp. 153–159.
28. "Is There Sense in Censorship." *Pageant,* March 1946, pp. 80–81, 147.
29. Johnston Alva. "Profiles: Public Relations—IV." *The New Yorker,* September 9, 1944, pp. 30–38.
30. Johnston, John LeRoy. "Stillmen Musn't Stand Still." *International Photographer* 11 (1), February 1939, pp. 9–12.
31. Johnston, John LeRoy. "Stills Must Have Action." *International Photographer* 11 (6), July 1939, pp. 12–16.
32. "Justice Dept. Sees Failure of Suit." *Motion Picture Herald* 163 (12), June 22, 1946, p. 15.
33. Kann, Red. "On the March." *Motion Picture Herald* 150 (8), February 20, 1943, p. 14.
34. Keat, Russell and John Urry. *Social Theory as Science*. London: Routledge and Kegan Paul, 1975.
35. Kindem, Gorham. "Hollywood's Movie Star System: A Historical Overview." In Gorham Kindem (Ed.) *The American Movie Industry*. Carbondale, IL: Southern Illinois University Press, 1982, pp. 79–93.
36. Klaprat, Cathy Root. "Back to Bette: The Star as Marketing Strategy." In Tino Balio (Ed.) *The American Film Industry*. Madison, Wisconsin: The University of Wisconsin Press, forthcoming.
37. McCarthy, John J. "Movie Advertising is Clean." *Printers' Ink*, November 15, 1934, pp. 31–36.
38. Motion Picture Association of America. *Annual Report* (*Twenty-fourth year*) *to the Motion Picture Association of America, Inc.,* March 25, 1946.

39. Motion Picture Association of America. "Motion Picture Advertising and Publicity Materials Serviced by Advertising Code Administration 1934–1951," *1951 Annual Report*, 1951, p. 32.
40. Motion Picture Producers and Distributors of America. *Seventeenth Annual Report on the Motion Picture Industry*, 1939.
41. Motion Picture Producers and Distributors of America. *Eighteenth Annual Report on the Motion Picture Industry*, 1940.
42. Motion Picture Producers and Distributors of America. *Nineteenth Annual Report on the Motion Picture Industry*, 1941.
43. Motion Picture Producers and Distributors of America. *Twentieth Annual Report on the Motion Picture Industry*, 1942.
44. Motion Picture Producers and Distributors of America. *Twenty-First Annual Report on the Motion Picture Industry*, 1943.
45. Motion Picture Producers and Distributors of America. *Twenty-Second Annual Report on the Motion Picture Industry*, 1944.
46. Motion Picture Producers and Distributors of America. *Twenty-Third Annual Report on the Motion Picture Industry*, 1945.
47. "MPA Tightens Advertising Code and Extends Scope." *Motion Picture Herald* 168 (5), August 2, 1947, p. 19.
48. Neale, Steve. "Poster-Film-Industry." *Selling Dreams: British and American Film Posters 1890–1976*, Welsh Arts Council, N.D.
49. Perkins, T. E. "Rethinking Stereotypes." In Michele Barrett, *et. al.* (Eds.) *Ideology and Culture Production*. New York: St. Martin's Press, 1979, pp. 135–159.
50. Peterson, Theodore. *Magazines in the Twentieth Century*. Urbana, IL: The University of Illinois Press, 1956.
51. Regan, Milton. "Constitutional Law—Monopoly—Right of a Private Association to Censor Movies of Voluntary Producer Members." *Texas Law Review* 25, 1947, pp. 537–538.
52. Rehm, John. "Inside Pitches: Sexy Movie Advertising Morally Wrong and Misleading." *Advertising Agency and Advertising and Selling* 43 (4), April 1950, p. 70.
53. Rovner, Samuel. "Movies' Face Washed in New P.R. Effort." *Editor & Publisher* 81 (43), October 16, 1948, p. 28.
54. Salierno, Frank and Lawrence Turner. "Injunction–Constitutional Law Monopolies—Contract." *Notre Dame Lawyer* 22, May 1947, pp. 224–226.
55. Sargeant, Winthrop. "The Cult of the Love Goddess in America." *Life*, November 10, 1947, pp. 81–96.
56. Scherman, David (Ed.) *The Best of Life*. New York: Time-Life Books, 1973.
57. Shurlock, Geoffrey. "The Motion Picture Production Code." *Annals of the American Academy of Political and Social Science: The Motion Picture Industry* 254, November 1947, pp. 140–146.
58. Staiger, Janet. "The Hollywood Mode of Production: the Construction of Divided Labor in the Film Industry." Ph.D. dissertation, University of Wisconsin–Madison, 1981.
59. "Studios' Still Photography Show." *International Photographer* 13 (3), April 1941, p. 6.
60. Theisen, Earl. "Photographs for a National Magazine." *International Photographer* 16 (5), June 1944, pp. 5–8.
61. Theisen, Earl. "Pictures for a National Magazine." *International Photographer* 16 (6), July 1944, pp. 7–11.
62. Theisen, Earl. "Photographs for a National Magazine." *International Photographer* 16 (7), August 1944, pp. 10–14.
63. Theisen, Earl. "Photographs for a National Magazine." *International Photographer* 16 (8), September 1944, pp. 9–13.
64. Theisen, Earl. "Photographs for a National Magazine." *International Photographer* 16 (9), October 1944, pp. 7–11.

65. Theisen, Earl. "Photographs for a National Magazine." *International Photographer* 16 (10), November 1944, pp. 9–11.
66. Theisen, Earl. "Photographs for a National Magazine." *International Photographer* 16 (11), December 1944, pp. 18–20.
67. Theisen, Earl. "Photographs for a National Magazine." *International Photographer* 16 (12), January 1945, pp. 16–23.
68. Theisen, Earl. "Photographic Glossary." *International Photographer* 19 (2), February 1947, pp. 4–8.
69. Theisen, Earl. "Photographic Glossary." *International Photographer* 19 (3), March 1947, pp. 14–17.
70. Theisen, Earl. "Photographic Vocabulary." *International Photographer* 19 (4), April 1947, pp. 11–14.
71. Theisen, Earl. "Photographic Vocabulary." *International Photographer* 19 (5), May 1947, pp. 13–16.
72. Theisen, Earl. "Photographic Vocabulary." *International Photographer* 19 (7), July 1947, pp. 10–12.
73. Theisen, Earl. "Photographic Vocabulary." *International Photographer* 19 (8), August 1947, pp. 10–13.
74. Theisen, Earl. "Photographic Vocabulary." *International Photographer* 19 (9), September 1947, pp. 22–23.
75. Theisen, Earl. "Photographic Vocabulary." *International Photographer* 19 (10), October 1947, pp. 10, 13.
76. Thomann, Louis F. "Hughes Fight Tightens Administration of Hollywood Code on Advertising." *Printers' Ink* 216 (11), September 13, 1946, p. 122.
77. Thompson, Kristin. "Cinematic Specificity in Film Criticism and History." *Iris* 1 (1), 1983, pp. 39–49.
78. "Urge All Exhibitors, Affiliated or Not, to Comply with Ad Code." *Exhibitors Herald-World* 99 (5), June 28, 1930, p. 9.
79. "Warner Bros. Magazine Photographers' Contest." *International Photographer* 13 (5), June 1941, p. 10.
80. Weaver, William. "Mr. Hughes Unveils His Maverick—And How." *Motion Picture Herald* 150 (7), February 13, 1943, p. 23.
81. Wood, James Playsted. *Magazines in the United States*. New York: The Ronald Press Company, 1971.

10

AB Svenska Biografteatern: Aspects of Production, 1912–1920*

John Fullerton

INTRODUCTION

This article is concerned with the film production interests of AB Svenska Biografteatern, the major production, distribution, and exhibition company in Sweden during the silent era. By concentrating on the period from 1912 to 1920, the article examines the development of Svenska Biografteatern from small company to corporate industry.

In the past a number of historians have addressed themselves to the history of early Swedish film (see 4, 5, 9). While acknowledging an indebtedness to their work, the present study sets for itself a rather different task. It seeks to attribute the success of Svenska Biografteatern to the financial management of the company, rather than to the work of distinguished directors such as Sjöström and Stiller. More particularly this article examines the financial management of the company's production interests. This area has been selected both to qualify previous representations of the history of Svenska Biografteatern, and to quantify, in financial terms, the company's production program. This objective is rendered feasible through the preservation of company ledgers at Svenska Filminstitutet.[1]

First, drawing upon the work of Idestam-Almquist (4, 5 in particular) a brief history of the company before 1912 will be presented. The establishing of

---

*An earlier version of this article was first presented at the East Midlands Arts/SEFT conference on film, *Putting Narrative in Place: the cinema 1906–1916,* at the Metro Cinema, Derbyshire College of Higher Education, Derby, England, December 10–12, 1982. I would like to thank Derbyshire College of Higher Education for their financial contribution to work I undertook at Svenska Filminstitutet, Stockholm during the summer of 1982.

[1]I would like to thank Torsten Jungstedt, former head of library and documentation at Svenska Filminstitutet, who first drew some of this material to my attention, and Margareta Nordström, currently head of library and documentation, for her help in giving me access to, in particular, documents nos. 214 (*Aktiebolaget Nordiska Filmsfabriken*), and 215 (*Inspelade filmer 1916–1919*), shelf location 9:6,1.

new production facilities on the island of Lidingö in that year affords us the opportunity of characterizing the material base for production before and after 1912. Second, in the main part of the article, the industrial base and financial strategies for production in the period from 1912 to 1920 will be examined. Last, by way of conclusion, a short section is presented which considers some limitations of the present analysis and indicates areas for future work.

Access to company ledgers enables us to quantify in human terms, as much as in financial terms, the operation of the company. These ledgers make available the names of individuals who worked for the company in production, distribution, and exhibition. Thus, we can establish detailed knowledge of company organization across its three areas of interest at an early point in its development from small company to corporate industry. But it would be naive to overemphasize the significance of these data in an article that cannot at the same time begin to evaluate the contribution made by hitherto unknown individuals. This task must wait.

Before we proceed, however, the analysis undertaken in this article should be qualified for it is less complete than I would like. Data in respect of the industrial base are only available for the period, defined at its broadest, between 1912 and 1916, and for films produced (from which we can deduce financial strategies) for the period 1914 to 1918. The company ledgers known to me at present give, unfortunately, little data after 1918. This study, therefore, although it confines analysis to the years 1912 through 1918 (for which data exist), is speculative inasmuch as it projects a policy for production two years beyond the period with which analysis can be supported by reference to known data. But speculation is mitigated by two factors. First, the production data that exist for the period 1914 to 1916 lead us to conclude that the financial and production strategies Svenska Biografteatern adopted in those years were broadly consistent with its policy between 1912 and 1914. Second, the data that exist for 1917 and 1918 indicate a considerable change in direction, which confirms that Svenska Biografteatern adopted different financial and production strategies in the years after 1916. Further, examination of its feature film output, although outside the scope of this present article, also supports this observation. But since, as is generally agreed, the success of Svenska Biografteatern's production program after 1916 gave the company sufficient capital by 1920 to establish new studios at Råsunda, and to take over studios at Långängen in Stockholm and in Hellerup, Denmark, the company's developing production program in this period can be regarded as one index to the nature of the company's corporate success.

Other approaches, however, could be used as indices to the company's corporate success. Approaches which considered the company's distribution and exhibition interests could be used to determine the development of Svenska Biografteatern, for, as with other corporations, the company was engaged not only in film production, but also in distribution and exhibition. In that this present study is confined to film production interests, our understanding of

Svenska Biografteatern's operation will be necessarily partial. At some future date attention must be paid to its other interests if a more complete picture of the company's operation is to be achieved.[2] But production data have been selected for analysis because they are the most complete and reliable source of information we have at present. Analysis of this material sheds light on the nature of corporate consolidation, and helps us understand more fully the operation of a successful medium-financed production base. Analysis of production data also clearly announces the initiatives that were taken in production during the period 1912 to 1920 by which date, as Sadoul has indicated (8, pp. 209–210), the merger of Svenska Biografteatern with Filmindustri AB Skandia (on December 27, 1919) formed a major European film corporation, Svensk Filmindustri, which has been a major force in the domestic Swedish film economy to the present time. The period, therefore, from 1912 to 1920 was critical to the development of a corporate film industry.

SVENSKA BIO BEFORE 1912

Svenska Bio, as its name implies, was first established as a film exhibition concern in 1905 by Gustaf Björkman and N. H. Nylander.[3] Based in Kristianstad in the southern province of Skåne (a province with a history closely connected with that of Denmark), the company was, in many respects, more an outpost of Danish exhibition than anything intrinsically Swedish in its first few years of operation. Kristianstads Biograf-Teater (by which name the company was initially known) was established at a time when Sweden, like many countries in Europe, was developing a film rental system. During the following four or five years the company developed a circuit of cinemas in the south of Sweden. When Björkman left the company, Nylander was backed by banker and town councillor, Carl Johan Arhén, who formed, on February 16, 1907, AB Svenska Biografteatern. In the following year the company established a new cinema in Kristianstad, the Cosmorama, which possessed a small production studio. Under Robert Ohlson, who is reputed to have previously worked for Charles Urban in England, the company ventured into producing short films. But it became clear that Svenska Bio required a production manager, and Charles Magnusson was recommended for the post. Appointed in 1909, he had previously owned a cinema in Göteborg. Moreover, he had connections with a film exporting busi-

[2]The article distinguishes between Svenska Biografteatern's interests as a whole (its *operation* as a company including production, distribution, and exhibition), and the company's work in film production proper. Ideally the two aspects should not be considered apart; production informs the operation of the company as a whole, and vice versa. But such an integrated approach is beyond the scope of this article, and, at present, awaits further research.

[3]To conform with widespread practice, Svenska Biografteatern is abridged hereafter to Svenska Bio, literally translated as "The Swedish Biograph-Theater Company."

ness, based in London, run by an émigré Swede, Oscar Rosenberg. A series of productions was initiated, some in the Film d'Art style (*Regina von Emmeritz,* 1910, directed by Gustaf Linden, adapted from Z. Topelius), some drawing upon popular literary and folk traditions (*Värmlänningarna,* 1910, directed by Carl Engdahl, adapted from C. F. Dahlgren; *Fänrik Ståls sägner,* 1910, directed by Carl Engdahl, adapted from J. L. Runeberg), and some melodramas of social injustice (*Järnbäraren,* 1911, directed by Ivan Hedqvist, adapted from A. Blanche).[4]

In many ways, although invoking Swedish traditions, these works reflect a more widespread ambition in the development of film: the adaptation of literary vehicles by directors and actors drawn from the world of the theater. Indeed, Idestam-Almquist (5, pp. 602–603, 605) cites competition from the Stockholm theater milieu (viz. Anna Hoffman-Uddgren's series of Strindberg adaptations for the screen), as much as the quality of competition from Denmark, as sufficient reasons in themselves to warrant Svenska Bio's move to the capital. Whatever the circumstances (competition from Denmark and Stockholm, and/or opportunities for company expansion in the capital), in 1911 work was started on constructing a new studio, and establishing the company as a whole in new offices in Stockholm. The capital's theater milieu could be enticed into film. Equally, Danish or Norwegian actors (viz. Lili Bech, or Gunnar Tolnaes) could be persuaded to work for the company. Among the new talent brought into film from the theater were Mauritz Stiller and Victor Sjöström, the two directors whose work is most closely associated with that of Svenska Bio.

PRODUCTION BEFORE AND AFTER 1912

As indicated earlier, the establishment of a new studio in 1912 affords us the opportunity of characterizing Svenska Bio's production facilities at Kristianstad and on Lidingö. Since primary source material for the period before 1912 is unavailable at present, many assertions cannot be adequately tested. But, given that this article is concerned primarily with the development of Svenska Bio's production interests after 1912, characterization of pre-1912 facilities is offered as a context in which to place the central concerns of this article.

The company's production interests before 1912 can be characterized in the following manner: (a) there was little industrial base for production in terms of plant and personnel; (b) there was a low output of low-financed one-reel or,

---

[4]Some authorities, unlike Idestam-Almquist, claim that *Järnbäraren* was directed by Gustaf Linden (see 1, 10). To conform with his work I have indicated that the film was directed by Ivan Hedqvist (see also 11). Some of these films, with other film fragments, can be viewed at Svenska Filminstitutet in a compilation film, *Kristianstad-Filmstaden.* Dates given in this instance are release dates. In the following sections, all dates refer to the year of production.

occasionally, two-reel dramas, with a screening time of between 15 and 30 minutes; (c) there was little differentiation in the division of labor—technician roles were often interchangeable, and the role of director (often a technician or leading player) was at an early stage of development; (d) production was a relatively undeveloped interest before Magnusson was appointed as managing director. Markets for the company's films were largely domestic in nature, and, inasmuch as little attention was given to product differentiation, marketing was undeveloped. Within the context of Sweden's national industry, as production, distribution, and exhibition were frequently discrete areas of activity, Svenska Bio, in common with other film companies, were not in a position to maximize its production, distribution, and exhibition interests.

After 1912 the company's mode of operation, as much as the national situation for production, distribution, and exhibition, quantifiably changed. Some aspects of that change, the subject of analysis in the following section of the article, can be characterized in the following manner: (a) there was increasing capitalization of the industrial base for production—in relative terms, a considerable outlay in studio facilities (both of plant and personnel); (b) films were longer (three, four, or five reels) with increasingly conspicuous production values (in terms of leading players, set design, lighting, etc.), and more ambitious in terms of literary pedigree; (c) the division of labor was more differentiated, and a production, distribution, and exhibition hierarchy instituted, which, in terms of remuneration, favored the production sector; (d) production was increasingly monitored and supervised through financial planning on the part of the studio head. In respect of the company's operation as a whole, we should also observe that products were increasingly differentiated (in terms of both the level of funding, and the strategies that were adopted in marketing); that the company was more concerned with identifying and reaching specific domestic markets; that attention was increasingly paid to achieving foreign sales (to which end an identifiable product for the international market was sought after); and that Svenska Bio consolidated its company interests through a more consistent policy of integrating production, distribution, and exhibition on a national basis.

To examine this development in its widest implications, we would need to attend to the company's full output (not just in feature films, but also its short film output and its newsreel *Veckorevy*), its studio organization, and we would need to give due emphasis to its other domestic and foreign interests. Furthermore, the company's operation would need to be examined in the context of its virtual monopoly status as a production base within the domestic Swedish film economy during the period 1912 to 1920. At a time when, according to other writers, Sweden's neutrality during the First World War assured Svenska Bio a reception in foreign markets that other national industries envied, we would wish to examine the development of the company's foreign interests in the light of these material considerations. But, limiting myself to an area of investigation that can be quantified, I shall now consider the industrial base for production in the years after 1912, and consider production strategies for the period 1914 to 1918.

SVENSKA BIO 1912–1920

In this section of the article Svenska Bio's production policy, as instanced in its industrial base, its script purchases record, and its production data, will be examined.

The Industrial Base

According to Werner (9, pp. 39–41), Svenska Bio's new studio on Lidingö measured 20 × 7 meters, and occupied a studio lot of some 1650 square meters. In 1914 this studio was extended, and in 1916 a further smaller studio was erected. This formed the physical base for Svenska Bio's production up to the merger of late 1919.

Document no. 214, *Aktiebolaget Nordiska Filmsfabriken,* provides data primarily for films that went into production in either 1914 or 1915. This document also provides data concerning leading player and directorial contracts, salaries for personnel in production, distribution, and exhibition (the last within the Stockholm first-run cinema circuit only), and listings of scripts purchased from 1914 through 1918. In the case of company personnel, with the exception of leading players and directors, it is difficult to be certain of the exact period for which data exist. But the data recorded in the ledgers represent a point of development that can be dated to the period 1913–1915. In other words, data for company personnel (other than for leading players and directors) cover a period broadly consistent with the production years that are quantified in the document *Aktiebolaget Nordiska Filmsfabriken.* There are additional data concerning foreign sales, particularly to Oscar Rosenberg in London, for most of the production ledgers give an indication of the countries to which prints were sold. But as far as I can ascertain, although Werner uses some of these data to construct his table of foreign distribution for the lost Stiller films, he also appears to have had access to data with which I am unfamiliar (9, pp. 341–343). Accordingly, in this article, I shall not devote attention to foreign distribution.

In the document, *Aktiebolaget Nordiska Filmsfabriken,* data concerning leading player and directorial contracts include information on the period during which a person was contracted to the company, and his or her salary on an annual or pro rata basis. From this material, we can see that Victor Sjöström, who was engaged as an actor-director as well as studio manager, received an annual salary of 15,000 Swedish Kronor during the period June 1, 1913, to August 15, 1914; Mauritz Stiller received an annual salary of 10,000 Swedish Kronor from May 15, 1912, to May 15, 1915; and Arvid Englind, contracted on a similar full-time basis, received 5,000 Swedish Kronor in the period May 1, 1914, to May 1,

1915. Edmond Hansen, engaged as an actor-director from the German-language theater in Riga, received 3,400 Swedish Kronor between June 28 and October 28, 1915, and would have been subsequently re-engaged at a similar rate during 1916 and 1917. However, there is no evidence that he took up these later contracts. Winquist and Jungstedt indicate that, during his four months with Svenska Bio in 1915, he directed seven films and acted in four (11, p. 378). We should further note that, with the exception of Arvid Englind (who only acted in *Högfjällets dotter,* 1914, directed by Sjöström), it was common practice for directors, during the Lidingö years, to be contracted as actor-directors. This practice (with the exception of Stiller who acted in only a few films in the period at Lidingö) continued beyond the merger of 1919.

However, a number of omissions, in respect of actor-directors, occur. In 1912, the earliest season of production, data on the salaries paid to Victor Sjöström, Axel Breidahl, and Georg af Klercker are unavailable. Similarly for directors working in or after 1915 (Fritz Magnussen, Konrad Tallroth, Egil Eide), data are not made available.[5] I conclude, therefore, that data for actor-directors in this ledger cover the period, more properly determined, between 1913 and 1915, even though some retrospective and projected salary figures are available outside this period.

If we compare, however, the salaries paid to leading actor-directors with those paid to leading players in this period, we can observe more clearly the growing division of labor within the company at this early point in its development. While a major actress from the theater such as Hilda Borgström received 3,000 Swedish Kronor for a month's work on two occasions in 1914 (in May and in August), regular leading players received considerably less. Greta Almroth received an annual salary of 3,000 Swedish Kronor between September 1913 and September 1914, rising to 4,200 Swedish Kronor per annum from September 1914 to September 1916; John Ekman received 4,200 Swedish Kronor between August 1913 and August 1914, rising to 5,000 Swedish Kronor per annum from August 1914 to August 1916, and Richard Lund, a major figure in the early years at Lidingö, received an annual salary of 4,000 Swedish Kronor from 1913 to 1914 rising to 8,000 Swedish Kronor in the period 1915 to 1916. Such salaries not only bear testimony to a growing differentiation in the roles of actor and actor-director (a differentiation, to some extent, qualified by the growing status of certain leading players in this period), but also evidence, as we might anticipate, discrimination in favor of male employees in the company.

[5]In a letter from Dr. Gösta Werner (Stockholm, August 2, 1983), Werner informs me that Magnussen and Eide received a fee of 900 Swedish Kronor for each film they directed, and Tallroth received a fee of 600 Swedish Kronor for his first directorial assignment with Svenska Bio. This fee was then raised to 900 Swedish Kronor for subsequent film work. In addition, both Tallroth and Eide were paid a fee for acting in the films they directed. I would like to thank Dr. Werner for his reading of my initial draft, and for the advice and information he generously gave me.

All those players discussed above, together with other players listed in *Aktiebolaget Nordiska Filmsfabriken,* had strong roots in the theater. The desire to consolidate cultural status for film (an aspect of Svenska Bio's operation which we have already noted, and which will be explored later in the article) is further evidenced in the number of established non-Swedish actors the company employed. Egil Eide and Gunnar Tolnaes were contracted from the National Theater in Kristiania (i.e., Oslo) at intervals during the period 1913 to 1916. Although the remuneration these actors earned is not clear from the ledgers, elsewhere the Danish vamp heroine Lili Bech is reputed to have earned 10,000 Swedish Kronor for six weeks work with Svenska Bio in 1912 (11, p. 85). But this figure is open to dispute, and it seems unlikely that she received such a substantial sum.

In respect of salaries paid to personnel across the three areas of Svenska Bio's operation, the ledgers evidence a well-developed hierarchical structure. Although detailed discussion of the personnel structure of the company lies outside the concerns of this article, when considering the industrial base for production in the Lidingö years, we should not lose sight of the company's staffing policy. Salaries paid to employees working in the studio ranged from 600 Swedish Kronor paid to Anna Carlsson (a cleaning lady) to 6,000 Swedish Kronor paid to Julius Jaenzon per annum as the company's leading cinematographer. Perhaps more typical of the remuneration studio employees received was the salary Hugo Edlund received, as cinematographer, of 3,000 Swedish Kronor per annum, or the remuneration assistants and stage hands (such as Erik Johansson or E. Hellstrand) received of between 1,200 and 1,800 Swedish Kronor per annum. Such incomes, however, should be contrasted with those of personnel employed in the distribution and exhibition sectors. While Lars Björck, distribution manager, received an annual salary of 4,200 Swedish Kronor, clerks employed in distribution or at Head Office earned as little as 900 Swedish Kronor in one instance. In exhibition, where employees were contracted on a weekly or even daily basis, salaries rarely went above 1,000 Swedish Kronor per annum, and regularly employees of the status of errand-boy (working by day at Head Office and by evening at a cinema as a program-seller) earned, in total, less than 900 Swedish Kronor per annum.

Using all available data in respect of salaries paid to company personnel (excluding leading players and actor-directors), the average monthly income in each area of company operation can be computed: in the production studio, monthly incomes averaged 173.23 Swedish Kronor; in the studio workshop, monthly incomes averaged 136.71 Swedish Kronor; in Head Office, monthly incomes averaged 162.08 Swedish Kronor; in distribution, monthly incomes averaged 140.56 Swedish Kronor; and in exhibition, monthly incomes averaged 92.76 Swedish Kronor. It should be noted that the above figure for Head Office does not include the salary Charles Magnusson, the managing director, received. His income, based on annual turnover commission, is not available in the ledgers, although we can be certain that it was a not inconsiderable sum.

We can observe, therefore, that in respect of the company's operation as a whole, the production sector of the company was favored in terms of both remuneration and, when compared with an area such as exhibition, job security. We can, therefore, not only identify that as early as the 1913–1915 period Svenska Bio had instituted a hierarchy in terms of company practice which, given its major organizational characteristics, had all the marks of a developing corporate industry, but we can also speculate in the matter. Given that the purpose of moving the company to Stockholm was to consolidate Svenska Bio's position within the domestic film economy (so initiating the organizational structure of the preceding discussion), we might legitimately expect to observe developments in production policy that respond to this ambition. Our attention, therefore, should be directed towards a discussion of Svenska Bio's production program in the years after 1912.

Production Program: Scripts

A total number of 208 scripts are listed in a ledger devoted to script purchases. Of this total, the ledger records that 63 scripts achieved production. This figure of 63 scripts is known to be inaccurate for there were a number of films produced for which production numbers do not appear in the script ledger (production nos. 12/1914, 14/1914, 15/1914, and 4/1916). Five further films (production nos. 9/1916, 26/1916, 1/1917, 5/1917, and 7/1917) were animated short films made by Victor Bergdahl, and shot from outlines not listed in this ledger. Unlike the ledgers used for the preceding examination of salaries which were difficult to date specifically, the period in which the company used the script ledger can be assigned with greater certainty. The ledger records that Svenska Bio purchased 162 scripts between 1914 and 1918. The remaining undated 46 scripts, the earliest entries in the ledger, are, therefore, presumed to have been purchased at some time before 1914.

The script ledger mandates close inspection because its data are a useful index to the development of production policy in the years 1914 to 1918. Data, on an annual basis, are summarized in Table 1.

Table 1 indicates that the purchase price for scripts was not subject to great fluctuation during the period from 1914 to 1916. But the total expenditure, in the same period, rose dramatically, even though the percentage of scripts that went into production declined. During the 1914–1916 period, the rate of return on capital invested in script purchases considerably declined. This might, of course, have been offset by annual box-office receipts. But at a time when, we may assume, the company was exploring avenues for production, we can conclude that, from data available after 1916, Svenska Bio initiated a considerable change in its purchasing policy. In the following two years (1917 and 1918), the company dramatically cut its total expenditure on script purchases to a level below that of 1914. This cut, allied to a marked increase in the percentage of scripts that went into production, and a significant rise in the unit purchase price per script, testifies to two major changes in the financial management of production. First,

Table 1
Annual Script Expenditure with Percentage Used in Production

Year of Purchase	Total Expenditure Per Annum (Kronor)	Number of Scripts Purchased	Average Purchase Price (Kronor)	% Used in Production[a]
1914	9,700	31	312.90	42
1915[b]	22,410	60	373.50	37
1916	20,800	61	340.98	33
1917	5,750	7	821.43	71
1918	5,200	3	1,733.33	100

[a]This last column—the percentage of scripts that were realized as films—is, in a number of instances, misleading, because the ledger from which the percentages are produced, does not list all the productions known to have been made. However, inaccuracies only occur in respect of the years 1914 and 1916. There are only four films (three made in 1914, one in 1916) that are not reflected in these percentages. The argument presented here, if these productions were taken into account, remains substantially unaltered.

[b]The data for 1915 are marginally inaccurate in respect to the total expenditure, and, hence, the average purchase price for scripts in this year. These calculations do not include an additional $25 paid to Whynne Johnson (June 15, 1915) for *Who will marry Fritz*. As this is the only instance of payment for a script being made in a foreign currency, it was not included in the computations.

the data reflect an increasing concern with the rate of return on finance invested in script purchases. Second, the dramatic unit cost rise in script purchases testifies to a management decision to purchase exclusively "quality" material. The decision to purchase "quality" material would appear, in the first instance, to be a management decision. But it was also defined, as we might anticipate, by the literary market, as a detailed discussion of the type of material purchased between 1914 and 1918 reveals.

A typical price paid for a script in the period before 1914 is exemplified by the film Sjöström directed, *Landshövdingens döttrar,* (produced as production number 1/1915, shot, according to a production ledger, from March 6, 1915, to March 20, 1915, and from April 11, 1915, to April 29, 1915) for which M. Stjernstedt received 300 Swedish Kronor. Some scripts were purchased for as little as 50 Swedish Kronor; others, notably those written by Peter Lykke-Seest, were bought for between 600 Swedish Kronor and 800 Swedish Kronor.[6] These latter prices, however, are exceptional for 1914. A more typical fee, paid in the early part of the script ledger, is the sum Carl Th. Dreyer received of 300 Swedish Kronor, (May 7, 1914) for *Döden forener* (never produced). Nils Krook, who sold a number of scripts (and whose work had been successfully used by Sjöström in *Ingeborg Holm,* 1913), rarely received more than 350 or 400

[6]Lykke-Seest directed a series of films in Norway between 1916 and 1919 for Christiania Film Compagni A/S (see 3, p. 10).

Swedish Kronor (for *Odets Vägar* or *I kamp för egen torfva,* neither of which were produced).

Both Sjöström and Stiller, as actor-directors, successfully adapted their own scenarios. Unfortunately the ledger does not record what either director received. So we are unable, in this early period, to draw some comparison between the fee regular contributors received, and the fee leading directors received. But Fritz Magnussen, who directed a number of films in 1915 and 1916, customarily received 500 Swedish Kronor or 600 Swedish Kronor for scripts he submitted in those years. Gustaf Molander, later to direct in his own right, received 250 Swedish Kronor (September 22, 1915) for *Barnhusbarnet* (never produced); 250 Swedish Kronor (October 26, 1915) for his treatment of Ibsen's poem *Terje Vigen* (directed by Sjöström, 1916); 250 Swedish Kronor (March 30, 1916) for *Millers dokument* (directed by Tallroth, 1916); and 500 Swedish Kronor (July 5, 1916) for *Stella, stjärnornas dotter* (never produced). By 1917 Molander was regularly receiving 800 Swedish Kronor for scripts and/or treatments. Such payments can be contrasted, indicative of the growing concern for literary pedigree, with the sum the Ibsen estate received of 4,000 Swedish Kronor for the rights to Ibsen's play, *Brand* (December 15, 1915, never produced).

Other established literary figures were increasingly used as the source of material in the period after 1915. The work of Selma Lagerlöf, a Nobel Prize winner, became much sought after as her earning power rose from 300 Swedish Kronor (December 31, 1915) for *En Herrgårdssägen* to 2,000 Swedish Kronor for *Tösen från Stormyrtorpet* (April 28, 1917), *Ingmarssönerna* (April 8, 1918), and *Herr Arnes Pengar* (April 8, 1918).[7] All these titles achieved production. Herman Bang, the Danish novelist, received 1,000 Swedish Kronor (June 9, 1916) for the rights to *Mikael* (directed by Stiller, and released as *Vingarne,* 1916). Johan Sigurjonsson, the Icelandic dramatist, received 800 Swedish Kronor (April 19, 1917) for the rights to *Berg-Ejvind och hans hustru* (directed by Sjöström, 1917).

Detailed discussion, therefore, of the script purchase ledger reveals that a new initiative was made in Svenska Bio's production program in 1916. In terms, specifically, of fiscal control, this initiative dates from 1917 (given the abrupt change in purchasing policy that Table 1 announces). But in terms of the type of material that Svenska Bio purchased, we can more precisely date this initiative to the production year of 1916 (which saw the production of *Terje Vigen* and *Vingarne*). We may speculate that in purchasing "quality" literary products (in

---

[7]Dr. Werner informs me that Selma Lagerlöf did not receive 300 Swedish Kronor for *En Herrgårdssägen.* Apparently, at a later date, when Svenska Bio negotiated its agreement with Lagerlöf, the rights to this work were bought for 2,000 Swedish Kronor in keeping with their agreement relating to her other literary properties. He also informs me that the 4,000 Swedish Kronor that was paid to the Ibsen estate for *Brand* included the film rights to *Terje Vigen.*

this case, specifically Scandinavian products), the company could achieve product differentiation on the international market, and also secure a middle-class, culture-oriented, domestic audience. But until we can corroborate such views in respect of domestic and foreign exhibition analysis, they remain, however credible, only a working hypothesis.

Production Program: Production Statistics

Our discussion of the company's production program in respect of scripts led us to conclude that the production years of 1916 and 1917 were central to a reformulation of Svenska Bio's production program. This reformulation was marked by an overall increase in the control of expenditure on scripts allied to a far greater concentration of capital in a greatly reduced number of products the company could put on the market. In other words, in producing fewer films per year, each film the company produced constituted a greater financial risk for the company when compared with its production program before the 1916–1917 initiative.

While the absence of information concerning domestic and foreign audiences for Svenska Bio's films means that we cannot readily discover if the initiative of 1916–1917 was profitable, we can be certain that if the initiative did not prove profitable, production statistics would reflect any subsequent change in production program. If, however, the 1916–1917 initiative proved profitable, its success, we can assume, would be reflected in the trend we can discern from examining the company's production statistics. Fortunately, the documents *Aktiebolaget Nordiska Filmsfabriken* and *Inspelade filmer 1916–1919*[8] make available production data for the crucial period with which we are concerned.

Aktiebolaget Nordiska Filmsfabriken and *Inspelade filmer 1916–1919* make available production data for the period 1914 to 1917. Both documents give a film's production number and year of production, and amongst much other data, the total cost of production and the final meter length of each completed film. From the production year of 1915, the ledgers also indicate the cost of production for each film on a unit meter length costing. From the point of view of financial management, the unit costing per meter length of each film produced would be an important statistic to have available to management in reviewing annual production expenditure. The availability to management of this statistic from the production year of 1915 was a significant development in the financial management of the company's production interests. A further section of the ledger is concerned with sales, and gives an indication of the number of prints that were prepared for domestic and foreign sales. Such data, however, as far as is ascertainable, are not complete.[9] Furthermore, from 1916, contrary to earlier

[8]The ledger *Inspelade filmer 1916–1919*, in point of fact, only gives data for films produced in 1916 and 1917.

[9]Werner (9, p. 327) uses these data to calculate the financial balance (loss/profit) for each

Table 2
Annual Review of Production Expenditure

Year of Production	Number of Films Produced	Total Length in Meters of Completed Films	Total Production Expenditure (Kronor)	Cost per Meter Length of Annual Production (Kronor)
1914	14	12,603	103,171.28	8.19
1915	25	20,569	255,993.58	12.45
1916	26	23,715	439,614.15	18.54
1917	7	8,891	353,598.24	39.77

company practice, later ledgers quantify and date (in some cases on almost a daily basis) the amount of film shot while a film was in production. Such data reflect not only a desire on the part of management to supervise expenditure during a film's production, but were, presumably, instituted as a means of monitoring expenditure at a time when film production was becoming increasingly more ambitious and, therefore, a high risk venture. Also dating from 1916, Svenska Bio instituted an annual survey of production expenditure so that, at the end of each production year, management had a reliable statistic reflecting the cost of one year's output compared with another.

While the company's annual survey was not conducted retrospectively, we can compute, in the manner of company ledgers from 1916 on, a table of annual expenditure. Table 2 presents an annual review of production expenditure for the period 1914 to 1917. Table 2 demonstrates development in the fiscal control of production complementary to that revealed in the script purchases ledger. We can observe that between 1914 and 1916 Svenska Bio increased its total expenditure on production more than fourfold, while almost doubling the number of products it could put on the market. The data that apply to the production year of 1917, however, mark a significant development. Far fewer films were produced, at a considerable saving in the total expenditure on production, with greater (and if the unit costing per meter length figure is a sufficient indicator, more conspicuous) production investment per film.[10]

These production figures, alongside the earlier observations concerning the development in script purchases, represent a considerable change in production

Stiller film during 1912–1916. His calculations are misleading since they do not take into account domestic box-office returns on films distributed in Sweden. As these data are only concerned with the *sale* of prints at home and abroad, his calculations do not fully represent the real profit or loss on each Stiller film. Until, therefore, adequate box-office returns are available for domestic exhibition, these data are insufficient to determine the financial balance of production.

[10]I am fully aware that the unit cost per meter length statistic is a poor index to an increase in production values. But without a close inspection of extant films, or an itemized account of additional expenses incurred in production, we can only speculate at present.

policy. The two developments would appear to indicate that Svenska Bio was able to concentrate its capital outlay (so satisfying purely financial interests) while acquiring a distinct production program that could give the company an edge on the international market. Moreover, these two mutually sympathetic goals could be realized at the same time as the company made an overall saving in production expenditure. We can surmise that this venture proved profitable since this form of production program was maintained until the mid-twenties, by which period Sjöström and Stiller had been attracted to Hollywood. Werner (9, p. 360), however, working from available data on the sale of prints, forms a rather different conclusion:

> Increased investment in production proved, therefore, to be a poor guarantee for a sufficiently large increase in the sale of prints at higher prices than before.

But, as I have indicated earlier (see footnote 9), Werner uses data only in respect of the sale of prints to domestic and foreign markets. His observation (which does not extend beyond 1916 and which concerns the films that only Stiller directed), furthermore, does not take into account domestic box office returns, which are relevant to considering the overall profitability of Svenska Bio's operation. Until, therefore, domestic exhibition data are consulted (if available), my conclusions, while strongly contesting that of Werner, must remain qualified.

What is clear from the preceding analysis is that the production year of 1917 was important in determining a new phase of production for Svenska Bio. We might more accurately date this phase (if we keep in mind the earlier observations concerning script purchases) to the production year of 1916, when Sjöström directed *Terje Vigen* (an Ibsen adaptation costing an unprecedented 59,734.65 Swedish Kronor), and Stiller directed the Herman Bang adaptation, *Vingarne*. But *Terje Vigen* would seem to have set the pattern for expenditure in 1917: *Berg-Ejvind och hans hustru,* 99,543.58 Swedish Kronor; *Tösen från Stormyrtorpet,* 87,771.76 Swedish Kronor; *Alexander den Store,* 83,068.89 Swedish Kronor; *Thomas Graals bästa film,* 76,799.01 Swedish Kronor. With the exception of Victor Bergdahl's animated short films, this pattern of production was maintained throughout the remaining years at Lidingö, and well into the 1920s.

More importantly, the preceding analysis begins to account for the international success of Svenska Bio's production in a different context to that of earlier histories of Swedish film (see 1, 2, 6). In 1917 Svenska Bio began to produce films which acquired (or have since acquired, through the writings of world histories of cinema) international status. In the main, international success has been attributed to a mixture of personal endeavor and vision on the part of a few individuals (Magnusson, Sjöström, Stiller). Although this article does not seek to evaluate their impressive contribution to the development of Swedish film, it places their endeavors, and the success of Svenska Bio, in a more materialist context. This context, moreover, requires that we appraise the nature of corporate consolidation in the history of film. Implicit in some writing on the consolidation of corporate film industries, is a belief that to be successful in the international and/or domestic market required that a company spend ever greater amounts on bigger and better productions.[11] While it would be interesting to enquire into other national industries to determine if such a policy was a prerequisite for domestic and/or international success, the present case study on Svenska Bio appears to indicate otherwise.

CONCLUSION

This article has demonstrated, using company ledgers, a policy for production whereby Svenska Bio maximized its return on capital invested in production. Argued here is that such concerns not only directly served financial interests but, in monitoring expenditure, actively promoted one type of production program in favor of another. Although further investigation into domestic box office returns and foreign distribution might provide a broader picture of the company's operation, the preceding analysis establishes the production year of 1917 as crucial to the success of its production interests. Further investigation into other aspects of company interest would likely determine more clearly the company's corporate success.

More broadly, in terms of a materialist analysis, the present case study can be characterized as a series of synchronic examinations. It can be likened to a series of production cross-sections, taken at annual intervals, wherein we can see production "frozen", as it were, at regular intervals. However, without company correspondence and other types of documentation which might help articulate the day-to-day *process* of the company (and highlight its contradictions), and without comprehensive data concerning foreign sales and domestic box office returns, this study is qualified in its ambition. We certainly cannot begin to consider broader issues such as the advantage a virtual monopoly status between 1914 and 1918 conferred on Svenska Bio in the Lidingö years.

Still, we have begun to construct a rationale for the films that came out of the company in these years. We have been able to qualify a number of previous approaches to early Swedish film history, and we can begin to understand the nature of Svenska Bio's international success without collapsing that understand-

[11]See Mitchell (7). Even though, quite rightly, Mitchell broadens the terms of the argument in respect of corporate consolidation, a more detailed examination of cost accounting, even in the American experience, might confirm my observation. We should not lose sight of the fact that the business of film production is to yield profit. If this means that prestigious productions can be made which also make an overall saving on production expenditure (particularly at a time when companies were keen to invest capital in the distribution and exhibition sectors), this would be doubly attractive to management and shareholders.

ing onto the figure of a few prominent individuals. We have, more generally, added to the literature on the nature of corporate consolidation in film history. We must now consider more closely the relationship between increasingly ambitious production programs and the nature of the funding of such output. We must consider, for example, if the experience of Svenska Bio was merely a localized phenomenon, or was typical of a more widespread development in the consolidation of corporate film industries. Only further work can shed light on these and other questions.

REFERENCES

1. Béranger, Jean. *La Grande Aventure du Cinéma Suédois*. Paris: Le Terrain Vague, 1960.
2. Cowie, Peter. *Sweden 2*. London: A. Zwemmer, 1970.
3. Holst, Jan Erik. *Norsk Filmografi 1908–1973*. Oslo, Norway: Norsk Filminstitutt, 1974.
4. Idestam-Almquist, Bengt. *Svensk Film före Gösta Berling*. Stockholm, Sweden: Pan/Norstedts, 1974.
5. Idestam-Almquist, Bengt. *När Filmen kom till Sverige*. Stockholm, Sweden: Norstedts, 1959.
6. Idestam-Almquist, Bengt. *Classics of the Swedish Cinema*. Stockholm, Sweden: The Swedish Institute/AB Svensk Filmindustri, 1952.
7. Mitchell, George. "The Consolidation of the American Film Industry 1915–1920." *Cine-Tracts* 6 (7 and 8), Spring, Summer, and Fall 1979, pp. 27–36, 63–70.
8. Sadoul, Georges. *Histoire Générale du Cinéma,* Vol. 5. Paris: Denoël, 1975.
9. Werner, Gösta. *Mauritz Stiller och hans Filmer 1912–1916*. Stockholm, Sweden: Norstedts, 1969.
10. Winquist, Sven G. *Svenska Stumfilmer 1896–1931 och deras Regissörer*. Stockholm, Sweden: Proprius, 1967.
11. Winquist, Sven G. and Torsten Jungstedt. *Svenskt Filmskådespelarlexikon*. Stockholm, Sweden: Forum, 1973.

11

Suppressing Controversial Films: From *Objective Burma* to *Monty Python's Life of Brian*

Ian Jarvie

> Censorship . . . can result from governmental decrees, from the pressure of powerful organizations (such as the Catholic Church) and from private arrangements (such as the MPAA Code). Whatever the source, censorship is an attempt to order men's affairs, to control their behavior—in this case, to regulate what they can see at the movies. Ayer *et al.* (1, p. 805)

This chapter offers case studies of non-governmental attempts to suppress two films; one campaign successful, the other unsuccessful. Analysis of the cases reveals that films still have the power to evoke private attempts at impeding their free circulation; this despite radical changes in their position in society.

METHODOLOGICAL AND THEORETICAL

In earlier work (16, chapters II and VIII; 17, chapter III; 19) I have shown that the position of the movies within Anglo-American social structure has completely changed in the last 30 years. Movies have shifted from being a centrally important mass medium to one which is a minority medium of marginal social importance. Yet culturally, and in the well-known dislocation between structure and culture (2), they retain for some groups an importance out of proportion to their structural position. This is illuminated by the fates of two movies—"controversial" in quite different ways—that were subject to attempts at "private ordering."

Lawyers distinguish between private ordering and public ordering in the matter of censorship (1). Public ordering includes legislation and administration by statutory bodies. Private ordering includes all kinds of regulation and certification carried out by non-governmentally owned and controlled bodies. Most of the literature on film censorship narrows and simplifies the topic by concentrating on the better-documented attempts at public ordering (4, 14, 27). Where private ordering is institutionalized, as it is in the United States and the United Kingdom, through the Motion Picture Association of America (MPAA) classification and the British Board of Film Censors' (BBFC) certificates, it is easy to study. However, attempts to impose private ordering by companies and lobbies, by activists and zealots, by consumer boycotts, by lenders and licensers, by foreign governments, diplomats and politicians is a much broader area, and one which is difficult to document. Still, such private ordering is important to study since it gives a far more detailed sense of the interface between films and the social groups that feel affected by them.

It is difficult to know where to begin. One approach is to study the careers of individual films as they encounter such pressures. For example domestic and foreign Muslim pressures on *Mohammed, Messenger of God* and *Death of a Princess* could be traced to discover what social functions were revealed by the pressure lines, what social results would flow from success or failure of the campaign. A full study of the career of the first widely popular pornographic feature, *Deep Throat,* would need to look at the many private ordering attempts it evoked in stimulating or extending its public ordering battles through the courts and with different levels of government. The finding might then link up with Zurcher and Kirkpatrick's study which followed not individual films but the emergence of antipornography crusades in two cities (32).

Another choice governing research is the nature of the ostensible "issue" which is to be ordered. Although efforts at censorship concerning sexual material are typically the most sensational, they are also perhaps the least sociologically interesting or important. Religion, politics, and other matters are much closer to "thought-control." The issues involved in the two films discussed here are international relations and religion.

I shall chronicle and discuss private attempts to suppress two Warner Brothers films released 34 years apart: *Objective Burma* (1945) and *Monty Python's Life of Brian* (1979). *Objective Burma,* an American picture, was subject to an intensely critical press campaign in Britain which led Warners to suspend its general release until 1952; *Monty Python's Life of Brian,* a British film, was subject to intense agitation by religious groups both in the USA and the UK, an agitation mostly not endorsed by the press, and Warners, while being apologetic in identical terms about no offense being intended, did little more than cry all the way to the bank.

Movies were once carefully regulated, especially during the war, by both public and private institutions; they were scrutinized on a variety of grounds. But in deciding on the degree of prior restraint an important estimate concerned the passions a film might unleash. In the case of *Objective Burma* both its American makers and their British distribution subsidiary seem to have underestimated its power to generate adverse reaction. Although Warner Brothers was a powerful company, they were sensitive enough about their image as responsible corporate citizens not meaning to offend to respond to the adverse reaction by withdrawing the film. The situation with *Monty Python's Life of Brian* was rather different. From the script stage there was nervousness about the subject; as a result it almost failed to get financing. Yet the film's makers, the Monty Python group, refused to cut it and Warner Brothers undertook to distribute it under no illusions about its capacity to generate adverse reaction. So, far from the company fearing damage to its image, they may well have calculated that ours are times when reactions of offense create public curiosity and probably box office.

These two films also illuminate new aspects of the problem of the effect films have on society. Hitherto, research in this area has concentrated on attempts to measure the effects, if any, films have on those who see them (9, 23), and on conjecturing the sorts of mechanisms responsible for the effects and so to further stimulate the search for such results. But society is not to be identified with its members. Certainly people are part of society; but society is not merely the sum of the people in it. Hence the effects of film on society are not exhausted by looking at how films affect people.

In what other dimensions, then, must research be pursued to study the impact of film on society? One is economic: the impact of the film industry as part of the economy in general; as one part of the economy of show business; as one part of the economies of Los Angeles and New York; and the impact of show business and the two coastal cities on the economy in general (e.g., as affecting patterns of internal migration). Another kind of impact on society comes from the fact that, for mass communication, people group themselves together in audiences to see films.[1] The make-up of these collective representations (7) as well as their content has yet to be seriously examined.[2] Further, there is the issue of film content: how content relates to society, whether movies are a mirror up to society, a window overlooking it, a hypodermic stuck into society's buttock, or what not (15, 16, 17).

My cases do not illuminate the economic, but they do reveal subtleties in the matter of content that complicate the concept of audience. It is easy to overdetermine audience and content in our specifications and hence to so narrow our investigation that it is crippled. A film's content is not a "given." For one thing, selective perception is at work and people see what is not there, as well as miss seeing what is. Less attended to is the fact that since films are so "visible" people receive information about their content and hence may decide what they

---

[1]Technically speaking a film audience is a quasi-group; that is, a body of persons physically present to one another and united by one purpose only, lacking other ties, structures, or traditions through time. Television audiences, by contrast, being predominantly familial, are primary groups proper, and quasi-groups only in bars, public lounges, etc.

[2]The military conducted some studies during the war (8, 13) and the Payne Fund Studies included research on children. But what one might call anthropological studies of the audience—microscale studies in the mode of Goffman or ethnomethodology or conversational analysis to flesh out the broad picture of Katz and Lazarsfeld (22) are still lacking.

think about them without having seen them. Not all such prior information is misinformation; not all selective perception is misperception. There are many people who dislike John Wayne's film *The Green Berets* because it was in favor of the Vietnam war; they know this even though they haven't seen the film; indeed, it was because they knew this that they did not go to see the film.[3] Similarly, protests against both *Objective Burma* and *Life of Brian* were entered by people who freely admitted they had not seen the film, did not feel obliged to do so, and might even refuse as a matter of principle.[4]

This sounds unreasonable but is not entirely so, as my examples show. You can know that *The Green Berets* took a certain stance on the Vietnam war, that *Objective Burma* exaggerated the American role in Burma and minimized the British role, that *Monty Python's Life of Brian* makes fun of the Cecil B. DeMille version of the life of Christ, all without actually having seen the film. Hence, if any of these ideas offends you, to protest, to refuse to contribute to them by buying a ticket, or to upset yourself further by actually seeing them, is not entirely unreasonable. This shows something sociologically important. The content of a film and its potential as a causal factor in society extends well beyond what its makers intended and works through many more people than ever constituted the film's paying audience. ''Content'' in the sense of social cause does not inhere in the film but is a social construct only disclosed by research.

Objective Burma illustrates how films can have effects because they touch on and hence stir up controversy on some socially sensitive topic. Whether the film itself is innocuous or offensive, the controversy takes on a life of its own because it involves wider social issues than movies, and the pressure generated can raise public consciousness, form images, and precipitate further events. Thus when controversy envelops a film much more than what is on the screen is involved and must be resolved.

The *Objective Burma* case illuminates a very wide range of issues from the position of the mass medium of movies in the English-speaking world in 1945 to the tensions in the Anglo-American alliance. It will be argued that *Objective Burma* manifested certain kinds of unwitting thoughtlessness and braggadocio in American popular culture that render American movies an inherently controversial export.

Monty Python's Life of Brian reveals just how far the process of dismantling and delegitimating the movies as a mass medium has gone in both countries, and how much less power the private ordering forces of organized religion

---

[3]See my discussion of the formation of a film's ''image'' (16, Chapter XIV).

[4]It is clear from his comments that Lord Denman, speaking in the House of Lords (*Hausard,* Vol. CXXXVII, 1945–1946, Columns 502–503), had not seen the film. The story in the *Los Angeles Times,* (August 31, 1979), Part IV, pp. 1, 15) reporting the visit of a priest and a rabbi to *Monty Python's Life of Brian* and describing their consternation about it, fails to mention that they had already joined the interfaith protests earlier in the week.

are able to wield over movies today. Whereas once, Catholic influence permeated the production code and its administration, whereas the production files on *Objective Burma* contain 25 letters from Joseph Breen, even quibbling over whether the word 'jerk' could be used, such surveillance totally overlooked what was to be the main issue of controversy around the film. For its part *Life of Brian* had frontal nudity, profanity, salaciousness, swearing, and blasphemy and was merely classified "R."

GREAT BRITAIN, 1945: THE *OBJECTIVE BURMA* CONTROVERSY

Objective Burma was suppressed in Great Britain for seven years. Warner Brothers suspended its release after seven days of showcasing in London and did not re-release it until 1952. The successful campaign against this film cannot be explained solely by its content, since its opponents described it as the last straw. The other straws are its contexts. At the very least other American war films are implicated. My research has led to still wider contexts: into the central role of movies in the popular culture and hence in wartime propaganda efforts (19, 18); relations between the allies; the centralized character of the British press; popular British sentiments towards America; and perhaps even British loss of a sense of world preeminence (18). To unpack and analyze these factors I must begin with the film.

Warner Brothers production number 629, *Objective Burma,* began as a fairly typical Hollywood war film of 1944.[5] It dramatized combat by concentrating on a small group of paratroopers. The group, as is usual in these films, was something of a cross-section of America: there is Captain Nelson, a disciplinarian, WASP-ish leader—played by Errol Flynn—whose toughness is later vindicated; the tough but tender war correspondent Williams (Henry Hull); a wiseacre sergeant; a talkative type; a Jewish type; a farmer type; an Italian type; a kid; a Ghurka; a Chinese; etc.[6] These men are dropped behind Japanese lines in Burma, to destroy a radar base in preparation for the invasion. The plan to extract them goes wrong, and they have to fight their way out, suffering heavy losses. The film is very long, well over two hours,[7] much of it involving depiction of jungle warfare.

---

[5]My information comes from the materials on this movie made available in the Special Collections room at the University of Southern California, at the Wisconsin Center for Film and Theater Research, Madison, and in the National Archives of the United States. There are snippets of information about it in Ministry of Information and Foreign Office files in Britain's Public Record Office.

[6]Utilizing a group that is a cross-section of American society can degenerate into a formula, as it did in countless war films; but it can also function as a convention to be exploited in the service of art, cf. *A Walk in the Sun* (1945).

[7]*Time* (February 25, 1945) gives the length as 144 minutes; *Monthly Film Bulletin* as 129 minutes.

The Warner Brothers production files on the film show no inkling whatsoever of the crucial issue that was to engulf the film in controversy. To put it simply: In actuality there was only a very small American ground presence in Burma; the overwhelming majority of troops there came from Britain, its dominions and colonies. The fighting was ghastly and costly. Why was Hollywood dramatizing that campaign through the exploits of a group of Americans? Malice was unlikely. Warner Brothers was the liberal studio in Hollywood, Democratic in politics, and noted for its dramatizations of social problems.[8] Jerry Wald, the film's producer, and the three main writers, Ranald MacDougall, Lester Cole, and Alvah Bessie, all had impeccable liberal credentials.[9] Nevertheless, these American liberals ended up making a film deeply offensive to the British ally. The film received a classic editorial denunciation in the London *Times;* it added fuel to the fire of British anti-Americanism; it made Errol Flynn and his heroic posturing a standing joke in England for many years; and it was such an embarrassment to Warner Brothers that they withheld it from general release in Britain for seven years.

Perhaps not surprisingly, the film's career in the U.S. market was uneventful. The previews were a success and the film was released in January 1945. Reviews in the *New York Times* (January 27, 1945), the *New York Herald Tribune* (January 27, 1945), and *Time* magazine (February 25, 1945) were all favorable, singling out the vigor of the direction by Raoul Walsh, and the authenticity of the jungle scenes photographed by James Wong Howe.[10] The film played in the United States through February and March, was a modest success, and was forgotten.[11]

The storm of controversy began on May 30, 1945, when Reuters carried a story from Advanced Headquarters, Burma, to the effect that the film had been described as a "travesty of the truth" by an American glider officer serving in Burma. Writing in the services' newspaper *Seac,* Lt. Colonel William H. Taylor, Jr., of the U.S.A. A.F. said in part:

> It is a disturbing thought that this meretricious hodge-podge, which implies that Burma was invaded and liberated by a force of American parachutists, American glider-borne troops, two Gurkha guides and a Chinese officer, will be seen by thousands of men of the 14th Army, who know better.

---

[8]Jerry Wald in a memo dated January 26, 1945, to Jack L. Warner says, "Warners have [*sic*] done more to encourage free expression of new ideas on the screen than any other studio." In his January 27, 1945, reply Warner comments, "we certainly can do a lot with the tools we use to help make this world a better one."

[9]Lester Cole and Alvah Bessie were among the "Hollywood Ten" jailed for contempt of Congress when they failed to cooperate with the Committee on Un-American Activities of the House of Representatives (3, 5, 6, 12, 20, 21, 26, 29).

[10]Raoul Walsh (30, p. 318) mistakenly attributes the photography to Sid Hickox.

[11]According to the *News Chronicle,* September 26, 1945.

> The thought that it has already been seen by millions of American civilians, whose impression of the Burma campaign must consequently be irreparably and viciously garbled, is enraging.
>
> The thought that it may be seen by the mothers, fathers, friends and relatives of the many Allied troops, British, West African and Burmese, who have lost their lives in the slow and painful struggle to clear Burma of the Japanese invader, is sickening.

Taylor suggests that the film would jeopardize inter-Allied relationships. Taylor's remarks, as reported by Reuters, were immediately picked up by British newspapers. The respected film critic of the *Daily Telegraph,* Campbell Dixon, had already written about what he called the "long series of affronts to truth and the Empire's fighting men" perpetrated by American war films (October 1, 1945). It had even become the practice, he suggested, for Hollywood to make two versions of its films, one for Britain, "shorn of criticism and embellished with references to British achievements, the other . . . for America and the rest of the world, in which British achievements are wholly or almost wholly ignored." The pot of controversy, then, was already boiling in May, four months before *Objective Burma*'s British release.

There are other factors intrinsic to the film. It purports to treat real events; makes use of genuine combat footage; focuses on American personnel (ostensibly for dramatic purposes); and mentions real persons like Mountbatten and Stilwell. As the war dragged on, the British became increasingly touchy about Yankee upstaging: i.e., they suspected the Americans were trying to grab the credit for winning the war. Summing up a strong feeling at the time, Dixon wrote:

> The distortion and denigration of the British Empire's efforts, in all theatres of war, is arousing natural resentment. There is a feeling that if Washington will not take action it is time London did. No one would welcome it more than serving Americans who know the facts. (May 31, 1945)

Warner's director of publicity in London said: "The picture is based on one incident in the Burma campaign. . . . It is not intended to present a complete picture of the Burma war." Yet defensive prefatory titles had been tacked onto the film very late in postproduction which stressed that the incident depicted was typical of many Allied efforts.

When the film opened, the London critics damned it to a man. They found its appropriation, even by suggestion, of a British dominated theater of war offensive. They sneered at the use of Errol Flynn. They found the simulated jungle resembled pleasant woodland glades, and that the atrocious fighting conditions were represented by the odd slap at an invisible fly. One or two found the action scenes effective. But interest centered around the felt slight to British efforts. So great was the hoo-hah that memory has exaggerated it. In his memoirs, Errol Flynn says that the Lord Chamberlain (the British theater censor) yanked the film after the first showing (10, pp. 252–253). Raoul Walsh in his memoirs suggests the film was banned by "England" after the first showing (39, p. 318). In fact, no British public ordering of any kind was attempted. Reminding us that he was himself an Australian whose education was completed in Britain, Flynn wrote:

> Actually *Objective Burma* ended with a shot showing a horde of American planes flying triumphantly over Burma. That might have been good for American morale at the time, but it sure made the English feel bad. (10, p. 253)

The critic of the *Daily Mirror,* the tabloid with the largest circulation, suggested that Warners withdraw the film. Stories surfaced that the head of The Associated British cinema chain was reconsidering whether to go ahead with the release. Critics of other newspapers reported letters arriving from soldiers and ex-soldiers of the China, Burma, and India theater protesting the film.[12] Some in the industry pointed to Warner Brothers' record as a reason for forgiving them this film.[13]

The trade press hinted that Associated British had decided not to risk a general release, and the easiest way to break the contract was for Warners to withdraw the film, which is what happened. Max Milder, Warner's managing director in London, issued a two-page press release which in one sentence noted the withdrawal from release of the film and used the remaining space to defend the company, the film, entertainment, the purity of intention and the fact that *Objective Burma* has "played to bigger audiences than any previous Errol Flynn picture. Probably forty percent of our patrons have been British soldiers—the largest troop percentage in the theater's history. Not one word of criticism or protest has been expressed by them. They have enjoyed the film as dramatic entertainment and have disregarded any suggestion of adverse propaganda."[14] Despite this uncompromising defense, Milder announced that *Objective Burma*'s release was to be suspended. Thirty-four years later Warners would defend *Life of Brian* equally spiritedly, but take no action on its release at all except where compelled by public ordering efforts at the local level (11).

As a postscript to the incident, the film was finally released in Britain in 1952 while Errol Flynn was over there shooting *The Master of Ballantrae.* Seven years after the furor, London's critics, many of them the same ones as before, could no longer quite see what all their fuss was about back in 1945. Although

---

[12]The *Daily Mirror* story is on September 21, 1945. On objections see *Daily Graphic* September 26, 1945; *News Chronicle* September 22, 1945 (and September 19, 1945); *Daily Telegraph* October 1, 1945. To my surprise, there were no letters about the film to *The Times.*

[13]Letter from Sidney Bernstein to *News Chronicle* October 1, 1945; *Daily Sketch* September 21, 1945.

[14]The text of this two-page press release is in the file on the film in the British Film Institute Library.

the film suggested a large American presence in Burma, by 1952 it could be seen as part of *genre* film-making: the all-male action film, derivative of the western, but often set in a theater of war. With the passage of time and removal of the real war context, they could also see that the genre conventions of the American war film were artificial and formulaic, either of the molding-the-raw GIs into-a-fighting unit formula, or the carrying-out-of a dangerous mission formula. Seen this way these films' intrinsic connection with Hollywood and its conventions was manifestly stronger than their extrinsic connection to any real war in the real world.

Objective Burma also shows just how readily American film-makers virtually cooperated with anti-American sentiment. Not just Hollywood, but the most liberal and socially conscious studio in Hollywood, spent thousands on research, re-takes, elaborate location work, weapons accuracy, and such to make a film certain to enrage influential and ordinary people alike in the closest allied nation. The warnings they received were either not dire enough, or were overridden, as we shall see. Anti-Americanism feeds where it is offered nourishment. America exported Coca Cola, chewing gum, war films like *Objective Burma* and it was, however unfairly, judged by such cultural objects. In those far-off days American movies were the foreigner's principal source of information about America (and who will say it is different now?). There can be little doubt that such was American self-confidence, such was the obliviousness to other people's national pride, that as Taylor predicted, such films helped sour Britain's attitude towards America.[15]

News of the controversy crossed the Atlantic. In the *New York Times* Sunday magazine there was an exchange between British commentator Dudley Carew and Bosley Crowther on the alleged artificiality, bad taste and self-congratulation of American war films.[16] *Variety* speculated that the clamor about American films might be an orchestrated campaign to give the British movie mogul J. Arthur Rank more leverage in his efforts to sell British films in the USA (October 30, 1945). But apart from Anglo-American relations in general, it was also pointed out in a magisterial editorial in London's *Times* (September 25, 1945) and by Campbell Dixon (August 27, 1945) that *Objective Burma* was disinforming. A Gallup poll revealed that many Americans were under the impression that their country fought alone in the S.W. Pacific, Burma, Tunisia, and Italy, making some observers wonder whether American films might be the sole source of all the contemporary history a great many Americans ever learn.[17]

[15]Lord Denman (n. 4 above) mentioned that *Objective Burma* was by no means the only film that offended in this way, reiterating the theme of Campbell Dixon. See also *Daily Mirror* (October 6, 1945) on *House on 92nd Street*. British ambivalence was nicely hinted at in *Yanks* (1979).

[16]*New York Times Magazine*, September 23, 1945. See the article the following week by Thomas M. Pryor, September 30, 1945, Section 2, p. 1.

[17]Not only Americans are so afflicted. In *Télérama* (December 15, 1963), there is a two page article on *Objective Burma* which opens: "Pendant la dernière guerre les troupes américaines ont été chassées de Birmanie par les Japonais. Le temps de la revanche est venu. L'invasion de la Birmanie se prépare."

Why should British press reaction have been so virulent, and why did Warner succumb? My argument is this. *Objective Burma,* like any film, is nested in a series of concentric contexts including: other films of its genre; other films of its period; other films of its country; other mass media products; the culture of the USA; and the cultural context shared by the USA with the UK. The single film can be treated as symptomatic of tensions between the two countries in each and every one of these contexts. It was one of a series of American war films that offended the British; it was a product of a mass culture, aspects of which offended the British; it was American. Films could focus such sentiments in 1945 because, although intellectuals disdained them, they were in fact the most visible and influential mass medium, securely placed at the center of the society (19, 28).

Appreciation of the above view is aided by noting the amount of effort that the Federal government invested in film matters during World War II. Both the War Department (WD) through its Bureau of Public Relations (WDBPR) and Signal Corps and the Office of War Information expended substantial resources in making films for the public and the troops about aspects of the war. Shortage of film stock and construction materials gave the government leverage to control the film industry, and war-related topics requiring military cooperation had to have War Department script and final approval. Hence there is a substantial file on *Objective Burma* in the National Archives. What we find there is painful. First the military tried to teach Hollywood about how the Army is run, and what would and would not transpire on such a mission. (An early script, for instance, had Nelson conducting a vote among his men about whether to kill POWs!) Further, there were simple factual points such as that there were no paratroops in Burma. Finally, there was the matter that Burma was a British ''show'' and the film used a unit of American troops. Minor WDBPR objections such as whether the film could depict Stilwell were resolved by using an unnamed look-alike.

Things came to a head when the Army finally got a look at the film. On March 31 an internal WDBPR memo had specified:

> This script is full of material which could be dangerous if improperly handled in production. Therefore, this office cannot approve it without assurance that an expert technical director be secured. . . . The touchiness of the subject makes it important that any revisions of the script be submitted for approval.

When the film was viewed we read:

> 6. In short, these Burmese activities have involved . . . Chinese . . . Indian . . . American . . . airborne . . . ground forces; Merrill's Marauders were Americans, Wingate's soldiers were English and Indian. These facts must be resolved in relation to the pictured presentation of the war being won by paratroopers—none of whom actually jumped in Burma. I recognize the fact that this is alleged to be a fictitious story, but its production is so authentic,

so vivid, and so realistic that a major part of the public is going to accept it as a record of events, especially in view of the announced cooperation of the Air Forces, the paratroopers and the War Department. Therefore, if we can bring its level of historical information up to its present level of authentic background, we will be serving the war effort well.

7. The epilogue infers that this picture is a record. This word should be abolished.

Hurriedly, the producer, director, writer and editor met with a WD representative and by January 11 Wald had devised the opening and closing narration and titles to try to give an allied context, getting WD final approval February 7.[18]

Materials are missing from both the Warner's and the National Archives files, materials that may be lost or may turn up and that would help explain how such strenuous objections were overridden. WDBPR ask that Under Secretary Patterson at State see the film, but there is no record of whether this happened or what his reaction was. The letter of approval interposes no objection to the film being shown at home or abroad. Whether doubts were genuinely resolved or whether the WD felt it had done all it could and no further delay of a costly film was justified, is unknown. But here we have attempts at public ordering failing in their purpose and private ordering attempts succeeding.

Meanwhile, throughout the war another context was developing: the making of official films about the war and its campaigns. Most ambitious and most fraught with difficulty of all these were attempts by allied teams to make movies about their joint efforts. Among the most acrimonious of all theaters was China–Burma–India where the contrasting flamboyances of Stilwell and Mountbatten had run into each other. Beginning with the formation of South East Asia Command in 1943, Mountbatten had requisitioned men and cameras for a filmed record of the campaign. But there was a severe lack of harmony between the allies in the historical interpretation of the war in that theater. To the Americans it was a campaign to relieve the pressure on China; to the British it was to reclaim lost parts of its Far Eastern Empire. Over this obstacle the joint film project was eventually abandoned, the footage pooled, and each side went on to make its own film *Burma Victory* (UK) and *The Stilwell Road* (USA).

A final context: whereas *Objective Burma* was shown in the USA in February and March 1945, it opened in London in September, when the war had been over for several weeks. A major public preoccupation at that time was one of accounting: counting the cost, taking the credit and laying the blame. In a Britain bombed, poor and exhausted there was more affect to this than detachment. Any credit-grabbing by America or suggestion that the British had not pulled their weight was nigh-intolerable. In its own curious way I think it was Warner's sensitivity to this that may have led to their shelving the film.

---

[18]Letter in the Records of the War Department Bureau of Public Relations RG 165, Objective Burma, National Archives.

USA AND UK, 1979: *MONTY PYTHON'S LIFE OF BRIAN*

The nested contexts surrounding *Monty Python's Life of Brian* are wholly different. That it was a British film seems to have concerned no one in either country. Its first context was as another product of the Monty Python comedy team, whose history includes many episodes of controversy and offense, some of which they consciously cultivated. Its second context was the tradition of religious satire, always weak in the Protestant countries. Part of this context was the overall decline of organized religion in general, but localized growth in new sects distinct from the established orthodoxies, and a secularizing trend in society. Another context is the dismantling of the systems of public ordering for films in the decades since World War II.

On both sides of the Atlantic, film censorship was mostly handled by forms of private ordering; the MPAA and the BBFC classify films, classification can be withheld (sometimes mis-described as a "ban") or classification negotiated (sometimes misdescribed as "cutting"). In both countries public regulation of showing is not beholden to these private initiatives. Local government licensing authorities and, in the US, state Laws and Censor Boards, and federal laws regulating interstate traffic, still apply. In the UK the 370-odd local authorities have the last word. In the USA *Brian* was suppressed, however briefly, in 13 states while in the UK it encountered difficulty by being banned or receiving an "X" certificate in more than 25 localities (11, pp. 81–83, 90).

Local licensing authorities were usually the problem in the UK, where there was no "voluntary" withdrawal by the exhibitor. In both countries prosecutions were rare because it was thought that juries would be reluctant to convict, and appellate courts would be highly sensitive to freedom of choice. The British Board of Film Censors had eased its classifications and rarely suggested cutting or banning (31). In the USA, *The Miracle* case had, in 1953, decisively decided against protecting religious sensibilities, giving films the status, and hence the protection, of "speech." Eccentric prosecutions such as of the lead actors in *Deep Throat* and *The Devil in Miss Jones* in Memphis Federal Court on charges of conspiracy to engage in interstate traffic in obscene materials seemed doomed to fail on their way through the appellate procedure (24). The MPAA Production Code Administration had ostensibly been altered from a prior censorship organization to a ratings administration.

Opening in mid-August of 1979 in the USA, *Life of Brian* got reviews that compared it with previous Python movies, mentioned the thick British accents, and warned the sensitive that it was in bad taste and liable to offend them. *Variety* (August 22) had already reported on the pre-release controversy surrounding the film in Britain and that it was being referred to the President of the British Board of Film Censors and to the Director of Public Prosecutions (roughly equivalent to the Attorney-General) to see whether its blasphemy was actionable. In the end the British classified it "AA," which admits anyone over 14.

What transpired in the US can only be called a wave of interfaith protests from Catholics, Protestants, and Jews. No doubt Christians were offended by such scenes as a squabble breaking out among listeners to the Sermon on the Mount because they can't hear what's being said, or the idea that the Biblical story might be a series of idiotic coincidences. Jews could take offense at the scene of stoning, arranged because someone had spoken the name of God, but which degenerates into a quarrel about what stones to use and who goes first.

The Conference Office for Film and Broadcasting of the Roman Catholic Church sent a formal complaint to the Motion Picture Association of America about the film having been given a rating. Jack Valenti, while acknowledging the tastelessness and the offense to religious sensibilities, had to remind the Rev. Sullivan, director of the Office, that the function of the rating system is to provide guidance to parents of a film's suitability for their children's viewing, not to place value or take a moral position (*Variety,* August 24, 1979).

True to form, Warner Brothers issued a statement on August 27 noting in part that Warners regretted that the film gives offense but "It was never our intention to offend anyone's beliefs." They comforted themselves that what they call a whimsical, friendly spoof had received critical acclaim—and lines at the box office. In its inimitable style *Variety* reported that the film racked up a boffo gross of $706,193 in 18 days.[19] A prominent Lutheran broadcaster termed the film blasphemous, crude, profane, and grossly offensive. "What is happening in a world where nothing is sacred anymore? Where faith is publicly ridiculed, mocked and scorned for the entertainment dollar?" The dilemma, of course, is that even to talk about the film in such terms these days may give it more publicity and hence success. Like the Catholics, what bothered the Lutherans is a world in which they no longer wield much power over movies, a world in which an affront like *Monty Python's Life of Brian* can thrive, and they have no recourse to either public or to private ordering. Prior censorship bodies are no longer in place, public authorities are wary of attempting prosecution. It is open to objectors to denounce and even to picket, but they know full well that this may pull down ridicule and resistance, as well as publicity, on their heads.

Rabbi Abraham Hecht, speaking on behalf of 1,000 rabbis of the Rabbinical Alliance of America, Union of Orthodox Rabbis of the United States and Canada and the Rabbinical Council of Near Eastern Sephardic Communities of America, found the film blasphemous, sacrilegious, and an incitement to possible violence. "Blasphemy and sacrilege are not protected by the First Amendment of the U.S. Constitution," he added a little ominously. Jewish groups rarely make a fuss about films, unlike Christian groups, the last being against *Jesus Christ Superstar*. In this film he singled out the stoning scene.

---

[19]*Variety,* September 5, 1979. Hewison (11, p. 83, 91) reports takings of $27 million in the USA, £4 million, in the UK.

The Catholics focused on the end-scene crucifixion; having the nihilistic song "Always look on the bright side of life," juxtaposed against "the very image of redemption (the cross) becomes something intolerable." The Roman Catholic Archdiocese of New York condemned it formally as blasphemy for holding the person of Christ up to ridicule (*Variety,* September 5, 1979). As might be expected, particularly vigorous campaigns were organized against the film in Utah, South Carolina, Louisiana, Georgia, and Tennessee, but also Maine, and sometimes with success, but not always. As with all humor, it is difficult to predict what will shock. Warners reported that at a special screening for the Provo district attorney he "laughed throughout" and found nothing criminally offensive (*Variety,* October 31, 1979). Basically the issue was resolved by protests and pickets on the one hand, and aroused curiosity on the other. Private ordering efforts failed and it was once more clear that for the moment the libertarian free speech argument rode high.

Surprisingly, although the scenario was different in detail, and despite recent successful prosecutions for blasphemy (11, pp. 60–63) the film's fate in its own country, the UK, was similar. Opening in the metropolis in November, it was tactfully sent to the provinces only after Christmas, and was withdrawn over Easter. Some of its opponents followed a tactic similar to those in the US of avoiding confrontation because they had observed the counterproductive effect of publicity in the USA (11, p. 84). Britain is a more closely-knit society than the US and has an established church, so perhaps a focused confrontation was unavoidable. It took place on national television between Pythons John Cleese and Michael Palin, broadcaster Malcolm Muggeridge, and Mervyn Stockwood, Bishop of Southwark—the latter assured the Pythons they would get their 30 pieces of silver (11, p. 87). In fact it was four million pounds sterling.

Fears were expressed of the bad effect on the religious upbringing and outlook of young people; there was the realization that "the entertainment industry will not likely prevent the creation of such material" (*Variety,* August 29, 1979) and that some people will do anything for money as long as it doesn't land them in jail. These are hardly earth-shaking lessons for the religious community to be learning at this late date.

Religious leaders who cited the biblical spectacle films of DeMille or those based on books by Lloyd C. Douglas as "the good old days" opened themselves to further ridicule. Using religion to serve Hollywood's commercial purposes is approved when the message is pro, despite the hokeyness; but when religion itself is satirized then the satirists' behavior is Judas-like.

But Monty Python define themselves by defying the establishment; indeed they initiated (but lost) a lawsuit to prevent editing selections of their original Flying Circus TV shows for US network television (11, pp. 41–56). So when three of them came to New York in October 1979 one could have predicted what would happen; they flatly denied that there was no intention to offend; affirmed a desire to be outrageous; affirmed that their target has not religion as such, but organized religion; exactly the sort of groups, indeed, that protested their film. Probed about their satire on Jews, director Terry Jones responded with an allusion to a deleted sequence, possibly apocryphal, in which a fascist Jewish group sets up a Jewish state with camps for the Samaritans. In the end, he said, we'd like to put back a scene that would have really offended the Jewish community.[20]

What general conclusions can we draw from this historical analysis of private ordering? For one, shrunken though it is, the medium of movies is still a target for declining and threatened groups to engage in what sociologists call status defense exercises (32). If such groups assert some control over a glamorous and visible product like movies, even if they can make some impact or draw some publicity from a campaign against a movie, they feel they have enhanced their status. Such desperate tactics are, naturally, the resort only of those groups that feel threatened or are actually on the decline. Thus, although the movies have shifted from the center to the periphery of our society (28), from a mass medium to a minority medium, there seems to be a lingering aura: they are still an attractive target because they attract greater attention than their actual importance as a socially integrating factor any longer warrants.

REFERENCES

1. Ayer, Douglas, Ray Bates, and Peter Herman. "Self-Censorship in the Movie Industry; An Historical Perspective on Law and Social Change." *Wisconsin Law Review* 1970, pp. 791–838.
2. Bell, Daniel. *The Cultural Contradictions of Capitalism.* New York: Basic Books, 1976.
3. Bessie, Alvah. *Inquisition in Eden.* New York: Macmillan, 1965.
4. Carmen, Ira H. *Movies, Censorship, and the Law.* Ann Arbor, MI: University of Michigan Press, 1966.
5. Ceplair, Larry and Steven Englund. *Inquisition in Hollywood.* New York: Anchor/Doubleday, 1980.
6. Cogley, John. *Report on Blacklisting. I: The Movies.* New York: Fund for the Republic, 1956.
7. Durkheim, Emile. *Elementary Forms of the Religious Life.* London: G. Allen and Unwin, 1915.
8. Fearing, Franklin. *Motion Pictures as a Medium of Instruction and Communication.* Berkeley, CA: University of California Press, 1950.
9. Fiske, Marjorie and Leo Handel. "Motion Picture Research: Content and Audience Analysis." *Journal of Marketing,* 11, October 1946, pp. 129–134.
10. Flynn, Errol. *My Wicked, Wicked Ways.* New York: Putnam, 1959. Reprinted New York: Berkeley Medallion, 1974.
11. Hewison, Robert. *Monty Python: The Case Against.* London: Eyre Methuen, 1981.
12. "Hollywood Blacklisting." *Film Culture* Nos. 50–55, Fall/Winter 1970.
13. Hovland, C. I., A. A. Lumsdaine, and F. D. Sheffield. *Experiments in Mass Communication.* Princeton, NJ: Princeton University Press, 1949.

---

[20]*Los Angeles Times,* October 23, 1979, Part V, p. 14. The sequence appears to be an allusion to pp. 125–131 of the printed script (25).

14. Hunnings, Neville March. *Film Censors and the Law*. London: Allen and Unwin, 1967.
15. Jarvie, I. C. *Window on Hong Kong: A Sociological Study of the Hong Kong Film Industry and Its Audience*. Hong Kong, China: Centre of Asian Studies, University of Hong Kong, 1977.
16. Jarvie, I. C. *Movies and Society*. New York: Basic Books, 1970. Reprinted New York: Garland, 1983.
17. Jarvie, I. C. *Movies as Social Criticism*. Metuchen, NJ: Scarecrow, 1978.
18. Jarvie, I. C. ''Fanning the Flames: Anti-American Reaction to *Objective Burma*.'' *Historical Journal of Film, Radio and Television* 1, 1981, pp. 117–138.
19. Jarvie, I. C. ''The Social Experience of Movies.'' In Sari Thomas (ed.), *Film/Culture*. Metuchen, NJ: Scarecrow, 1982, pp. 247–268.
20. Kahn, Gordon. *Hollywood on Trial*. New York: Boni and Gaer 1948.
21. Kanfer, Stefan. *A Journal of the Plague Years*. New York: Atheneum, 1973.
22. Katz, Elihu and Paul Lazarsfeld. *Personal Influence*. Glencoe, IL: Free Press, 1955.
23. Klapper, Joseph. *The Effects of Mass Communication*. Glencoe, IL: Free Press, 1961.
24. Mayer, M. F. ''New Approach to Obscenity: The Conspiracy Doctrine.'' *St. Louis University Law Journal* 21, 1977, pp. 366–373.
25. *Monty Python's Life of Brian*. New York: Ace Books, 1979.
26. Navasky, Victor. *Naming Names*. New York: Viking, 1980.
27. Randall, Richard S. *Censorship of the Movies. The Social and Political Control of a Mass Medium*. Madison, WI: University of Wisconsin Press, 1968.
28. Shils, Edward. *Center and Periphery*. Chicago, IL: University of Chicago Press, 1975.
29. Vaughn, Robert. *Only Victims*. New York: Putnams, 1972.
30. Walsh, Raoul. *Each Man in His Own Time*. New York: Farar Strauss and Giroux, 1974.
31. Williams, Bernard. *Report of the Committee on Obscenity and Film Censorship*. London: HMSO, 1979.
32. Zurcher, Jr., Louis A., and R. George Kirkpatrick. *Citizens for Decency: Antipornography Crusades as Status Defense*. Austin, TX: University of Texas Press, 1976.

12

Public Nuisance Laws: A New Mechanism for Film Censorship*

Denise M. Trauth
John L. Huffman

Since its very inception in this country, film has been a target for censorship. "No sooner had the first prototypes of the movies been introduced than they were under attack for being 'immoral and offensive to public taste.' " (11, p. 109) From the first official court case in 1897 (16) until the present, litigation—based upon presumed effects of the medium—continues, centering on two intertwined issues. The first involves First Amendment protection for film; the second, censorship (i.e., prior restraint) of film exhibition.

During the last 80 years the debate over whether and how to control film has been addressed by Congress, state, and municipal governments; however, the major struggle was and continues to be the struggle for local control, and it is in this arena where litigation has been the most prolific (11, p. 109).

In recent years, local communities have found a new device—the public nuisance law—to aid in their battle for control over one particular type of motion picture—the pornographic film. Although in the past communities have used a variety of methods to control outlets for pornographic material, including film censorship boards (19) and zoning law (18, 25), the use of the public nuisance law is a fairly new strategy. Local communities have found an ally in the U. S. Court of Appeals for the Fourth Circuit, which in April 1982 upheld the state of North Carolina's obscenity nuisance statutes. This was the first time such public nuisance laws were found to be a Constitutional exercise of power in the control of obscenity. This article traces the evolution of these censorship laws and discusses the impact they may have on film in America.

---

*This article was made possible in part by a grant from the Faculty Research Committee of Bowling Green State University. An earlier version of this article was presented at the Speech Communication Association conference, Louisville, Kentucky, November 1982.

HISTORY OF FILM CENSORSHIP

In 1907 Chicago passed the first municipal ordinance which empowered a police department to issue motion picture exhibition permits. This ordinance was upheld by the Illinois Supreme Court in 1909. Four years later the City of New York followed suit and passed the first comprehensive municipal law for the regulation of film (11, p. 116).

The first state to legislate official censorship was Pennsylvania in 1911, followed by Ohio in 1913. In addition, Ohio had the distinction of being the first state to have its law reviewed and upheld by the United States Supreme Court. In a 1915 case, *Mutual Film Corp.* v. *Ohio* (14), the Court faced the issue of whether motion pictures were protected by the First Amendment. The Court answered negatively, comparing the communication function of film not to newspapers or books but rather to "the theater, the circus and all other shows and spectacles" (14, p. 243) and stressing that "the exhibition of moving pictures is a business pure and simple, originated and conducted for profit" (14, p. 244). The state's motivation in passing its law—the assumption that the new medium was "capable of evil"—was also sustained by the Court (14, p. 244).

The holding of *Mutual* became the principle courts used during the next 30 years when litigating cases involving film censorship. It was not until 1948 that the Supreme Court suggested that film had constitutional protection. In that year the Court heard the *Paramount* case (23) which involved a suit initiated by the U.S. Department of Justice charging the major film production companies with violating the Sherman Antitrust Act.

Almost as an aside in *Paramount,* the high Court noted "We have no doubt that moving pictures, like newspapers and radio are included in the press whose freedom is guaranteed by the First Amendment" (23, p. 166). However, since the issue being litigated involved monopoly in the motion picture industry and not First Amendment protection, the Court's ruling did not extend constitutional protection to film and did not overrule *Mutual*. That had to wait until 1952.

In that year the Supreme Court granted *certiorari* for the first time since 1915 to a case involving film censorship. The case grew out of New York State's banning of the Italian film *The Miracle* because it was "sacrilegious." In this case, *Burstyn, Inc.* v. *Wilson* (10), the high Court included film in the constitutional protection afforded other media. As the unanimous Court noted, "the present case is the first to present squarely to us the question whether motion pictures are within the ambit of protection which the First Amendment . . . secures to any form of 'speech' or 'the press' " (10, p. 501).

Although the high Court answered this question affirmatively, and struck down the New York law which permitted the ban, it went on to note:

> To hold that liberty of expression by means of motion pictures is guaranteed by the First and Fourteenth Amendments, however, is not the end of our problem. It does

not follow that the Constitution requires absolute freedom to exhibit every motion picture of every kind at all times and all places. . . . Nor does it follow that motion pictures are necessarily subject to precise rules governing any other particular method of expression. (10, pp. 502–503).

Thus, while the Court extended First Amendment protection to film in *Burstyn,* and struck down sacrilege as a basis for censorship, it also intimated that censorship might be allowable for other reasons.

Based upon the holding of *Burstyn,* during the next nine years, in a series of six decisions (five of which were *per curiam*) the Supreme Court struck down six statutes authorizing censorship (see 3, 6, 8, 12, 20, 21). As a result of these cases, "harmful" and "immoral" were disallowed as standards for censorship, and banning a film due to "sexual immorality" was considered to be barring discussion of ideas and thus not permitted. Gradually, in both state and federal courts, the only basis for prior restraint of film exhibition became obscenity, as defined by the Supreme Court in the 1957 case *Roth* v. *United States* (17), and applied to film that year by the Court in *Times Film Corp.* v. *Chicago* (21).

However, the important underlying issue that had been smouldering since *Burstyn*—the constitutionality of prior restraint in the form of film licensing—was not resolved in any of the aforementioned cases. That had to wait until 1961 when the Supreme Court heard *Times Film Corp.* v. *Chicago* (22).

This case gave the high Court the opportunity to confront a question "never having been specifically decided by this Court" (22, pp. 44–45): whether First Amendment protection of motion pictures includes absolute freedom to exhibit a film at least once. The negative answer, coming from a five-to-four Court, was based on two themes reminiscent of *Burstyn:* that films may have a "capacity for evil" (22, p. 49) and that First Amendment protection of film is not absolute (22, p. 48).

Although *Times Film* did present the Court with an issue it had not previously adjudicated, the decision did not set a clear precedent for two reasons. First, the facts of the case were highly abstract, leading the lower courts to disregard the decision for lack of a justiciable controversy; applying the *Times Film* holding to any other set of facts was difficult. Second, the justices were badly divided. Chief Justice Warren wrote a strong dissent, signed by four members of the Court, favoring limitations on licensing. Thus, even though *Times Film* held that film licensing was not a violation of the First Amendment per se, it said little about the constitutionality of any particular system of licensing, and signaled even less about directions the Court might take in the future.

CENSORSHIP SYSTEMS

The articulation of a set of principles governing licensing systems was accomplished in the 1965 case *Freedman* v. *Maryland* (5). Here Justice Brennan delivered the opinion of the Court, which held that the First Amendment was violated by a Maryland motion picture censorship statute. That law required film exhibitors to submit movies to a state Board of Censors for the Board's approval *before* any showing would be allowed. The law also placed the burden of seeking judicial review of any Board decision upon the exhibitor.[1]

The appellant challenged the Maryland law by exhibiting a film, *Revenge at Daybreak,* at his Baltimore theater without first getting a clearance from the Maryland Board. Maryland conceded that the picture was by no stretch of the imagination pornographic, but Freedman was convicted because he did not apply for the required license.

Essentially, the reasoning of the Court revolved around the concept of prior restraint. The Court repeated the oft-cited principle of *Bantam Books, Inc.* v. *Sullivan* (2) that "any system of prior restraints of expression comes to this Court bearing a heavy presumption against its constitutional validity." However, the Court took cognizance of the legal fact that while prior restraints were normally constitutionally repugnant, *Near* v. *Minnesota* (15) and subsequent cases had demonstrated that prior restraints and censorship were permissible when dealing with legally defined pornographic material.

The Court noted that any censorship system presented special dangers for constitutionally protected speech, in that such speech might be suppressed along with unprotected speech. Rather than holding that censorship systems were unconstitutional, the Court decided to shift the burden of proving whether a particular film is a protected or unprotected expression (legally obscene, that is) from the exhibitor of the film to the censorship board. In addition, the Court held that only a judicial determination in an adversary proceeding would suffice to prove that a film was legally obscene.

After *Freedman* v. *Maryland,* a censorship board, in order to be "legal," had to operate under certain set rules. Within a specified "brief period," the censor was required to either issue a license for a particular film or else go to court to restrain showing of the film. The Court also mandated that any censorship law had to provide for a "prompt final judicial decision" as to whether or not the film was obscene. The Court specified in *Freedman* that the emphasis on speed was crucial, since without such an emphasis exhibitors and distributors would not be likely to challenge the censor's decision because of a reluctance to engage in protracted litigation over a single film.

---

[1]Maryland Law (Md. Ann. Code, 1957, Art. 66A) stated in section 2: "It shall be unlawful to sell, lease, lend, exhibit or use any motion picture film or view in the State of Maryland unless the said film or view has been submitted by the exchange, owner or lessee of the film or view and duly approved and licensed by the Maryland State Board of Censors, hereinafter in this article called the Board." In section 6 the law stated: "The Board shall examine or supervise the examination of all films or views to be exhibited or used in the State of Maryland and shall approve and license such films or views which are moral and proper, and shall disapprove such as are obscene, or such as tend, in the judgment of the Board, to debase or corrupt morals or incite to crimes."

Freedman, with its emphasis on procedural due process, remains the standard against which censorship boards are to be compared. Following this case the demise of a number of these bodies occurred.

In addition to censorship boards, some states and localities had boards that were involved not in censoring films but in classifying them. This latter function was reviewed by the Supreme Court in 1967 in *Interstate Circuit* v. *Dallas* (9). In this case the Court held that a Dallas ordinance which established the Motion Picture Classification Board and charged it with determining if a film was "not suitable for young persons" violated the First Amendment. The violation occurred not because of its application to youth as a class but because of the vagueness of the statute which, according to the Court, lacked "narrowly drawn, reasonable and definite standards for the officials to follow" (9, p. 690). (However, the ordinance was not rescued by an appeal to the fact that it was aimed at the protection of juveniles, *Ginsberg* v. *New York* (7), notwithstanding.)

Again, as in *Burstyn* and *Freedman,* the high Court did not totally outlaw these boards but rather established stringent guidelines for them to follow.

Interstate Circuit is noteworthy for yet another reason. In it the Court displays a sensitivity to the havoc local classification boards could wreak on Hollywood's production and distribution companies. This point will be returned to later during a discussion of the potential impact of various laws on the film industry.

In 1980 the U.S. Supreme Court again took up the question of what are allowable prior restraints in the area of obscenity in *Vance* v. *Universal Amusement* (24). At issue in this case were Texas "public nuisance" laws that authorized a prior restraint of indefinite duration on the exhibition of motion pictures. The laws provided for no final judicial determination of obscenity, nor did they guarantee any prompt review of a preliminary finding of probable obscenity.

Universal Amusement operated an indoor, adults-only motion picture theater. Its manager filed suit in U.S. District Coutt seeking an injunction to forestall any application of state "nuisance laws" to his place of business. The District Court concluded that the nuisance statutes operated as an invalid prior restraint on the exercise of First Amendment rights. The first nuisance statute authorized injunction suits in the name of Texas against alleged nuisances. If successful, judgment was to be rendered "abating said nuisance and enjoining the defendants from maintaining the same, and ordering that said house be closed for one year." The second nuisance statute provided that certain habitual uses of premises would constitute a public nuisance and could be enjoined at the suit of either Texas or one of its citizens. Among the prohibited uses was "the commercial manufacturing, commercial distribution, or commercial exhibition of obscene material." In finding for Universal Amusement, the three-judge District Court held that both of these laws authorized Texas state judges, on the basis of a showing that obscene films had been exhibited at a particular theater in the past, to prohibit the future exhibition of motion pictures that had not yet been found to be obscene. To the District Court, this clearly constituted an impermissible prior restraint.

The state of Texas appealed to the Fifth Circuit Court of Appeals. A divided panel of that court reversed the lower court and held that the Texas laws were "basically sound." The same Court of Appeals then granted rehearing *en banc* and, in an eight-to-six decision, reversed its own panel's holding and ruled that the statutes were objectionable because they "would allow the issuance of an injunction against the future exhibition of unnamed films that depict particular acts enumerated in the state's obscenity statute." In light of the divided opinions and contrary findings of the Court of Appeals, the case was obviously ripe for a Supreme Court determination, and the state of Texas appealed.

In a *per curiam* opinion (with four members of the Court dissenting) the Supreme Court upheld the Circuit Court's decision. The high Court limited its review to two arguments advanced by the state of Texas: first, that an obscenity injunction constituted no greater a prior restraint than any criminal statute; and, second, that the Court of Appeals had erroneously held that no prior restraint of possibly First Amendment protected materials was possible.

The Supreme Court's *per curiam* opinion stated that the Court of Appeals had been quite correct in concluding that the regulation of any communication activity such as motion pictures must adhere to more narrowly drawn procedures than would be necessary for the abatement of an ordinary nuisance (e.g., one that had no Constitutional implications). Further, the Court stated that the burden of supporting an injunction against a future exhibition should be even heavier than the burden of justifying a criminal penalty for a past communication. In an explanatory footnote, the Court expanded upon this philosophy:

> The presumption against prior restraints is heavier—and the degree of protection broader—than against limits on expression imposed by criminal penalties. Behind this distinction is a theory deeply etched in law: a free society prefers to punish the few who abuse rights of speech *after* they break the law than to throttle them and all others beforehand. It is always difficult to know in advance what an individual will say, and the line between legitimate and illegitimate speech is often so finely drawn that the risks of freewheeling censorship are formidable. (24, p. 2556)

The Supreme Court pointed out that under the Texas laws, film exhibitors would have to obey a restraining order pending a review of a film's merits, and, if they chose to violate the order and show the film before such a review, they would be subject to contempt proceedings, even if the film were ultimately found non-obscene. According to the Court, this would be more onerous and more objectionable than the threat of criminal sanctions after a film had been shown, since, obviously, nonobscenity would be a defense in any criminal prosecution.

The Supreme Court saw no special merit in the fact that a state judge, rather than an administrative censor as in *Freedman* v. *Maryland,* was the person who would determine probable obscenity and issue the temporary injunction:

"That a state trial judge might be thought more likely than an administrative censor to determine accurately that a work is obscene does not change the unconstitutional character of the restraint if erroneously entered" (24, p. 2556).

The Supreme Court quickly dismissed the state's second argument, finding that the Court of Appeals had not held that there can never be a valid prior restraint on communication, and that Texas had misinterpreted that part of the Circuit Court's judgment.

Arising out of *Freedman* and *Vance,* then, is the current position of the U.S. Supreme Court regarding prior restraints imposed on obscene and pornographic materials. A prior restraint of such materials is permissible. However, the prior restraint must be very carefully drawn. The burden of proving obscenity must rest with the censor, not the burden of proving non-obscenity with the person being censored. The censor, within a specified brief period, must go to court and obtain a restraining order. And, again within a specified short period, a final judicial decision as to whether the material is in fact legally obscene must result from an adversary proceeding. Finally, the person being censored should be able to defeat criminal contempt proceedings if s/he violates the restraining order and the material is ultimately judged to be non-obscene.

THE NORTH CAROLINA NUISANCE LAWS: LEGAL PRIOR RESTRAINT?

Fehlhaber v. *North Carolina* (4) was decided by the U.S. Court of Appeals for the Fourth Circuit on April 15, 1982. The Fourth Circuit found a North Carolina obscenity nuisance statute not in violation of the First Amendment, despite the fact that the statute authorized a permanent injunction against adult theaters and adult bookstores.

Senior Circuit Judge Haynsworth began his decision by immediately revealing where he stood on the issue. He said:

> This is another skirmish in the battle of the purveyors of hard core pornography seeking the protection of the precious values of the First Amendment, and legislative bodies, seeking to lend protection to other societal values supportive of morality and decorous communities. (4, p. 1609)

The question before the Circuit Court was whether an injunction issued in accordance with the nuisance law was invalid because it applied to materials not yet judicially determined to be obscene—materials that might be non-obscene and therefore Constitutionally protected.

The North Carolinian obscenity statute was directed only at "pictorial" obscenity, and not at written material. The statute applied only if the exhibition of obscene films was a "predominant and regular course of business" or if other obscene pictorial materials were a "principal or substantial part of the stock in trade'' (4, p. 1610). Thus, the law was directly aimed at adult theaters and adult bookstores. The ''lewd matter'' the law sought to enjoin was defined in terms of *Miller* v. *California* (13), which set the present standards for obscene materials.[2]

The process by which the nuisance statute was to be enforced was as follows. The attorney general or a local district attorney would file in superior court a verified complaint alleging the facts constituting the nuisance. An application for a preliminary injunction could be made at this time, and a permanent hearing time would then be set within 10 days. In the meantime, a judge could issue an *ex parte* temporary restraining order, but solely for the purpose of preserving the evidence. The order could not restrict the sale of any stock in trade. It could only require that a full accounting be kept of all transactions in materials specified in the complaint. The permanent hearing would, according to the law, be given priority on the docket over virtually all other civil matters. A jury was to be provided if the defendant requested one. If, at the permanent hearing, the existence of a nuisance was established, the court was directed by the law to enter an order of abatement to ''perpetually enjoin the defendant and any other person from further maintaining the nuisance at the place complained of, and the defendant from maintaining such nuisance elsewhere within the jurisdiction of the State.'' An enjoined defendant would be responsible for court costs, any gross income received for selling obscene materials after the entry of the preliminary injunction, and attorneys' fees and damages.

Once an abatement injunction had been issued, a defendant was subject to a trial on a criminal contempt charge for any violation of the injunction. The law specified penalties for the contempt charge: a fine of no less than $200 nor more than $1,000, or imprisonment in the county jail for no less than three nor more than six months. According to the law, the contempt proceeding had to be held according to plenary procedures, meaning that the state had to prove all elements of the offense (including obscenity) beyond a reasonable doubt.

In Judge Haynsworth's opinion, the above procedure is more gentle than ordinary criminal sanctions. He pointed out that if the defendant is initially found to be selling obscene materials, s/he is not sent to jail as s/he would be in many jurisdictions. Instead, the defendant is simply ''told'' by injunction to go and sin no more. Judge Haynsworth concluded his opinion with the following:

> If any prior restraint is ever justified, the area of pictorial obscenity is the place. With all of the safeguards in the statute, as interpreted and applied by North Carolina courts, we conclude that it meets federal requirements. (4, p. 1610)

---

[2]The test of obscenity is that a work is obscene if (a) the average person applying contemporary community standards would find that the work, taken as a whole, appeals to prurient interest; (b) the work depicts or describes, in a patently offensive way, sexual or excretory conduct specifically defined by the applicable state law; and (c) the work, taken as a whole, lacks serious literary, artistic, political or social value. For the purpose of the test, ''community'' is defined as ''local community'' where a film is screened or material is sold.

And, indeed, the North Carolina nuisance law does seem to meet the rule of *Freedman* and *Vance*. The prior restraint is very carefully drawn, both by statute and by judicial gloss. The burden of proving obscenity falls on the state. The state must go to court in order to obtain a restraining order. Within a brief time, an adversary proceeding must be held and a final judicial decision rendered on whether the material is legally obscene. If a defendant is enjoined from ever operating a nuisance (e.g., an adult theater or bookstore) again, and s/he then violates the injunction, s/he is penalized only if the materials sold are once again adjudged legally obscene. Technically, the North Carolina law seems to be in compliance with the dictates of the U.S. Supreme Court.

However, this is not the end of the question. It must be remembered that the key feature of the North Carolina law, as pointed out by Circuit Judge Phillips in his dissent in *Fehlhaber,* is the power it gives to the state's courts to *permanently* enjoin, under threat of contempt, the sale of materials that have not yet been determined to be legally obscene. Although the U.S. Supreme Court has never upheld such a law, an insight into how the high Court would deal with it was provided by that body in November 1982 when it denied *certiorari* in an Ohio case dealing with an adult theater and bookstore.

In this case, *Avenue Bookstore* v. *Tallmadge* (1), the Supreme Court declined to review an Ohio appeals court decision upholding, in a city's public nuisance action against a theater and bookstore, an injunction that permanently prohibited the store from using its rear section to display and sell obscene materials.

The Ohio Court of Appeals held that the injunction was not a prior restraint of protected communication "in violation of the First and Fourteenth Amendments because 'no punishment will be imposed until it is proven that obscene material was indeed involved' " (1, p. 2453).

However, in a dissent to the Supreme Court's *per curiam* denial of *certiorari,* Justice White, who was joined by Justices Brennan and Marshall, pointed out that despite Ohio's claim that the injunction was not an unconstitutional prior restraint, there remained an unresolved issue:

> The Court has never determined, however, whether abatement orders, such as the one involved in the present case, will pass constitutional muster when they permanently enjoin the use of a business premises for the sale or display of obscene material, but do not subject the owner to contempt sanctions unless there has been a judicial determination of obscenity. (1, p. 2453)

Justice White and his two colleagues conclude that since the Supreme Court has never confronted questions regarding the extent to which states may use nuisance statutes to control legally obscene material and the procedural safeguards necessary to avoid constitutional problems, the case should be accepted for review by the Court and these important unsettled issues addressed. In

Tallmadge, then, the Supreme Court tacitly permitted states to use public nuisance laws to enjoin the sale or display of obscene materials. By contrast, it should be noted that in *Fehlhaber,* North Carolina proscribed materials that had not yet been found to be legally obscene. Thus *Tallmadge* is not necessarily a sign that the North Carolina law will be upheld should it be appealed.

CONCLUSION

One final issue remains: the impact these recent cases may have on the American film industry. As has been pointed out, attempts to inhibit film exhibition by state and local governments are not new. The industry has learned to live with them. What is new is the position of the Supreme Court relative to censorship. For the last 30 years, during which film has been considered protected by the First Amendment, the Court has maintained a consistent posture, generally allowing censorship systems but strictly enforcing procedural safeguards. In part this posture has been motivated by the realization, articulated by the Court in *Interstate Circuit* v. *Dallas,* that censorship and classification systems may have a negative impact upon film producers and exhibitors:

> It may be unlikely that what Dallas does in respect to the licensing of motion pictures would have a significant effect upon film makers in Hollywood or Europe. But what Dallas may constitutionally do, so may other cities and States. Indeed, we are told that this ordinance is being used as a model for legislation in other localities. Thus, one who wishes to convey his ideas through that medium, which of course includes one who is interested not so much in expression as in making money, must consider whether what he proposes to film, and how he proposes to film it, is within the terms of classification schemes such as this. If he is unable to determine what the ordinance means, he runs the risk of being foreclosed, in practical effect, from a significant portion of the movie-going public. Rather than run that risk, he might choose nothing but the innocuous. . . . Moreover, a local exhibitor who cannot afford to risk losing the youthful audience when a film may be of marginal interest to adults . . . may contract to show only the inane. The vast wasteland that some have described in reference to another medium might be a verdant paradise in comparison. The First Amendment interests here are, therefore, broader than merely those of the film maker, distributor, and exhibitor. (9, pp. 683–684)

The sensitivity not only to the realities of the film industry but also to the needs of the audience that the Supreme Court displays in this passage seems to have been lost in *Tallmadge* and so the question remains: Is *Tallmadge* a sign of things to come? It should be stressed at this juncture that not only has the Supreme Court never upheld a law such as the one at issue in *Fehlhaber,* it has countless times over the years warned of the "chilling effect" of prior restraints on materials not yet determined to be outside the ambit of the First Amendment.

Up until 1982, the Supreme Court has, in the area of obscenity, allowed injunctions only against materials judicially found to be obscene or injunctions that were strictly limited as to duration. In *Tallmadge* we see for the first time the high Court disregarding, albeit in a *per curiam* decision, this "chilling effect" and allowing a law to stand which would certainly force adult theater and bookstore owners into a more conservative posture, the posture *Interstate Circuit* deemed conducive to a "wasteland." Whether the U.S. Supreme Court has reached the point where it can finally put behind it decades of Blackstonian antipathy to censorship and prior restraint remains to be revealed in future cases.

REFERENCES

1. *Avenue Bookstore* v. *Tallmadge,* 8 Med. L. Rptr. 2452 (1982).
2. *Bantam Books* v. *Sullivan,* 372 U.S. 58 (1963).
3. *Commercial Pictures Corp.* v. *Regents of the University of New York,* 346 U.S. 587 (1954).
4. *Fehlhaber* v. *North Carolina,* 8 Med. L. Rptr. 1608 (1982).
5. *Freedman* v. *Maryland,* 380 U.S. 51 (1965).
6. *Gelling* v. *Texas,* 343 U.S. 960 (1952).
7. *Ginsberg* v. *New York,* 390 U.S. 629 (1968).
8. *Holmby Productions, Inc.* v. *Vaughn,* 350 U.S. 870 (1955).
9. *Interstate Circuit* v. *Dallas,* 390 U.S. 676 (1968).
10. *Joseph Burstyn, Inc.* v. *Wilson,* 343 U.S. 495 (1952).
11. Jowett, Garth. *Film: The Democratic Art.* Boston: Little, Brown and Company, 1976.
12. *Kingsley International Pictures* v. *Board of Regents,* 360, U.S. 684 (1959).
13. *Miller* v. *California,* 413 U.S. 15 (1973).
14. *Mutual Film Corp.* v. *Industrial Commission of Ohio,* 236 U.S. 230 (1915).
15. *Near* v. *Minnesota,* 383 U.S. 697 (1931).
16. *People* v. *Doris,* 14 App. Div. 117, 43 N.Y.S. 571 (1st. Dep't 1897).
17. *Roth* v. *U.S.,* 354 U.S. 476 (1957).
18. *Schad* v. *Mount Ephrain,* 101 S.Ct. 2176 (1981).
19. *Star* v. *Preller,* 419 U.S. 956 (1974).
20. *Superior Films, Inc.* v. *Dept. of Education of Ohio,* 346 U.S. 587 (1954).
21. *Times Film Corp.* v. *Chicago,* 355 U.S. 35 (1957).
22. *Times Film Corp.* v. *Chicago,* 365 U.S. 43 (1961).
23. *United States* v. *Paramount Pictures,* 334 U.S. 131 (1948).
24. *Vance* v. *Universal Amusement,* 5 Med. L. Rptr. 2553 (1980).
25. *Young* v. *American Minitheaters,* 427 U.S. 50 (1976).

Author Index

Italic page numbers indicate bibliographic citations.

Subject Index

T